北京仲裁

BEIJING ARBITRATION QUARTERLY

BIAC
北京仲裁委员会
Beijing Arbitration Commission
北京国际仲裁中心
Beijing International Arbitration Center

第 122 辑（2022年第4辑） Vol.122（2022,No.4）

主　办：北京仲裁委员会／北京国际仲裁中心
协　办：中国国际私法学会

编委会

主　任：王利明
编　员：William Blair　陈　洁　黄　进
　　　　Michael Hwang　姜丽丽　李曙光
　　　　Loukas Mistelis　Michael J. Moser
　　　　师　虹　宋连斌　Thomas Stipanowich
　　　　陶景洲　王贵国　易继明　郑若骅

编辑部

主　编：陈福勇
副主编：张皓亮
编　辑：林晨曦　沈韵秋　赵菡清　徐　畅

中国法制出版社
CHINA LEGAL PUBLISHING HOUSE

本书所刊载的文章只代表作者个人观点,不必然反映本书编辑部或其他机构、个人的观点,谨此声明!

目录

编者按

获奖论文

005 境外仲裁机构在中国内地仲裁裁决的法律性质
　　——兼论"仲裁地"法律概念在我国的发展 / 高　杨

027 反复指定对仲裁员资格的影响
　　——兼论北仲《行为守则》/ 邓芷珊

043 从"自治"归于"他治"的空中楼阁
　　——论当事人共同选定仲裁员制度中的意思自治 / 陈令祚

077 从裁决到协商：我国国内 ISDS 机制的新趋势
　　——兼议外商投资投诉制度 / 刘子婧

113 诉仲间主管竞择的规制盲区及应对
　　——以《仲裁法（修订征求意见稿）》第40条后段为中心 / 张世超

140 按小时费率计收仲裁员报酬的优缺点与监督机制研究 / 黄　帆

158 《仲裁法》修改背景下的仲裁裁决撤销程序：立法检视、性质定位与规则建构 / 张喜彪

178 论上诉机制与 ICSID 公约和 UNCITRAL 仲裁规则的兼容性 / 刘文慧

Contents

Editor's Note

Award-Winning Papers

005 The Legal Nature of Arbitral Awards Made by Foreign Arbitration Institutions in Mainland China—With a Discussion of the Development of the Legal Concept of "Arbitral Seat" in Chinese Law Gao Yang

027 Effect of Repeat Appointment on Qualification of Arbitrator—on Code of Conduct Deng Zhishan

043 From "Self-Governance" to "Other-Governance" —On Party Autonomy in Joint Appointment of Arbitrators Chen Lingzuo

077 From Adjudication to Negotiation: New Trend in China's Domestic ISDS Mechanisms—Also Discussing the Foreign Investment Complaint Mechanism Liu Zijing

113 Regulatory Blind Spots and Countermeasures in Arbitral Forum Shopping— Centering on the Latter Paragraph of Article 40 of the Arbitration Law (Revised Draft for Public Comments) Zhang Shichao

140 Implementing Hourly Rate System for Arbitrator's Remuneration in China: Challenges and Solutions Huang Fan

158 The Procedure of Revocation in Arbitration under the Backdrop of Amendment Arbitration Law: Legislation View, Orientation of Character and Rules Construction Zhang Xibiao

178 The Compatibility of an Appellate Mechanism with the ICSID Convention and the UNCITRAL Arbitration Rules Liu Wenhui

编者按

商事仲裁作为一种现代商事争议解决机制，正处于蓬勃发展的阶段。优秀的青年法学学子是推动中国商事仲裁未来发展的重要力量。为了鼓励高校法学专业学生熟悉仲裁、研究仲裁，培养更多青年学子成为仲裁事业的推动者和接班人，北京仲裁委员会/北京国际仲裁中心（BAC/BIAC，以下简称北仲）秉持"弘扬仲裁文化、培育仲裁新人"的宗旨，自2013年起每年举办一届"北仲杯"全国高校商事仲裁有奖征文大赛，得到众多高校法学学子的关注和参与。

第十届"北仲杯"全国高校商事仲裁有奖征文大赛于2022年6月6日启动，现已圆满结束。本届大赛面向国内外高校法学专业学生，以商事仲裁或其他多元争议解决方式（相关的实体或程序法律问题）为征文主题。参赛论文题材依然保持着前九届涵盖范围广、涉及主体多的特点，既有关注国内仲裁制度的，又有对国际仲裁以及仲裁中涉及的实体法律问题展开研究的。不少论文观点新颖，研究深入，体现了我国法学学子更加广阔的学术视野和日益精进的研究水平。

经过初审、复审、答辩三个环节的筛选，本届大赛共评选出一等奖一名、二等奖三名、三等奖四名、优秀奖五名。具体获奖论文作者、院校及论文题目如下：

一等奖：

高　杨（澳洲国立大学）：《境外仲裁机构在中国内地仲裁裁决的法律性

质——兼论"仲裁地"法律概念在我国的发展》

二等奖：

邓芷珊（广东外语外贸大学）：《反复指定对仲裁员资格的影响——兼论北仲〈行为守则〉》

陈令祚（中国人民大学）：《从"自治"归于"他治"的空中楼阁——论当事人共同决定仲裁员制度中的意思自治》

刘子婧（中国政法大学）：《从裁决到协商：我国国内 ISDS 机制的新趋势——兼议外商投资投诉制度》

三等奖：

张世超（清华大学）：《诉仲间主管竞择的规制盲区及应对——以〈仲裁法（修订征求意见稿）〉第 40 条后段为中心》

黄　帆（澳门大学）：《按小时费率计收仲裁员报酬的优缺点与监督机制研究》

张喜彪（中央财经大学）：《〈仲裁法〉修改背景下的仲裁裁决撤销程序：立法检视、性质定位与规则建构》

刘文慧（莱顿大学）：*The Compatibility of an Appellate Mechanism with the ICSID Convention and UNCITRAL Arbitration Rules*

为了满足读者需要，进一步丰富和繁荣商事仲裁理论研究成果，本辑《北京仲裁》作为第十届"北仲杯"全国高校商事仲裁有奖征文大赛的获奖论文专刊，在经获奖作者授权后，将其中 8 篇获奖论文予以刊载。这些论文的研究题材主要围绕仲裁裁决撤销中的公共利益、快速程序、国际投资仲裁等业界广泛关注的实务问题，从程序及实体多维度就仲裁行业前沿热点进行了富有探索性的研究。这些论文充分体现了作者们独到的学术视角和活跃的学术思维。需要说明的是，在论文答辩过程中，评审专家针对部分论文指出了一些问题，提出了一些修改意见或研究建议，部分作者在参加完论文答辩后对论文的内容或标题进行了完善，并向大赛组委会提供了修改后的论文，本辑刊载的即为修改后的论文。

"北仲杯"全国高校商事仲裁有奖征文大赛采用公正严格的评审机制，力求为广大关心仲裁发展、热爱仲裁事业的青年法学学子提供学术研究的机会、与专家交流的渠道以及施展才华的平台。在前九届大赛的基础上，第十届大赛继续在高校中保持着较广泛的影响力，继续贯彻大赛以征文形式推动宣传仲裁、以奖助方式鼓励研究仲裁、以锁定学生实现培育新苗、以严格评审达到公平择优之旨的比赛模式，为今后大赛积累了更多宝贵的经验。大赛将继续把"推进仲裁研究，培养仲裁人才"作为一项目标，推动北仲成为多元争议解决人才培养中心，助力中国仲裁事业的传承与发展。同时，北仲另设有"科研基金项目""北仲争议解决新探索文库项目""北仲争议解决新视野译丛项目"等，用于鼓励资助争议解决理论及实务研究，欢迎读者继续关注。

"北仲杯"征文大赛组委会

《北京仲裁》编辑部

2023 年 12 月 31 日

境外仲裁机构在中国内地仲裁裁决的法律性质

——兼论"仲裁地"法律概念在我国的发展

高　杨[*]

● **摘　要**

当事人约定将商事争议提交境外仲裁机构在中国内地仲裁的现象日益普遍，由此在我国司法实践和学术讨论中引起了诸多争议。我国法院在对该类案件进行司法审查的实践中往往面临复杂的法律问题，尤其是如何判断裁决的籍属，以及我国法院应该适用什么法律依据来对裁决进行司法审查。围绕境外仲裁机构在中国内地仲裁裁决的法律性质，本文深度分析了相关的法律问题，梳理了我国近期司法实践的重要发展。

我国立法长期以来并没有确立"仲裁地"的法律概念。虽然在大部分国内仲裁机构的仲裁实践中，是否适用"仲裁地"的法律概念似乎无关紧要，但在涉及境外仲裁机构在我国内地仲裁裁决的司法程序中（包括对裁决的执行及司法审查），适用"仲裁地"还是"仲裁机构所在地"的标准，会让法院对该类裁决的籍属作出不同的认定，从而导致在此问题上适用不同的法律依据。

在就此问题的司法实践中，我国法院的认定标准经历了从"仲裁机构所在地"标准到"仲裁地"标准的转变。在过去长期主导的

---

[*] 高杨，现供职于中山大学法学院。

"仲裁机构所在地"标准下,境外仲裁机构在我国内地仲裁裁决的性质遭遇了尴尬的境地:此类裁决既不属于《纽约公约》下的"外国裁决",也不属于中国法项下传统的"涉外裁决"。对此,学理上和部分法院倾向于将其认定为《纽约公约》项下的"非内国裁决",由此产生了诸多法律问题和困境。这种局面直到最近才被我国法院在典型案件"布兰特伍德案"中得到解决,该判决颇具开创性地适用"仲裁地"标准,将国际商会仲裁院在广州作出的仲裁裁决,认定为我国民事诉讼法项下的"涉外裁决"。由此,我国法院认定仲裁国籍的标准逐渐向"仲裁地"标准转变,这不仅与国际仲裁实践接轨,还清晰地体现了我国法院支持仲裁的司法政策。

2021年7月底司法部颁布的《仲裁法(修订)(征求意见稿)》(以下简称《仲裁法修订草案》)正式确立了"仲裁地"的法律概念。这个转变是对近期司法实践的立法确认,体现了司法和立法在此问题上的良性互动。若其通过立法程序,则代表着我国法律正式确立"仲裁地"标准认定境外仲裁机构在我国内地仲裁裁决的籍属。通过修订成文法的法律渊源,将我国司法实践经验予以"法典化",明确境外仲裁机构在我国内地仲裁的相关法律规则,可以实现我国立法与国际主流立法的接轨,有利于加强我国仲裁制度的国际化,增强我国仲裁制度的吸引力。

● **关键词**

境外仲裁机构 裁决籍属 外国裁决 非内国裁决 涉外裁决

Abstract: It is increasingly common for parties to submit commercial disputes to foreign arbitration institutions to render an arbitral award in Mainland China, a phenomenon that has triggered many controversies in Chinese judicial practices and scholarly debates. To handle this practice, Chinese courts have been grappling with complex legal issues, particularly how to determine the nationality of these arbitral awards and how to apply Chinese law to conduct judicial review on them. Focused on the legal nature of arbitral awards made by foreign arbitration institutions in Mainland China, this article provides an in-depth analysis of relevant legal issues, and reviews important recent development of Chinese judicial practices.

Under Chinese law, the concept of "arbitral seat" has not been established for a long time. While this notion seems irrelevant in most domestic arbitrations, the case is quite different in the judicial review process over arbitral awards made by foreign arbitration institutions in Mainland China. Importantly, based on whether to apply the criteria of "arbitral seat" or the "location of the arbitration institution", Chinese courts would be led to different conclusions as to the nationality of these arbitral awards, and may accordingly apply different rules on this matter.

To determine the legal nature of arbitral awards made by foreign arbitration institutions in Mainland China, the standards of Chinese courts have shifted from a test of the "location of the arbitration institution" to "arbitral seat". Ironically, under the longstanding standard of the "location of the arbitration institution" that remained prevalent in the past, arbitral awards made by foreign arbitration institutions in Mainland China were caught in a legal dilemma: these awards were neither "foreign arbitral awards" made in another country under the New York Convention; nor did they constitute "foreign related arbitral awards" under Chinese law. In this regard, some Chinese scholars and courts tended to consider these awards as "non-domestic arbitral awards" under the New York Convention, which caused numerous legal problems and controversies. However, this problem has been resolved by Guangzhou Intermediate Court in the recent landmark case of Brentwood Industries, Inc. (U.S.A.), whose decision innovatively applied the standard of "arbitral seat" to recognize an award made by ICC International Court of Arbitration in Guangzhou as a "foreign related arbitral award" under Chinese Civil Procedure Law. This decision represents an important shift of Chinese courts to embrace the standard of "arbitral seat" to determine the nationality of arbitral awards, which not only aligns with international arbitration practices but also clearly indicates the pro-arbitration stance of Chinese judiciary.

Subsequently, in the proposed amendments of Arbitration Law issued by the Department of Justice, the concept of the "arbitral seat" has been formally established, which seems to be a legislative confirmation of recent judicial practice mentioned previously, and suggests a productive interaction between the judiciary and the legislature. If this draft passed the legislative process, it will mark the formal recognition by Chinese law of the notion of "arbitral seat". As such, this proposed amendment of statutory law will codify the lessons learned from Chinese judicial practices, clarify the relevant rules for foreign arbitration institutions practising in Mainland China, and align Chinese law with mainstream international standards, all of which can make China a more attractive place of arbitration for various stakeholders.

Key Words: foreign arbitration institutions, nationality of arbitral awards, foreign arbitral awards, non-domestic arbitral awards, foreign-related arbitral awards

一、引言

商事仲裁作为一种基于当事人意思自治的替代性争端解决方式正在跨国商事纠纷中发挥着不可替代的重要作用。随着中国经济的迅速发展及世界经济全球化深化，不仅我国仲裁机构管理的仲裁案件数量和争议标的金额迅速增长，由境外仲裁机构在中国内地仲裁商事纠纷的实践也日益增多。相关的法律问题随之而来：针对境外仲裁机构在中国境内进行的仲裁程序而言，其产生的仲裁裁决的法律性质、裁决的籍属及司法审查的法律依据是什么？这些问题曾引发我国仲裁立法、司法和学界的长期争议。本文以这些问题为导向，梳理了我国立法和司法实践对于这些问题的态度及其演变、发展，并展开讨论。

二、问题的产生

（一）境外仲裁机构在中国内地仲裁的含义

总体而言，境外仲裁机构在中国内地进行仲裁主要有两种方式。

一是由境外仲裁机构在我国内地境内设立分支机构，通过跨境商业存在的形式提供仲裁服务。例如，由某境外机构在上海自贸区设立分支机构，从而和内地仲裁机构一样为当事人提供仲裁服务。[1]显然分支机构的设立需要我国政府有关部门依照法定程序和条件予以行政审批或授权。

在此方面，2015年国务院发布《进一步深化中国（上海）自由贸易试验区改革开放方案的通知》（以下简称《通知》），首次提出支持国际知名商事争议解决机构入驻，并将其提升至"推动权益保护制度创新"的层面。[2]此后，境外仲裁机构先后在上海自贸区设立代表处或办公室：2015年11月，香港国际仲裁中心在上海自贸区设立代表处；2016年2月，国际商会仲裁院在上海自贸区设立仲裁办公室；2016年3月，新加坡国际仲裁中心在上海自贸区设立代表处。[3]2019年，国务院出台《中国（上海）自由贸易试验区临港新片区总体方案》，提出允许境外知名仲裁及争议解决机构在临港新片区开展仲裁业务，则标志境外仲裁机构内地仲裁的市场准入和机制改革进一步取得了实质性进展。[4]随着改革的深化，相信境外仲裁机构在中国设立的分支机构管理仲裁案件也会在不远的将来实现。

二是不设立分支机构，通过自然人流动的形式，由境外仲裁机构适用其仲裁规则并在中国内地提供仲裁服务，以解决国际商事争议。既可以是当事人在仲裁协议中直接约定仲裁地在中国，也可以是仲裁协议未明确指定仲裁地，但约定的外国仲裁机构依据其仲裁规则的要求，认为中国是仲裁地的情况。[5]例如，当事人约定将某争议提交国际商会仲裁院依据其仲裁规则在上海仲裁，国际商会虽然未在上海设立分支机构，但可以委派仲裁秘书及相关工作人员协助当事人选定或仲裁院指定的仲裁员在上海完成开庭、审理、合议等仲裁工作；而该仲裁协议也明确约定中国上海为仲裁地，从而将仲裁程序和仲裁裁决置于中国法律和相关法院的管辖之下。本文所讨论的境外仲裁机构在我国

---

[1] 赵秀文：《中国仲裁市场对外开放研究》，载《政法论坛》2009年第6期。

[2] 2015年4月，国务院《进一步深化中国（上海）自由贸易试验区改革开放方案的通知》，第11点。

[3] 李庆明：《境外仲裁机构在中国内地仲裁的法律问题研究》，载《环球法律评论》2016年第3期。

[4] 刘晓红、冯硕：《制度型开放背景下境外仲裁机构内地仲裁的改革因应》，载《法学评论》2020年第3期。

[5] 刘彤、杜菁：《外国仲裁机构在中国仲裁的相关问题探讨》，载《北京仲裁》2017年第2期。

内地仲裁，主要是指这种形式的仲裁实践。

（二）中国仲裁市场的开放

对于境外仲裁机构在中国内地仲裁是否具有可能性的问题，在2015年国务院《通知》出台前，学界曾长期存在诸多不同观点。一种观点认为，中国在2001年加入世界贸易组织（WTO）时没有承诺开放商事仲裁服务；而国内法层面，我国《仲裁法》和《民事诉讼法》长期以来亦未授权允许境外仲裁机构在中国内地提供仲裁服务，故这种实践缺乏国际法和国内法的依据。而该问题解决的关键仍需中国立法机构在《仲裁法》的修订中予以解决。[6] 另一种观点认为，仲裁本身即当事人自愿解决争议的一种替代性纠纷解决途径，即使未开放市场，如果当事人选择某境外仲裁机构在中国仲裁，那么这种操作也不应存在问题。[7]

对于这两种观点，本文认为都应该辩证地看待。对于第一种观点，诚然，虽然中国加入世贸组织的协定书的附件关于法律服务的内容没有明文提及境外商事仲裁机构提供仲裁服务的内容，而我国《仲裁法》和《民事诉讼法》也并未直接对此规定。但是也应看到：至少中国法律对此并不存在禁止性规定。虽然境外仲裁机构在我国内地设立分支机构并开展仲裁业务需要有关部门的审批，但是跨境自然人流动形式的仲裁活动依据是当事人的仲裁协议，应属于当事人意思自治的范畴。[8] 在私法领域，商事仲裁的权力依据来自当事人将争议提交仲裁解决的合意，源于当事人的意思表示，属于民事主体意思自治，无须得到行政授权。在不违反法律和行政法规关于效力性的强制性规定、我国司法主权及公序良俗时，没有理由不允许其存在。此外，允许境外仲裁机构在我国内地提供仲裁服务，也可以促进我国仲裁实践与国际仲裁接轨，实现争议解决途径的多元化，并发展我国涉外法律市场。

第二种观点强调当事人的合意可以授权境外仲裁机构在我国进行仲裁，但

---

[6] 李健：《外国仲裁机构在中国内地仲裁不可行》，载《法学》2008年第12期（认为国际商事仲裁属于商事性的法律服务，而非公共服务）；赵秀文：《中国仲裁市场对外开放研究》，载《政法论坛》2009年第6期；刘彤、杜菁：《外国仲裁机构在中国仲裁的相关问题探讨》，载《北京仲裁》2017年第2期。

[7] 赵秀文：《中国仲裁市场对外开放研究》，载《政法论坛》2009年第6期；刘彤、杜菁：《外国仲裁机构在中国仲裁的相关问题探讨》，载《北京仲裁》2017年第2期。

[8] 刘彤、杜菁：《外国仲裁机构在中国仲裁的相关问题探讨》，载《北京仲裁》2017年第2期。

是同时也需看到，境外仲裁机构在中国仲裁仍需得到仲裁地法院的支持和认可，否则难免成为"无本之木"，从而难以得到长远发展。这可以体现在以下三个主要方面。一是当事人约定提交境外仲裁机构在中国仲裁的仲裁协议的效力可能需要我国法院的认可和确认。否则一旦被法院确认为协议无效，如果一方当事人向我国法院提起诉讼，可能会实质性"剥夺"仲裁庭对该争议的管辖权。二是境外仲裁机构在我国作出的仲裁裁决可能需要得到我国法院的承认和执行。如果不能实现这点，那么输掉仲裁的当事方可以拒不履行裁决义务，进而"剥夺"仲裁程序的"胜利果实"。三是对于仲裁程序可能出现的严重影响程序公正和实体正义的事项（如仲裁员带有明显偏见、存在受贿、文书送达出现重大纰漏、一方当事人合理陈述案情的权利严重受侵害等），可能需要仲裁地法院对该裁决行使审查和监督职能，在符合法定条件时进行撤销。值得注意的是，这些方面，对于境外仲裁机构依靠自然人流通形式在我国提供的仲裁服务而言依然适用。而对于设立分支机构的方式提供仲裁，则面临更直接的市场准入问题，显然需要国家有关主管机关和部门的审批或授权。

总之，境外仲裁机构通过自然人跨境流动形式在我国内地进行仲裁属于当事人意思自治的私法领域，在不违反我国法律的前提下应无须行政审批。但是，该形式的实践在中国仲裁的市场中能走多远、能在多大程度上高效地解决跨境争议，不仅依赖于当事人的自主选择，而且在很大程度上还依赖于中国立法和司法的"配套机制"的保驾护航。因此，仲裁市场对外开放程度越高，立法和司法越能为境外机构在中国仲裁提供法律支持，这种争议解决的实践则可在越大程度上发挥最大功效，并不断发展、普及和完善。

（三）裁决的分类和困境的产生

随着境外仲裁机构在我国内地开展仲裁实践的发展，在裁决的承认和执行层面上产生的重要法律问题是：如何判断其裁决的法律性质，如何认定裁决的籍属，以及我国法院应该适用什么法律依据来对裁决进行司法审查。

《仲裁法》生效长期以来，我国并未如《纽约公约》和国际商事仲裁惯例一样依据仲裁裁决作出地（即"仲裁地"）来认定仲裁裁决的国籍问题，而是采取了"仲裁机构所在地"为标准，将仲裁裁决分为外国仲裁裁决、国内仲裁裁决、涉外仲裁裁决（包括涉港澳台地区的仲裁裁决）三大类，对每一类均适用不同的法律依据进行司法审查。[9] 虽然在大部分国内仲裁机构的仲裁实践中,是否适用"仲裁地"的法律概念似乎无关紧要,但在涉及境外仲裁机构在我国内地仲裁裁决的司法程序中(包括裁决的执行、司法审查),适用"仲裁地"还是"仲裁机构所在地"的标准,会让法院对该类裁决的国籍作出不同的认定,从而导致在此问题上适用不同的法律依据。

所谓的"外国仲裁裁决",按照我国《民事诉讼法》第304条规定,是指在中华人民共和国领域外作出的发生法律效力的仲裁裁决,主要依据《纽约公约》的规定或者按照互惠原则予以承认和执行。涉港澳台地区的仲裁机构作出的仲裁裁决,应按照双边互相承认和执行仲裁裁决的安排予以承认和执行,包括《最高人民法院关于内地与香港特别行政区相互执行仲裁裁决的安排》(以下简称《关于内地与香港相互执行仲裁裁决的安排》)、《最高人民法院关于内地与澳门特别行政区相互认可和执行仲裁裁决的安排》和《最高人民法院关于认可和执行台湾地区仲裁裁决的规定》。[10] 所谓的"涉外仲裁裁决",是指"中国国际经济贸易仲裁委员会及其分会、中国海事仲裁委员会以及依照仲裁法规定组建的仲裁委员会作出的具有涉外因素的仲裁裁决"。[11] 其执行依据是《民事诉讼法》第291条、《仲裁法》第71条的规定。而无论是对国际仲裁裁决还是对涉外仲裁裁决,我国法院均只审查裁决存在的程序问题(如仲裁协议的效力瑕疵、仲裁程序瑕疵等事项),不审查实体问题。[12] 所谓的"国内仲裁裁决",指的是我国的仲裁机构(包括涉外仲裁机构)作出的没有涉外因素的仲裁裁决,其执行的依据主要是《民事诉讼法》第248条和《仲裁法》第63条的规定,法院在司法审查中需审查裁决的实体问题和程序问题。

境外仲裁机构在中国内地仲裁的裁决性质在我国法律的这种分类下曾一度面临较为尴尬的境地。首先,我国《仲裁法》以仲裁机构所在地为标准来判断仲裁裁决的国籍。根据此标准,因为境外仲裁机构的机构所在地在境外

---

[9] 李庆明:《境外仲裁机构在中国内地仲裁的法律问题研究》,载《环球法律评论》2016年第3期;李霁:《论国际商会示范仲裁条款在中国的效力——实证分析和理论探讨》,载《北京仲裁》2007年第2期。

[10] 法释〔2000〕3号、法释〔2007〕17号、法释〔2015〕14号。

[11] 最高人民法院《关于人民法院处理涉外仲裁及外国仲裁案件的若干规定(征求意见稿)》第38条。

[12] 李霁:《论国际商会示范仲裁条款在中国的效力——实证分析和理论探讨》,载《北京仲裁》2007年第2期。

（其亦未在我国境内设立分支机构），境外仲裁机构在我国内地仲裁的仲裁裁决显然难以认定为我国国内裁决。

其次，境外仲裁机构通过跨境自然人流动形式在我国境内作出的仲裁裁决显然也不属于"涉外仲裁裁决"，因为境外仲裁机构并非在我国依法组建的仲裁机构。总之，不论是"国内仲裁裁决"还是"涉外仲裁裁决"，依照《民事诉讼法》和《仲裁法》的规定，都指由我国成立的仲裁委员会在我国境内作出的仲裁裁决，不包括境外仲裁机构在内地作出的裁决。

最后，《纽约公约》项下的外国裁决是指在被请求承认与执行仲裁裁决的国家以外的领土内作出的仲裁裁决。[13]这显然也不包括境外仲裁机构在中国内地仲裁的裁决，因为其裁决是在我国境内作出。《纽约公约》还规定：对于依照缔约国法律不被视为是国内裁决的仲裁裁决（arbitral awards not considered as domestic awards），缔约国也应承认和执行（即应执行"非内国裁决"）。[14]公约对"非内国裁决"没有直接定义，国际上也尚不存在统一的认识，故"非内国裁决"的判断主要取决于被申请执行地之法律。[15]而中国法下，境外仲裁机构在内地仲裁的裁决，既不是我国裁决（因为我国裁决是我国仲裁委员会在我国境内作出），也不是在我国境外作出的《纽约公约》项下的"外国裁决"，故应认定为《纽约公约》项下的"非内国裁决"。[16]

而问题在于：依据全国人大常委会关于我国加入《纽约公约》时曾作出"互惠保留声明"："中华人民共和国只在互惠的基础上对在另一缔约国领土内作出的仲裁裁决的承认和执行适用该公约。"[17]因为境外仲裁机构在我国内地作出的裁决显然不属于在"另一缔约国领土内作出的仲裁裁决"，故在《纽约公约》项下申请承认和执行该类仲裁裁决的法律依据阙如。

由此，该类裁决能否在我国法律下被法院承认和执行，显然面临法律的

---

[13] 《纽约公约》第1条第1款。

[14] 《纽约公约》第1条第1款。

[15] ICCA's Guide to the Interpretation of the 1958 New York Convention, 20-21, https://cdn.arbitration-icca.org/s3fs-public/document/media_document/judges_guide_nyc_english_2018_reprint.pdf.

[16] 赵秀文：《论非内国仲裁项下的浮动仲裁与〈纽约公约〉项下的非内国裁决》，载《国际经济法学刊》2009年第16卷第1期，第7—8页。

[17] 参见1986年《全国人民代表大会常务委员会关于我国加入〈承认及执行外国仲裁裁决公约〉的决定》。

不确定性所带来的困境。时任最高人民法院副院长的万鄂湘曾就此指出:"国外的仲裁机构在中国内地裁决的案件,是属于国外裁决还是国内裁决,目前还没有明确规定,这将必然导致裁决执行时的麻烦。"[18]

三、长期以来的我国学界争议和典型司法案例

(一)学者观点:"非内国裁决"和"涉外裁决"

就此问题,我国学者展开了长期的学术争论,大体上,可分为认为该类判决属于"非内国裁决"和"涉外裁决"两派观点,就是否应该承认和执行观点又有细分。总体上存在三种具有代表性的典型观点。

第一种观点认为,境外仲裁机构在我国内地仲裁的裁决,属于《纽约公约》项下的"非内国裁决",应当依据《纽约公约》第1条第1款的规定予以承认和执行。虽然我国在《纽约公约》项下作出了互惠保留(故该类裁决不能通过我国互惠保留的规定予以承认和执行),但是《纽约公约》第1条第1款规定:针对执行地国按照当地法律不认为是在其境内作出的当地裁决的非内国裁决,公约对其承认与执行同样适用。[19]换言之,"我们认为可以适用公约承认与执行非内国裁决的法律依据当然不是互惠保留声明,而是《纽约公约》本身的规定"。[20]

具体而言,鉴于公约所适用的仲裁裁决包括"外国仲裁裁决"和"非内国裁决","互惠保留"的效力应限于《纽约公约》项下的"外国仲裁裁决"而言,强调的是"缔约国"之间的互惠(reciprocity),但对"非内国裁决"并不适用。否则,如果认为只要缔约国作出"互惠保留"即可完全排除"非内国裁决"的适用,则《纽约公约》对"非内国裁决"的规定会变得毫无意义,因为大多数缔约国均作了"互惠保留"的声明。[21]

第二种观点认为,虽然国际商会仲裁院在中国内地仲裁的裁决属于《纽约公约》项下的"非内国裁决",但是我国法院并没有义务对其予以承认和执行。按照国际条约解释的基本规则,缔约国对条约的保留应理解为是对整个

---

[18] 万鄂湘:《〈纽约公约〉在中国的司法实践》,载《法律适用》2009年第3期。
[19] 《纽约公约》第1条第1款。
[20] 赵秀文:《中国仲裁市场对外开放研究》,载《政法论坛》2009年第6期。
[21] 刘晓红:《非内国仲裁裁决的理论与实证分析》,载《法学杂志》2013年第5期。

条约适用对象的保留，而不是对条约适用对象某一部分（即"外国裁决"）的保留。既然我国在《纽约公约》项下作出互惠保留，即是针对"外国裁决"和"非内国裁决"的保留，故理应排除"非内国裁决"。因此，我国在《纽约公约》项下没有义务执行"非内国裁决"。但是也应看到，假如我国法院在某些案件中执行了此类裁决，既不能推导出我国在《纽约公约》项下存在该义务，也并非与我国在《纽约公约》项下的义务相矛盾：因为"无义务"不等于"不能做"。换言之，我国法院在此类案件中享有自主决定是否承认与执行裁决的自由裁量权（discretion），具有灵活性；至于是否选择承认与执行，一个重要的考量因素是我国的公共政策。[22]

第三种观点认为，此类仲裁裁决应属于中国法下的"涉外裁决"。境外仲裁机构在内地仲裁的仲裁协议中，当事人约定中国内地为仲裁地，故应当以仲裁地为标准判断仲裁裁决的国籍。依据仲裁地判断仲裁裁决国籍符合国际仲裁的通常惯例，也为大多数国家的司法实践所普遍接受。而该类裁决本身具有涉外因素，应依据《仲裁法》和《民事诉讼法》对"涉外仲裁裁决"执行的相关规定对其进行承认和执行。同时，我国法院作为仲裁地法院，有权力对该类涉外仲裁裁决行使司法监督，享有依照法定条件和程序撤销裁决的权力。[23]

就此问题，学界尚未达成一致。问题的关键在于应当依据"仲裁机构所在地"还是"仲裁地"标准来判定此类裁决的国籍，以及宜对《纽约公约》项下的"互惠保留"作宽泛的广义解释还是严格的狭义解释。

（二）我国初期的相关司法实践

1. 2008年宁波工艺品案

在此问题上的标志性案件，是2008年的宁波市中级人民法院审理的瑞士德高钢铁公司（DUFERCO）与宁波市工艺品进出口有限公司合同争议案（以下简称宁波工艺品案）。本案中，瑞士德高钢铁公司以宁波市工艺品进出口有限公司（以下简称宁波工艺品公司）为被申请人，向法院申请承认与执行国

---

[22] 吕炳斌：《论外国仲裁机构到我国境内仲裁的问题——兼析我国加入〈纽约公约〉时的保留》，载《法治研究》2010年第10期。

[23] 宋连斌、王珺：《国际商会在中国内地仲裁：准入、裁决国籍及执行——由宁波中院的一份裁定谈起》，载《西北大学学报（哲学社会科学版）》2011年第41卷第3期。

际商会第14006/MS/JB/JEM号仲裁裁决案。本案中，双方当事人2003年在宁波签订了买卖合同，其中仲裁条款规定，将争议"提交给仲裁地位于中国的国际商会仲裁委员会"进行仲裁。仲裁程序中，国际商会仲裁院确认北京为仲裁地。之后，申请人瑞士德高钢铁公司提起请求承认与执行仲裁裁决的司法程序。[24]

宁波市中级人民法院经审理后认为：国际商会仲裁院在北京作出的仲裁裁决属于《纽约公约》项下的"非内国裁决"，应依据《纽约公约》裁定执行该仲裁裁决。值得注意的是，该院并没有讨论我国在《纽约公约》项下所作出的"互惠保留"的相关规定，只是提到"本案不存在拒绝承认和执行所涉仲裁裁决的理由"，也没有提到不将该裁定认定为"外国裁决"的理由。[25]而本案"非内国裁决"的认定，也引发了我国学界对此问题的广泛讨论。[26]

此外，依据最高人民法院确立的"报送制度"，下级法院仅在对涉外或国外仲裁裁决裁定不予执行前，须报送辖区内高级人民法院审查，如果后者同意不予执行，则须报送最高人民法院批准。[27]因为该案最终裁定承认并执行涉案裁决，故宁波市中级人民法院并没有将本案上报至最高人民法院审核，后者的正式态度未知。最高人民法院并未就此问题的司法审查作出具有指导意义的司法解释。

2. 其他将国际商会仲裁院在法国以外作出裁决认定为法国裁决的案件

本阶段我国法院对境外仲裁机构在我国作出裁决的国籍认定并不一致。在宁波工艺品案之外，司法实践中不乏将国际商会仲裁院在法国以外的地区作出的仲裁裁决认定为法国裁决的情况，即视为《纽约公约》项下的"外国裁决"（而非"非内国裁决"）。

例如，2004年，在山西天利实业有限公司案（以下简称山西天利案）中，最高人民法院在复函中认为，该案属于国际商会仲裁院在香港仲裁，因为国

---

[24] 浙江省宁波市中级人民法院民事裁定书，（2008）甬仲监字第4号。参见赵秀文：《从宁波工艺品公司案看我国法院对涉外仲裁协议的监督》，载《时代法学》2010年第8卷第5期。

[25] 浙江省宁波市中级人民法院民事裁定书，（2008）甬仲监字第4号。

[26] 参见前文所述三种不同代表性观点。

[27] 最高人民法院《关于人民法院处理与涉外仲裁及外国仲裁事项有关问题的通知》，法发〔1995〕18号。

际商会仲裁院属于在法国设立的仲裁机构，因此应适用《纽约公约》的规定进行承认和执行的司法审查，而不应适用《关于内地与香港相互执行仲裁裁决的安排》。[28] 可以看出，此时最高人民法院判断该仲裁裁决的标准在于仲裁机构所在地，因为国际商会仲裁院是总部设在法国的仲裁机构，故其作出的裁决应属于法国裁决，即使该程序的仲裁地在香港。[29]

此外，在 2003 年成都华龙汽车公司案中，当事人签订的仲裁协议约定："根据国际商会仲裁院的仲裁规则在洛杉矶进行"仲裁。尽管仲裁协议约定美国洛杉矶为仲裁地，但成都市中级人民法院认为，国际商会仲裁院在美国洛杉矶作出的裁决应当属于法国裁决（而非美国裁决），并依据《纽约公约》承认并执行了该裁决。[30]

（三）问题、困境与成因

总体而言，可以看出在这一时期我国学界和司法实践在对境外仲裁机构在我国内地仲裁裁决的性质认定上出现了较大争议，并未形成统一的标准和广泛的共识。究其原因，首先在于对仲裁裁决国籍的认定标准。虽然国际惯例和大部分国家的司法实践采纳了"仲裁地"标准，但"仲裁地"在我国相关立法中却是一个陌生的概念。这是因为我国《仲裁法》并没有规定什么是"仲裁地"，而是创设、适用了"仲裁委员会（机构）所在地"这一法律概念。[31] 而《民事诉讼法》依据仲裁机构的所在地和涉外性关于"国内裁决"、"涉外裁决"和"外国裁决"的划分方法并不合理，也欠缺周延性。[32]

而我国现行立法采用的"仲裁机构所在地"的判断标准，与《纽约公约》和多数国家采用的"仲裁地"标注的主流实践相左，导致我国法院在司法实践中对仲裁裁决国籍的认定存在与国际仲裁实践的偏差。同时，还在仲裁案

---

[28]《最高人民法院关于不予执行国际商会仲裁院 10334/AMW/BWD/TE 最终裁决一案的请示的复函》，(2004) 民四他字第 6 号。

[29] 杨炎龙、颜鸿杰、王骁：《仲裁地的概念及裁决的执行》，载《商法（China Business Law Journal）》2017 年 10 月 16 日。

[30] TH&T 国际公司与成都华龙汽车配件有限公司申请承认和执行国际商会国际仲裁院裁决案，(2002) 成民初字第 531 号裁定书。

[31] 参见《仲裁法》。参见瑞生国际律师事务所争议摘要《仲裁地的概念及裁决的执行》。

[32] 宋连斌、王珺：《国际商会在中国内地仲裁：准入、裁决国籍及执行——由宁波中院的一份裁定谈起》，载《西北大学学报（哲学社会科学版）》2011 年第 41 卷第 3 期。

件司法审查中产生一些难以克服的实践难题,[33]造成境外仲裁机构在中国内地仲裁的案件中对仲裁裁决国籍的认定上的不确定性,并容易因概念的混淆而影响裁决执行的法律依据,由此产生承认和执行裁决的困境。例如,在宁波工艺品案和山西天利案中,宁波市中级人民法院和最高人民法院在认定裁决国籍上,适用了不同的认定标准。

其次,争议的关键还在于对《纽约公约》项下"互惠保留"的解释和适用究竟应当从严还是从宽,以及我国法律中对《纽约公约》项下的"非内国裁决"的认定标准及执行问题。对此,我国法律均未作出明确规定,尚依赖于我国法律制度和最高人民法院相关司法解释的规定。整体看来,宁波工艺品案中宁波市中级人民法院首次承认与执行"非内国裁决"属于孤立的个案(事实上,该案也似乎是唯一一个将该类裁决作为"非内国裁决"执行的案例),[34]可能不宜"夸大其对我国仲裁和司法实践的普遍指导意义"。[35]

同时,虽然宁波工艺品案因为将国际商会仲裁院在我国内地仲裁裁决作为《纽约公约》项下"非内国裁决"予以承认和执行得到了许多我国学者的认同,[36]但深入分析后可以看出这种方式依然存在诸多问题。

首先,将当事人约定在我国境内进行仲裁的案件认定为"非内国裁决",最大的问题是忽视了当事人约定仲裁地的意思表示,从而与国际商事仲裁的国际惯例和普遍实践相左。国际仲裁的一般性原则是仲裁地决定了仲裁裁决的"国籍",例如,当事人选择在巴黎仲裁,则该仲裁程序所产生的裁决应为法国仲裁裁决。在国际仲裁中,仲裁地是指"仲裁的法律地或司法管辖地,它决定了管理仲裁程序所适用的法律为仲裁地法(lex arbitri),以及仲裁地法院对仲裁的支持管理或监督介入的范围和程度",更多地属于一个法律上而非

---

[33] 万鄂湘、于喜富:《论仲裁地的概念及其法律功能》,载《中国仲裁与司法》2004年第2期。

[34] 曾有记者就此问题询问过最高人民法院审理此类案件的法官,后者答复宁波中级法院属于个案,并不代表中国立法及最高司法机关对类似裁决的态度。参见王婧:《外国仲裁机构或将撕开最高仲裁市场一角》,载《法治周末》2009年6月25日。

[35] 刘晓红:《非内国仲裁裁决的理论与实证论析》,载《法学杂志》2013年第5期。

[36] 赵秀文:《中国仲裁市场对外开放研究》,载《政法论坛》2009年第6期;刘晓红:《非内国仲裁裁决的理论与实证论析》,载《法学杂志》2013年第5期;李雯:《论国际商会示范仲裁条款在中国的效力——实证分析和理论探讨》,载《北京仲裁》2007年第2期;刘彤、杜菁:《外国仲裁机构在中国仲裁的相关问题探讨》,载《北京仲裁》2017年第2期。

纯地理上的概念。因此，既然当事人选择在我国内地仲裁，则基于当事人的[37]这种意思表示，应该将该仲裁裁决视为受我国法律管辖、支配、管理及监督的仲裁裁决，即成为中国法下的仲裁裁决（同时具有涉外因素）。而将其裁决认定为"非内国裁决"，明显不符合以仲裁地判定裁决国籍的基础性内在逻辑，也与国际仲裁的普遍惯例不符。

其次，如前文所述，将该类裁决认定为"非内国裁决"，随之而来的问题就是如何解决《纽约公约》项下我国所作"互惠保留"的法律解释问题。对此，学界没有定论，最高人民法院或相关立法机关也没有给出具体的意见以解决此问题。虽然宁波工艺品案作出了承认和执行该裁定的决定，但该案的法律论证和适用并不清楚，对其他法院也没有必然的约束力，而且与最高人民法院在相关决定中将国际商会仲裁院在法国以外作出裁定认定为法国裁定的判断标准相左。因此，该案恐怕并不具有普遍的参考或指导意义。在司法实践中，不同地区、层级的法院可能对裁决的国籍、对《纽约公约》项下的"互惠保留"及"非内国裁决"存在不同理解，从而在法律适用和法律解释上导致存在不确定性和不可预见性，这不仅会导致当事人依据类似仲裁条款获得的仲裁裁决仍存在不被认可或无法执行的风险，从而造成个案中此类裁定面临的法律困境，而且也难以给外界稳定的预期，无益于中国仲裁的整体形象。

最后，将此类裁决认定为"非内国裁决"，会造成我国法院对当事人约定在我国境内作出的仲裁程序和裁决丧失审查、监督的管辖权，从而造成该类案件对裁定行使撤销职权的仲裁地法院的阙如。国际仲裁中，通常由仲裁地法院对仲裁裁决行使审查、监督的管辖权，其法院可以有权依法撤销该裁决。而此类案件中，一方面，当事人约定仲裁地为中国内地；另一方面，我国法院不认为该类裁决属于我国法律管辖下的仲裁裁决，会导致实际上没有法院对裁决行使审查、监督的管辖权。例如，国际商会仲裁院在我国内地仲裁的案件，法国法院会认为仲裁地在中国内地，故其无权撤销该裁决。而中国法院也会认为该裁决并非我国法律下作出的裁决，故不会行使审查、监督的管辖权。

有学者指出，将该类裁决认定为"非内国裁决"，并不是我国法院不能对此裁决"行使撤销权的司法监督"，而是属于"我国法院依照我国现行法律主

---

[37] 参见瑞生国际律师事务所争议摘要《仲裁地的概念及裁决的执行》。

动放弃此项司法监督"。[38] 如果是为了保障该类仲裁裁决的承认和执行而作出的利弊权衡（trade-off），未免代价过大而得不偿失。

此外，在此类案件中，倘若出现了严重的程序问题，例如仲裁协议的效力问题、仲裁员对一方当事人带有明显的偏见从而影响其客观性、出现严重的程序性文书送达问题从而影响一方当事人合理地陈述案情的权利，也不存在相应的法院可以对仲裁裁决行使撤销权。此时，如果胜诉当事人同时向多个司法辖区申请执行该裁决，则败诉方并不能向对裁决的仲裁地法院申请撤销该裁决，这可能会造成十分严重的不利后果。

总之，宁波工艺品案中法院将该类裁决认定为"非内国裁决"的认定，属于立法未完善之前、出于便于该类裁决承认和执行的权宜之计，不能从根本上解决其国籍认定问题。[39] 此外，还会带来上述的诸多问题。比较而言，依据"仲裁地"标准认定此类裁决的国籍，从而将其认定为中国法下的"涉外裁决"，不仅有利于对裁决的承认和执行，还可以避免这些问题，因此是个性价比更高的"更优解"。

四、我国法院承认和执行境外仲裁机构在内地裁决的新发展

（一）我国法院从"仲裁机构所在地"向"仲裁地"标准的逐渐转变

在2004年山西天利案之后，我国法院在认定仲裁裁决的国籍问题上呈现出一种逐渐明朗的趋势：即从早期依赖"仲裁机构所在地"的标准逐渐转变为依据"仲裁地"作为判断标准。[40]

在2006年邦基农贸新加坡私人有限公司案（以下简称邦基农贸案）中，当事人选择将争议提交国际油、油籽和油脂协会（FOSFA）在伦敦仲裁，最高人民法院的复函中认为FOSFA的仲裁员在英国伦敦所作出的仲裁裁决属于英国裁决，对其裁决的承认与执行应适用《纽约公约》的规定。[41]

---

[38] 赵秀文：《中国仲裁市场对外开放研究》，载《政法论坛》2009年第6期。

[39] 宋连斌、王珺：《国际商会在中国内地仲裁：准入、裁决国籍及执行——由宁波中院的一份裁定谈起》，载《西北大学学报（哲学社会科学版）》2011年第41卷第3期。

[40] 宋连斌、王珺：《国际商会在中国内地仲裁：准入、裁决国籍及执行——由宁波中院的一份裁定谈起》，载《西北大学学报（哲学社会科学版）》2011年第41卷第3期。

[41] 《最高人民法院关于邦基农贸新加坡私人有限公司申请承认和执行英国仲裁裁决一案的请示的复函》，（2006）民四他字第41号。

在 2008 年济南永宁制药股份有限公司案（以下简称济南永宁案）中，当事人在合同的仲裁条款中约定，将争议"提交巴黎国际商会仲裁委员会，根据该会的仲裁程序暂行规则进行仲裁"。山东省高级人民法院在对裁决申请承认和执行的司法审查中认为，因作出涉案裁决的国际商会仲裁院确定法国巴黎为仲裁地，故裁决应视为在法国作出，本院应依据《纽约公约》的规定对裁决的申请承认和执行进行审查。[42]

在这两个案件中，最高人民法院和山东省高院在裁定中并没有提及仲裁机构所在地，而是均强调了仲裁地，并据此认定裁决的国籍，此判断方法显然区别于山西天利案中依赖"仲裁机构所在地"以判断裁决籍属的标准。

2009 年，最高人民法院公布了《最高人民法院关于香港仲裁裁决在内地执行的有关问题的通知》，首次提出应以仲裁地来确认仲裁裁决的国籍，规定当事人向我国法院申请执行在香港作出的临时仲裁裁决、国际商会仲裁院等国外仲裁机构在香港作出的仲裁裁决的，应按照《关于内地与香港相互执行仲裁裁决的安排》（而非《纽约公约》）的规定进行司法审查。[43] 由此可看出，针对国际商会仲裁院在香港作出的裁决，最高人民法院在该通知中明确指出，应采纳"仲裁地"标准认定其属于香港裁决，从而正式改变了山西天利案中依据"仲裁机构所在地"认定其为法国裁决的做法。值得注意的是，该通知作为最高人民法院发布的规范性文件，对全国各级法院处理同类案件中认定类似仲裁裁决的国籍问题提供了明确指引。但是同时也应看到，该文件的适用范围局限于在香港作出的仲裁裁决，最高人民法院并没有明确指出所有境外进行的仲裁产生的裁决均须按照仲裁地标准认定国籍，更没有说明对境外仲裁机构在我国内地作出的裁决也应按此标准认定为我国的裁决。

在该通知出台之后，最高人民法院在对广东省高院（2010）粤高法民四他字第 2 号判决请示的复函中，同样适用"仲裁地"标准，将国际商会仲裁院在新加坡作出的裁决，认定为新加坡裁决（而非法国裁决）。[44] 虽然这裁决并非境

---

[42]《最高人民法院关于不予承认和执行国际商会仲裁院仲裁裁决的请示的复函》,（2008）民四他字第 11 号。

[43] 2009 年《最高人民法院关于香港仲裁裁决在内地执行的有关问题的通知》。

[44]《最高人民法院关于申请人 DMT 有限公司（法国）与被申请人潮州市华业包装材料有限公司、被申请人潮安县华业包装材料有限公司申请承认和执行外国仲裁裁决一案请示的复函》（2010 年 10 月 12 日）。

外仲裁机构在中国内地作出，但最高人民法院的认定标准显然是"仲裁地"标准（而非"仲裁机构所在地"标准）。与之类似的，还有最高人民法院关于不予执行国际商会仲裁院第18295/CYK号仲裁裁决案。该案中，当事人向泰州市中级人民法院申请执行国际商会仲裁院指定的独任仲裁员在香港作出的裁决，最高人民法院在复函中确认了在香港作出的仲裁裁决应当依照《关于内地与香港相互执行仲裁裁决的安排》进行司法审查，而非依据《纽约公约》。[45]

近期的案件还表明，针对于贸仲委境外仲裁分支机构在境外作出的裁决，部分地方法院在司法实践中认为该通知关于"仲裁地"的判断裁决籍属标准同样适用。例如，在2016年12月，南京市中级人民法院在我国内地首例执行贸仲委香港仲裁中心在香港作出的仲裁裁决，依据《关于内地与香港相互执行仲裁裁决的安排》的规定对裁决进行司法审查，并将贸仲委香港仲裁中心管理的仲裁程序作出的仲裁裁决作为香港裁决进行审查。[46]这表明，如果当事人选择中国内地仲裁机构在境外（香港）仲裁，部分地方法院依然选择以仲裁地（而非仲裁机构总部所在地）作为判断仲裁国籍的依据。

可见，在这一阶段，我国最高法院和地方法院的司法实践中明显注重以"仲裁地"为标准确定境外（包括香港）作出的仲裁裁决的国籍，明显有别于上一阶段依赖"仲裁机构所在地"（特别是仲裁机构总部的所在地）确立裁决籍属的标准。我国法院在当事人约定在伦敦、巴黎、香港由国际商会仲裁院管理仲裁的裁决中，均改变了山西天利案的做法，在此方面开始与国际仲裁的主流实践接轨。但是，这些案件并没有直接涉及境外仲裁机构在我国内地仲裁的情形。

（二）2020年布兰特伍德案

在2020年广州市中级人民法院审理的布兰特伍德案中，我国法院首次在受理申请承认和执行仲裁裁决的民事裁定书中明确提出：境外仲裁机构在内地仲裁作出裁决可以视为我国的"涉外裁决"。本案中，合同当事人签订的合同的仲裁条款约定，将争议"提交国际商会仲裁委员会"在项目所在地（即广州）进行仲裁。2014年国际商会仲裁院指定独任仲裁员作出案号为18929/CYK的仲裁裁决。2012年，广州市中级人民法院作出裁定确认涉案仲裁条款

---

[45]《最高人民法院关于不予执行国际商会仲裁院第18295/CYK号仲裁裁决一案请示的复函》。

[46]《贸仲香港裁决获内地人民法院强制执行》，载中国国际贸易促进委员会广西分会及广西国际商会网站，https://www.ccpitgx.org/webcpitgx/2017/yujing_0109/9588.html，最后访问时间：2022年8月10日。

有效。[47]2015 年，申请人布兰特伍德公司向广州市中级人民法院申请承认并执行该裁决。本案中申请人认为，根据中国法院以仲裁机构所在地为仲裁裁决国籍地的司法实践，因裁决为总部设在巴黎的国际商会仲裁院作出，应属于法国仲裁裁决，按照《纽约公约》进行承认和执行。而如果法院认为该裁决是由国际商会仲裁院在香港的分支机构作出，也应依据《关于内地与香港相互执行仲裁裁决的安排》予以认可并执行。[48]

2020 年该院作出裁定，认为该裁决是国际商会仲裁院指定的独任仲裁员组成的仲裁庭在仲裁地广州作出的裁决，属外国仲裁机构在中国内地作出的仲裁裁决，可以视为中国"涉外仲裁裁决"。故本案不应作为"外国裁决"进行承认和执行，申请人应参照《民事诉讼法》第 273 条（现为第 290 条）的规定申请执行，而非《纽约公约》或《关于内地与香港相互执行仲裁裁决的安排》，属于援引的法律依据错误。经多次释明后申请人均未纠正，该院据此驳回申请，并指出申请人可依法另行提起执行申请。[49]

（三）本阶段我国法院司法态度之评析

综上所述，相比于上一个阶段，本阶段我国法院在处理仲裁裁决的国籍认定时明显呈现出一种趋势，逐渐改变了过去依赖"仲裁机构所在地"的标准，转而采用与国际仲裁实践接轨的"仲裁地"标准。对于当事人约定在国外仲裁的情形，最高人民法院和山东省高院在邦基农贸案和济南永宁案中开始以仲裁地（而非仲裁机构所在地）为标准判断裁决国籍。对仲裁地为香港的仲裁，通过最高人民法院《关于香港仲裁裁决在内地执行的有关问题的通知》到 2016 年南京市中级人民法院执行贸仲委香港仲裁中心作出的仲裁裁决，我国法院对该类仲裁裁决的国籍认定逐渐统一标准，采取仲裁地的判断标准逐渐清晰。而这股趋势更在 2020 年布兰特伍德案中得到彰显，至此，我国法院首次在民事裁定书中明确：对境外仲裁机构在我国境内作出的仲裁裁决，也应该采取仲裁地标准认定其国籍，这进一步拓宽了以仲裁地标准判断裁决国

---

[47] （2011）穗中法仲异字第 11 号民事裁定书。

[48] 王长生：《从"龙利得案"到"布兰特伍德案"：境外仲裁机构在中国内地仲裁的突破》，载微信公众号"仲裁研究院"2020 年 10 月 23 日。

[49] 王长生：《从"龙利得案"到"布兰特伍德案"：境外仲裁机构在中国内地仲裁的突破》，载微信公众号"仲裁研究院"2020 年 10 月 23 日。

籍的案件范围。

值得注意的是，布兰特伍德案具有特殊的标志性意义。第一，该案中，我国法院首次在民事裁定书中明确境外仲裁机构在中国内地作出具有涉外性质的裁决，可以视为我国的涉外仲裁裁决。对于此类裁决在申请承认和执行中面临的困境，该案无疑是我国司法实践的一个重大突破和最新发展，有利于减轻该问题在法律上的不确定性和风险。第二，该决定的内在逻辑在于坚持仲裁地标准认定裁决国籍，体现了对当事人约定仲裁地意思表示的尊重：既然当事人约定中国内地为仲裁地，即作出了选择中国法支配仲裁程序和仲裁裁决的意思表示，故应当属于我国法律管辖的裁决（而该类裁决又具有涉外因素，故可以视作我国涉外仲裁裁决）。这种坚持仲裁地判定裁决国籍的标准，不仅尊重了当事人进行仲裁的意思表示，也符合国际仲裁的普遍实践和主流观点。第三，认定为我国涉外仲裁裁决，没有遵循宁波工艺品案提出的"非内国裁决"观点，也避免了将裁决认定为"非内国裁决"可能存在的诸多问题。前文所述，将该类裁决认定为"非内国裁决"不仅有悖于国际仲裁的通常实践，也可能因《纽约公约》项下的"互惠保留"声明产生执行的不确定性和困境，还可能造成对该类裁决进行司法监督的管辖问题，意味着我国法院主动地放弃作为仲裁地的法院对撤销裁决享有的司法管辖权。涉外裁决的认定，则可以在很大程度上解决这些问题。第四，将该类裁决视为涉外仲裁裁决，也意味着明确了对其进行司法审查的法律依据，即可以比照《民事诉讼法》第291条关于"我国涉外仲裁机构作出的裁决"的规定进行司法审查。该标准主要审查程序问题（类似于《纽约公约》第5条的规定），相比于国内裁决审查程序和实体问题的标准，显然更有利于裁决的执行，故可以提高该类裁决在我国得到承认和执行的效率和概率。

但是同时也应看到，布兰特伍德案仅是广州市中级人民法院作出的一个民事裁定，并非最高人民法院作出的批复或具有普遍指导意义的司法解释。考虑到我国不同地区和层级的法院不必然会直接遵循该案的决定，因此，严格意义上，涉外仲裁机构在我国内地仲裁裁决的法律性质、国籍的认定、承认和执行的法律依据上依然存在"法律空白"。对此，最根本的长远之计还是修改《仲裁法》，以全面坚持仲裁地原则认定此类裁决的籍属。同时，考虑到修订法律的难度，次优解应是由最高人民法院出台相关的司法解释，从而以最高人民法院释法的形式对该问题加以系统性解决。

五、《仲裁法修订草案》正式确立"仲裁地"的法律概念

以上讨论可知，在原有《仲裁法》框架下，如何认定境外仲裁机构在我国内地作出的仲裁裁决的法律性质，存在诸多争议并产生了复杂的法律问题。这反映的深层问题是：在我国法律不承认"仲裁地"法律概念的前提下，如何认定该类仲裁裁决的籍属，并对裁决的执行或撤销程序适用相应的法律依据。要从根本上解决此问题，除了开拓性的司法实践，还需要立法机关适时通过正式的法律渊源对此问题予以解决。

2021年7月底司法部颁布《仲裁法修订草案》首次正式确立了"仲裁地"的法律概念。第27条规定，"当事人可以在仲裁协议中确定仲裁地"（无约定或约定不明确的，视为"管理案件的仲裁机构所在地"），"仲裁裁决视为在仲裁地作出"，"仲裁地"不影响当事人约定、选择仲裁庭对案件开庭、审理、合议的地点。第七章"涉外仲裁的特别规定"第91条规定，"当事人没有约定仲裁地或者约定不明确的，由仲裁庭根据案件情况确定仲裁地"。由此，境外仲裁机构在我国内地进行仲裁程序，仲裁地应当原则上为我国。据此，布兰特伍德案中，当事人约定将争议"提交国际商会仲裁委员会"在广州仲裁的约定，应视为约定仲裁地在广州的合意。因此，该类裁决的性质为"涉外裁决"应不再有争议。

结合上述司法实践，可以看出这个重要转变是对近期司法实践中逐步放弃"仲裁机构所在地"标准、适用"仲裁地"标准的立法确认。如果顺利通过立法程序，则代表着我国法律正式确立以"仲裁地"作为认定境外仲裁机构在我国内地仲裁裁决籍属的法律标准，并解决了应适用何种法律依据对此类裁决予以执行及司法审查的法律问题。这体现了"司法先行""立法确认"的良性互动，不仅可以解决我国仲裁实践中长期富有争议的境外仲裁机构在我国内地仲裁裁决的法律性质和适用的难题，还可以促使我国立法与国际主流立法接轨，增强我国仲裁法律体系的国际化和专业化。

六、结论

就境外仲裁机构在我国仲裁产生的裁决性质问题，本文概述了相关的主要争议，分析了其面临的法律困境，重点梳理并总结了相关仲裁和司法实践的最新发展。在认定裁决籍属问题上，我国法院的司法实践近期体现了从过

去的"仲裁机构所在地"到"仲裁地"标准转变的趋势,并在布兰特伍德案中打开了新局面。该案具有标志性意义,我国法院首次明确境外仲裁机构在内地仲裁作出裁决应按仲裁地标准认定为我国的"涉外裁决",这避免了过去"非内国裁决"所可能带来的诸多问题,并与国际仲裁的主流实践所接轨。

这些司法实践的新发展,均体现了我国法院在司法实践中通过法律解释和司法适用积极弥补仲裁立法方面的不足,基于支持仲裁的司法政策,灵活地解决《仲裁法》相关的空缺问题,从而对仲裁裁决的性质、国籍的判断和司法审查的法律依据予以明确。这尊重了当事人选择仲裁的意思自治,体现了我国法院支持、促进、保障仲裁的政策,也顺应国际仲裁主流观点和普遍实践。此外,通过修订、调整《仲裁法》的相关规定,正式确立"仲裁地"的法律概念,有利于明确境外仲裁机构在我国内地仲裁的相关法律规则。

综上,对境外仲裁机构在境内仲裁裁决的法律性质的认定,我国司法和立法机关经历了从"仲裁机构所在地"标准向"仲裁地"标准的转变。这不仅解决了我国仲裁实践中长期争议的裁决国籍问题,还为此类裁决的执行及司法审查提供了逐渐清晰的法律依据。这种"司法先行""立法确认"的良性互动模式,以修订成文法的法律渊源,将我国司法实践经验予以"法典化",明确境外仲裁机构在我国内地仲裁的相关法律规则,可以实现我国立法与国际主流立法的接轨,有利于加强我国仲裁制度的国际化、专业化、法治化,增强我国仲裁制度的吸引力,为我国仲裁事业的长足发展保驾护航。

反复指定对仲裁员资格的影响

——兼论北仲《行为守则》

邓芷珊[*]

- 摘　要

    国际仲裁要求仲裁员保持公正与独立。然而，随着国际经贸来往的频繁以及争议数量的增加，反复指定是否对仲裁员公正性与独立性产生影响以及采取何种判断标准成为亟须解决的问题。由于仲裁员行为接受市场规律调整，以及仲裁员高标准的任职资格使其具有思辨能力以及保持中立的倾向，宜确定反复指定本身不构成影响仲裁员公正性与独立性的因素，须结合其他因素综合判断，在判断时宜采取合理怀疑标准而非明显缺乏标准。北仲《国际投资争端仲裁员行为守则》强调仲裁员公正性与独立性，对反复指定现象做到必要提醒，采取合理怀疑标准判断仲裁员公正与独立，符合仲裁实践趋势，但反复指定纳入法定披露义务范围不符合经济原则。

- 关键词

    反复指定　公正性　独立性　《国际投资争端仲裁员行为守则》

    Abstract：International arbitration mechanism requires arbitrators to be impartial and independent. With the development of international

---

[*] 邓芷珊，广东外语外贸大学法学院2021级国际法研究生。

economic, problems of whether repeat appointment affects the impartiality and independence of arbitrators and what criteria should be adopted arise. Repeat appointment alone shall not constitute the factors affecting the impartiality and independence of arbitrators. But rather, it should be determined combining with other factors. It is not only because arbitrators behavior is subject to market adjustment, but also because arbitrators high standard of qualification. Reasonable doubt standard rather than manifest lack standard should be adopted when judging repeat appointment's effect on arbitrators qualification. The Code of Conduct for Arbitrators in International Investment Dispute emphasizes the significance of impartiality and independence of arbitrators and adopts reasonable doubt as a standard, which is in line with the trend of arbitration practice. Moreover, it makes necessary reminders of repeated appointment. However, it is inconsistent with the economic principle to obligate arbitrators to disclose repeat appointment.

Key Words: repeat appointment, impartiality, independence, Code of Conduct for Arbitrators in International Investment Arbitration

引 言

无论在国际仲裁、国内仲裁，抑或是商事仲裁、投资仲裁中，仲裁员公正性和独立性均作为一种强制性规定和基本要求被普遍遵循和践行着。国际专业服务机构——Pinsent Masons 的国际仲裁专家 Richard Dickman 认为，仲裁最重要的两块基石，一是当事人意思自治，二是仲裁员公正性。"仲裁的好坏取决于仲裁员的好坏"，是仲裁界经久不衰的名言。[1]因此，实践界和学术界普遍强调并要求仲裁员具有公正性和独立性。当今，随着国际仲裁制度（包括国际商事仲裁和国际投资仲裁）的兴起、完善与进一步推广，仲裁员在国际争议解决方面发挥着举足轻重的作用，各国普遍重视仲裁人才的培养，提

---

[1] Stephen R Bond, The International Arbitrator: From the Perspective of the ICC International Court of Arbitration, 12 Nw. J. Int'l L.&Bus. 1(1991), p.1.

高自身在仲裁界的话语权和影响力。虽然仲裁人才层出，但同一仲裁员被同一当事人在相关案件中反复指定的情况或引发另一方当事人以及公众对该仲裁员公正性和独立性的质疑，本文称这种情形为反复指定。反复指定是否会影响到仲裁员的公正性和独立性？相应主体（如国内司法机构、仲裁机构的行政委员会等）应当持何种标准作出审查和判断？本文从现有国际投资仲裁规则、国际商事仲裁实践和国际投资仲裁实践分析入手，尝试阐述和澄清反复指定对仲裁员公正性和独立性造成的影响，并提出符合经济最大化原则的解决方案和思路。

一、问题的提出：仲裁员公正性和独立性的影响因素和审查标准

第二次世界大战之后，全球化浪潮加快，各国政治、经济、文化、金融等交流日益加深，经济全球化更是成为其中发展最为迅猛的分支。即使是现在，逆全球化的话题时有提起，但全球化的大方向没有改变，经济发展的齿轮未曾停止。各国经济交流加深的同时，私人之间、私人与国家之间的纠纷日益凸显。在国际争议解决方面，诉讼、仲裁、调解"三驾马车"中，国际仲裁因其高度契约性、自治性和准司法性一直以来备受国际商事主体的青睐，成为解决跨境贸易与投资纠纷的首选方式。选择仲裁作为解决纠纷的方式，是国际商事交往中较为频繁的做法。也正因如此，同一仲裁员被反复指定的情况时有发生，引发公众对该仲裁员公正性和独立性的质疑。

仲裁员的公正性和独立性也是仲裁获得长足发展的重要因素之一。独立性，是指仲裁员与双方当事人之间不存在会影响裁决的连带关系；公正性，是指仲裁员对当事人或争议诉求不偏颇且无明显倾向性。[2]

（一）影响因素的模糊性："反复指定"不必然影响仲裁员公正性和独立性

本文所称"反复指定"，是指同一仲裁员被同一当事人在多个相关案件中指定的情形。"相关案件"，一方面指的是案件涉及的争议问题、案件事实等可能存在重合的情况，另一方面指的是案件当事人存在重合但并非完全相同的情况。例如，在争议方 C 和争议方 R 的案件中，争议方 C 指定 A 为仲裁员，涉及的法律问题是 L，而在争议方 C 和争议方 D 的案件中，同样地，争议方

---

[2] ［英］艾伦·雷德芬、马丁·亨特：《国际商事仲裁法律与实践》，林一飞、宋连斌译，北京大学出版社 2006 年版，第 215 页。

C指定A为仲裁员，涉及的法律问题同样是L。在这种情况下，则存在争议方D或争议方R质疑仲裁员A的中立性、独立性的可能，因为被反复指定的仲裁员可能会被认为其功能在于为实现当事人利益提供更好的服务，而非作为中立第三方解决争议。

  显然，从上述公正性、独立性的定义出发，无法明确回答哪位仲裁员足够公正和独立以及哪位仲裁员不然。要做到这一点，还必须明确影响仲裁员公正性和独立性的事实因素。在这一方面，国际律师协会（International Bar Association，以下简称IBA）做了非常全面而细致的工作。IBA在2014年10月23日修改通过了《国际律师协会关于国际仲裁中利益冲突的指南》（IBA Guideline on Conflicts of Interest in International Arbitration，以下简称《利益冲突指南》），为全球各仲裁机构保障和审查仲裁员公正性和独立性、确定仲裁员信息披露义务范围、判断当事人质疑申请等提供了较为详细的指引。具体而言，为了促进解释的统一性和非必要的质疑申请，《利益冲突指南》列举了被指定的仲裁员应当披露、可以披露和无须披露的红色清单、橙色清单、绿色清单。其中，针对橙色清单下的事项，仲裁员承担的是"可以披露"的义务，即原则上，仲裁员无须披露，但仍然需要根据个案情况分析，如果该情况足以引起对该仲裁员公正性和独立性的合理怀疑，则仲裁员需承担披露义务。[3] 根据《利益冲突指南》橙色清单，其中一项包括"某仲裁员在过去三年中被同一争议方或其附属机构指定两次或以上"，同时，《利益冲突指南》的脚注还说明，无论是在海事仲裁、体育仲裁抑或是商事仲裁中，只要该仲裁员被同一个当事人指定两次以上，均纳入橙色清单之中，是否承担披露义务，属于仲裁机构的"个案审查"范围。[4] 这种情况即为本文所言"反复指定"。可见，《利益冲突指南》并不认为反复指定必然引起相应仲裁员失去中立性和独立性，这也符合当今国际仲裁通说。接下来的问题是，既然反复指定对公正性和独立性的影响属于"个案审查"范围，那么审查的标准为何？

（二）审查标准的不一致："合理怀疑"标准抑或"明显缺乏"标准
  在规范和实践两个视角下，对仲裁员公正性和独立性的审查标准有两个：

---

[3] IBA Guideline on Conflicts of Interest in International Arbitration, Part II, Section 6, p.18.

[4] IBA Guideline on Conflicts of Interest in International Arbitration, p.22.

"明显缺乏"标准和"合理怀疑"标准。

"明显缺乏"标准体现在《关于解决国家与他国国民之间投资争议公约》（以下简称《ICSID 公约》）中，常见于 ICSID 仲裁庭。《ICSID 公约》第 14 条体现了负责争议解决的仲裁员应当满足的条件：一是高尚的道德品质；二是在法律、商业、产业和金融领域有公认的能力；三是为当事人所信任能够作出独立判决。学者普遍认为第三点则是对仲裁员独立性和公正性的要求，尽管只提到了"独立判决"（independent judgement）一词。[5] 同时，《ICSID 公约》第 57 条规定，一方当事人认为仲裁员"明显缺乏"（manifest lack）第 14 条规定的品质时，得以向委员会或仲裁庭提出质疑。值得注意的是，规定中所使用的措辞是"明显缺乏"（manifest lack），这种修饰在法条之中并不常见，说明起草者意图提高仲裁员被质疑成功的门槛，从而提高纠纷解决的"结案率"和保证仲裁高效性。虽然《ICSID 公约》及其评注均没有阐明何为"明显缺乏"，但是仲裁庭或委员会显然注意到这一修饰性措辞，在一些案例中解释和适用"明显缺乏"标准，其中最具有代表性的、同时也是饱受争议的案件是 Suez v. Argentina 案（Suez 案）。Suez 案仲裁庭所采用的是高度可能性标准（highly probable standard），沿用了 Amco Asia Corp v. Indonesia 案仲裁庭的决定，指出提出质疑的当事人须证明仲裁员缺乏独立性的事实是"明显的"（manifest）、"高度可能的"（highly probable），而非仅仅是"可能的"（possible）或者"准确定的"（quasi-certain）。[6]

"合理怀疑"标准则广泛运用于商事仲裁、投资仲裁实践和规范中。《利益冲突指南》规定，如果某种情况足以引起对该仲裁员公正性和独立性的合理怀疑，则仲裁员需承担披露义务。[7] 显然，这里采用的是"合理怀疑"标准（justifiable doubt standard）。《联合国国际贸易法委员会（UNCITRAL）仲裁规则》（以下简称《UNCITRAL 仲裁规则》）中亦包含更为明显的规定。《UNCITRAL 仲裁规则》第 12 条规定，若存在可能对独立性或公正性产生有

---

[5] 于湛旻：《论国际投资仲裁中仲裁员的回避》，载《武大国际法评论》2014 年第 1 期。

[6] Suez, Sociedad General de Aguas de Barcelona S.A., and InterAgua Servicios Integrales del Agua S.A. v. The Argentine Republic, ICSID Case No. ARB/03/17, Decision on a Second Proposal for the Disqualification of Gabrielle Kaufmann-Kohler, 12 May 2008, para.29.

[7] IBA Guideline on Conflicts of Interest in International Arbitration, Part II, Section 6, p.18.

正当理由怀疑的情况，即可要求仲裁员回避。[8]学者认为，相较于"合理怀疑"（justifiable doubt）而言，"明显缺乏"（manifest lack）给举证者施加了更重的举证责任和举证难度，提高了举证门槛。[9]例如，在 Blue Bank v. Venezuela 案中，ICSID 行政委员会在处理投资者对东道国指定仲裁员提出的质疑时，指出"一个具有主观判断能力的合理客观第三方基于常识性认知对此案的评价，都可以得出该仲裁员明显缺乏合格性的结论"。[10]可见，该案行政委员会舍弃前述严苛的"明显缺乏"标准，而提出以第三方对证据的合理评估为基础的客观标准（objective standard）。该标准不再要求质疑方证明存在切实的不公正或不独立，仅需证明有足以确定不公正或不独立的表象（appearance）即可。[11]后续案件基本沿用此标准，采取合理怀疑标准的案件在发生时间上较采取明显缺乏标准的案件而言更为新、近。[12]

二、反复指定的不可避免性使其不宜列入红色清单

仲裁员在多个相关案件中被同一当事人指定的情况具有客观性和不可避免性。在国际仲裁实践中，除独任仲裁员以外，争议当事人都有权利指定特定仲裁员共同组成仲裁庭，此属于选择仲裁作为争议解决方式的争议当事人享有的权利，故而，当事人重复指定同一名其信任、熟悉的仲裁员，同样属于当事人的权利之一，是"当事人意思自治的核心"。[13]实践中，反复指定问题频繁出现，引起联合国国际贸易法委员会的高度关注。但即使如此，没有一个仲裁规则、司法机构持当事人不可指定同一仲裁员的观点，而是通过个

---

[8] UNCITRAL Arbitration Rules, Article 121. Any arbitrator may be challenged if circumstances exist that give rise to justifiable doubts as to the arbitrator's impartiality or independence.

[9] 于湛旻：《论国际投资仲裁中仲裁员的回避》，载《武大国际法评论》2014年第1期。

[10] Blue Bank International & Trust Ltd. v. Bolivarian Republic of Venezuela, ICSID Case No. ARB/12/20, Decision on the Parties' Proposals to Disqualify a Majority of the Tribunal, 12 Nov 2013, para.60.

[11] Blue Bank International & Trust Ltd. v. Bolivarian Republic of Venezuela, ICSID Case No. ARB/12/20, Decision on the Parties' Proposals to Disqualify a Majority of the Tribunal, 12 Nov 2013, para.59.

[12] 张榆钧：《国际投资仲裁中仲裁员重复委任问题的评价标准研究》，载《中山大学青年法律评论》（第5卷），法律出版社2020年版，第30—49页。

[13] ［美］加里·B.博恩：《国际仲裁：法律与实践》，白麟、陈福勇等译，商务印书馆2015年版，第173页。

案分析与反复论证的方式探讨反复指定是否影响被反复指定仲裁员的公正性和独立性。

实践中频繁出现反复指定引起当事人质疑仲裁员公正性和独立性的案例，仲裁庭的论证趋势表明，反复指定并不必然导致仲裁员的不公正和不独立，对这一问题应当审慎对待，进行个案分析。在 Universal Compression v. Venezuela、OPIC Karimum v. Venezuela、Tidewater v. Venezuela 和 Urbaser v. Argentina 四个案件中，仲裁庭一致驳回了取消仲裁员资格的申请。以 Tidewater 案为例，投资者对委内瑞拉指定的 S 教授作为仲裁员提出质疑，认为 S 教授在过去六年中被委内瑞拉任命为其他三个 ICSID 仲裁庭的成员，因而无法公正独立地解决眼前这一同样涉及委内瑞拉的案件。[14]其余两位仲裁员则认为，被任命的次数需要结合其他因素才会对仲裁员公正性和独立性产生影响，[15]仲裁员在不同的案件中须履行同样的中立性功能。[16]在 OPIC Karimum v. Venezuela 案中出现了同样的情况——投资者质疑委内瑞拉指定的仲裁员。另外两位仲裁员的态度值得考究，一方面，另两位仲裁员提出，多次指定一名仲裁员客观地表明了当事各方及其律师的观点，即相比之下，在多次被指定者担任仲裁庭成员的情况下，争议的结果更有可能取得成功。[17]另一方面，另两位仲裁员从事实出发，认为没有充足证据表明此仲裁员在经济上依赖争议当事人，因此驳回了投资者的质疑。

上述两个案件反映实践的一个共识：反复指定本身并不必然影响仲裁员的公正性和独立性，必须结合其他因素进行综合审查。其他因素既可能是该仲

---

[14] Tidewater Investment SRL and Tidewater Caribe, C.A. v. Bolivarian Republic of Venezuela, ICSID Case No. ARB/10/5, Decision on Claimants' Proposal to Disqualify Professor Brigitte Stern, Arbitrator, 23 Dec 2010, para.14.

[15] Tidewater Investment SRL and Tidewater Caribe, C.A. v. Bolivarian Republic of Venezuela, ICSID Case No. ARB/10/5, Decision on Claimants' Proposal to Disqualify Professor Brigitte Stern, Arbitrator, 23 Dec 2010, para.59.

[16] Tidewater Investment SRL and Tidewater Caribe, C.A. v. Bolivarian Republic of Venezuela, ICSID Case No. ARB/10/5, Decision on Claimants' Proposal to Disqualify Professor Brigitte Stern, Arbitrator, 23 Dec 2010, para.60.

[17] OPIC Karimum Corporation v. The Bolivarian Republic of Venezuela, ICSID Case No. ARB/10/14, Decision on the Proposal to Disqualify Professor Philippe Sands, Arbitrator, 5 May 2011, para.47.

裁员以往审理案件涉及的法律问题与当前案件是否以及多大程度上具有相似性，也可能是该仲裁员与当事人在经济上的依赖关系。总而言之，反复指定不构成影响仲裁员公正性和独立性的独立因素。

三、仲裁员公正性与独立性的保障机制分析

仲裁员公正性和独立性需要有法律和制度上的形式理性的保障，才符合现代法治的要求。在国际仲裁中，保障仲裁院公正性和独立性的机制包括外部保障机制和内部保障机制。

外部保障机制包括仲裁员披露义务和撤销仲裁裁决制度，前者是事前预防机制，后者则属于事后救济措施。如果当事人觉得仲裁员无法做到公正、独立地审理案件争议，可以在作出裁决前对仲裁员资质、合格性提出异议和质疑，同样地，如果裁决已经作出，当事人可以申请撤销仲裁裁决，以免不公正、不独立的裁决被执行，得出不公正的结果。

然而，无论是披露义务或是撤销仲裁裁决制度，都可以说是从仲裁员本身以外的保障，而且有赖于当事人的观察了解、提出质疑以及启动相关程序，具有一定的限制性。相反，如果能从仲裁员本身出发，要求仲裁员保持公正和独立，则可以克服上述弊端，本文称为内部保障机制，包括仲裁的服务性质和仲裁员自身的自律。

（一）仲裁的市场化服务性质促使仲裁员保持公正独立

不少评论认为，被指定的仲裁员与指定者之间的关系使仲裁员难以保持公正与独立。本文认为，从仲裁服务的市场化视角出发，这种情况或许不会发生。

商事仲裁是一种专业化服务，仲裁员的裁判行为是向市场所提供服务的一种形式，接受市场经济规律的调整，决定了仲裁员无法与某一方当事人形成紧密的联盟关系。商事仲裁是商事主体自主采取的解决自身争议的方式，是一种商事救济行为，其本质属性是专业化的服务，属于市场经济中的法律服务范畴和一个专门行业。[18]根据法律市场理论，公众个体的行为可以对生产者产生激励作用。[19]仲裁员作为商事仲裁中的服务提供者，其行为接受市场经

---

[18] 康明：《论商事仲裁的专业服务属性》，对外经济贸易大学2004年博士论文。

[19] 刘双舟：《法律市场视野中的制度竞争与立法行为选择》，载《政法论坛》2010年第3期。

济规律的支配。因为优秀仲裁员是一种稀缺资源，特别是想要寻找一些在技术或者经济方面符合要求的仲裁员更是困难。[20] 仲裁员在仲裁活动中投入了大量的智力劳动，时间、精力、金钱等直接成本，也放弃了通过其他活动获得更大收益的机会成本。这些成本都具有经济学意义上的价值。因而，仲裁员也将根据自身条件、报酬多少、精力投入大小、获得收益大小自由决定是否参与仲裁活动。资源的稀缺性与参与人的个体偏好，决定了仲裁员行为必然接受市场经济规律的支配。同时需要注意到，仲裁制度的适用基础是当事人的意思自治，也就是说，相对于其他法律市场（如实体法的法律市场）而言，仲裁制度的法律市场更接近完全竞争市场，因为人们在这一市场中的选择自由度更高。[21] 在一次次的选择与被选择中，经济资源向被选择的商品（即仲裁员的裁判行为）流动并为商品生产方（仲裁员）带来利益，商品生产方（仲裁员）也因此具有充分的动机去不断改良更新自己"产品"（公正、独立的裁判行为），从而提高对买方的吸引力并获得更多被选择的机会，进而获取更多资源的倾斜。[22] 因而，如果仲裁员由于长期为某一当事人指定而与其结成"同盟"，沦为"某些人"利益的代表者，会受到其他人的排斥，[23] 使得仲裁员在国际仲裁界的声誉、能力和道德评价受到贬损，进而降低其他当事人指定其为仲裁员的欲望。即是说，仲裁员与某一当事人结成同盟的行为不符合市场经济规律，也不符合个人利益最大化原则。

由此，有学者批驳道，仲裁员意欲被反复选任，会通过裁决结果满足投资者诉求的方式，以期达到被反复选任之目的。[24] 实际上，仲裁员作为一个理性第三人，自然明白公正独立的裁判行为、良好的声誉将最终被保留并成为仲裁法律市场上的长期产品。

---

[20] Bernhard F. Meyer and Jonatan Baier, Arbitrator Consultants—Another Way to Deal with Technical or Commercial Challenges of Arbitrations, ASA Bulletin, 33 (2015), p.37.

[21] 田雨酥:《从法律市场视角看国际商事仲裁制度的未来——兼论仲裁机构的改革方向》，载《商事仲裁与调解》2021年第1期。

[22] 田雨酥:《从法律市场视角看国际商事仲裁制度的未来——兼论仲裁机构的改革方向》，载《商事仲裁与调解》2021年第1期。

[23] 谭立:《商事仲裁程序问题的经济分析》，武汉大学2015年博士论文。

[24] Gus Van Harten, Investment Treaty Arbitration and Public Law, Oxford University Press, 2007, pp.172–173.

（二）高标准的任职资格条件为公正独立争议解决提供保障

高标准的任职资格条件在很大程度上为公正独立争议解决提供保障。国际仲裁普遍要求高标准的仲裁员任职资格条件。《ICSID 仲裁规则》规定仲裁员必须具有高尚道德操守以及具备法律、商业、工业或金融领域的公认能力。挑选仲裁员时还通常考虑到仲裁员的语言资格、担任仲裁员的经验、国际法知识等。此外，各国国内法也通常规定仲裁员的任期资格，如我国《仲裁法》规定，仲裁员须从事律师工作满 8 年，或是曾任法官或仲裁员满 8 年，或是具有高级职称，或是具有法律知识、从事经济贸易等专业工作并具有高级职称或者同等专业水平等。实际上，仲裁员群体由法律行业的资深从业者组成，对专业水平和实务经验均有要求，真正加入仲裁员队伍的群体大多为资深公司法务、大学教授、退休法官、知名律师等，在业界具有一定知名度和影响力。这通常意味着，仲裁员本身具有足够的思辨能力保持自身的中立和客观，具有充足的独立思考、不盲目相信权威或者当事人、习惯的自由意志，是接受精英教育熏陶和具有丰富阅历经验的理性人。学者也认同，对仲裁员小组而言，在法律方面的资格尤为重要，ICSID 对资格的要求实质上确保了仲裁员"独立判断"的能力。[25]

综上所述，仲裁作为一种专业化且市场化服务，仲裁员的声誉对其职业发展尤其重要，仲裁员的声誉积累来自其公正与独立，因此，为在仲裁行业获得可持续发展，仲裁员会自觉调整自身可能带有的偏见。另外，鉴于仲裁员基本上都接受过良好的教育，培养出良好的思辨能力，也能确保自身保持公正与独立。

四、判断"反复指定"对仲裁员公正性和独立性影响宜采取"合理怀疑"标准

（一）晚近 ICSID 仲裁实践表明其已经转向"合理怀疑"标准

《ICSID 仲裁规则》中对仲裁员公正性和独立性的判断采取的是"明显缺乏"标准，同时，仲裁庭或委员会在一些案例中解释和适用"明显缺乏"标准，其中最具有代表性的、同时也是饱受争议的案件是 Suez v. Argentina

---

[25] 孙南翔：《国际商事仲裁员资格特征研究——兼评我国贸仲委选聘仲裁员之实践》，载《国际经济法学刊》2013 年第 1 期，第 139—159 页。

案（Suez案）。Suez案仲裁庭所采用的是高度可能性标准（highly probable standard），沿用了Amco Asia Corp v. Indonesia案仲裁庭的决定，指出提出质疑的当事人须证明仲裁员缺乏独立性的事实是"明显的""高度可能的"，而非仅仅是"可能的"或者"准确定的"。[26]由于这一严苛的标准，2013年之前，在40余起对仲裁员质疑的案件中，仅有一起被支持，使得这一标准饱受批评。2013年，Blue Bank v. Venezuela案拒绝采用如此严苛的标准，首次采用较之前案证明门槛更低的以第三方对证据的合理评估为基础的客观标准（objective standard）。该标准不再要求质疑方证明存在切实的不独立或不公正，仅须证明有足以确定存在不独立或不公正的表象（appearance）。从该案开始至今，后续案件基本沿用此标准，该标准也被视为回归以2001年Vivendi v. Argentina案为代表所采用的"合理怀疑"标准（reasonable doubts standard）。

因此，尽管《ICSID仲裁规则》中并没有改变"明显缺乏"这一措辞的使用，但从实践上看，晚近的国际投资仲裁案件大多数从"明显缺乏"标准转向"合理怀疑"标准，为"合理怀疑"标准提供了丰富的国际法渊源。

（二）国际投资仲裁的公共属性对仲裁员的公正性和独立性提出更高要求

"明显缺乏"标准给举证者施加了更重的举证义务，使得当事方质疑获得成功变得更加困难，变相降低了仲裁员保持公正和独立的要求，不利于国际投资争议的妥善解决。数据显示，自2001年至2018年1月，在确实涉及一项或多项仲裁员回避申请的33起案件中，有52份回避通知要求60名不同仲裁员回避，[27]而国际投资争端解决中心申请回避成功率约为3%，伦敦仲裁院商事仲裁申请回避成功率为22%。[28]伦敦仲裁院商事仲裁大多适用英国上议院在

---

[26] Suez, Sociedad General de Aguas de Barcelona S.A., and InterAgua Servicios Integrales del Agua S.A. v. The Argentine Republic, ICSID Case No. ARB/03/17, Decision on a Second Proposal for the Disqualification of Gabrielle Kaufmann-Kohler, 12 May 2008, para.29.

[27] 联合国贸法会第三工作组：《投资人与国家间争议解决制度的可能改革：国际政府间组织提交的材料和补充材料：指定仲裁员（秘书处的说明）》，http://undocs.org/en/A/CN.9/WG.III/WP.146，最后访问时间：2022年8月10日。

[28] 联合国贸法会第三工作组：《投资人与国家间争议解决制度的可能改革：确保投资人与国家间争议解决制度中仲裁员和裁定人的独立性和公正性（秘书处的说明）》，http://undocs.org/en/A/CN.9/WG.III/WP.151，最后访问时间：2022年8月10日。

Porter v. Magill 案中确立的"合理怀疑"标准，即"一名公平的并且通情达理的旁观者在考虑了事实之后，是否会得出结论，认为法庭有存有偏见的真实可能性"[29]。可见，在国际商事仲裁中，"合理怀疑"标准是质疑仲裁员资格普遍适用的审查标准，较好地保障了国际商事纠纷的公正及独立解决。相反，国际投资仲裁中对仲裁员资格的质疑频频因为证明标准门槛过高而不成立，导致本身可能不公正、不独立的仲裁员作为仲裁庭一员参与案件审理。然而，需要注意到，几乎没有评论否认国际投资仲裁中所包含的公共利益属性较国际商事仲裁而言更为明显和敏感，由此可推理出，在国际投资纠纷解决程序中，对仲裁员公正性和独立性的要求应当更高。然而，现实状况是质疑商事仲裁员的标准比质疑投资仲裁低，这着实与国际投资仲裁的公共利益属性不相符。

对此，有学者考虑到现实情况以及《ICSID 仲裁规则》起草者当初选择"明显缺乏"标准的目的意图，认为对当事人指定的仲裁员采取"明显缺乏"标准，对首席仲裁员采取"合理怀疑"标准。[30] 本文认为，这种"双重标准"的做法不具有合理性。从现实情况出发，国际商事仲裁历来采取"合理怀疑"标准作为审视仲裁员资格的判断依据，并没有使得商事仲裁"丧失存在的基础"，[31] 内含更多公法要素的国际投资仲裁想必也不会因仲裁员更容易被成功质疑而被挫败。从"明显缺乏"标准的目的——确保投资仲裁的权威性和稳定性——出发，达成这一目标的途径有多种，其中最重要的即为仲裁裁决的执行无须经过国内法院的承认，而并非必须通过稳固仲裁员任职资格来实现。

因此，考虑到国际投资纠纷所涉及的公共利益因素，解决国际投资纠纷的仲裁员更应当保持公正独立，审理案件。

---

[29] 黄子宜:《仲裁员质疑裁量标准初探——基于英国伦敦商事仲裁院（LCIA）仲裁员质疑数据库的分析》，载《法律适用》2019 年第 17 期。

[30] 丁夏:《谁之公正与何种独立——ICSID 仲裁员公正性标准研判》，载《国际经济法学刊》2013 年第 3 期。

[31] 丁夏:《谁之公正与何种独立——ICSID 仲裁员公正性标准研判》，载《国际经济法学刊》2013 年第 3 期。

五、北仲《国际投资争端仲裁员行为守则》对仲裁员公正性和独立性要求的讨论与思考

北京仲裁委员会/北京国际仲裁中心于2021年12月30日发布了包括100余名仲裁员在内的《国际投资争端仲裁员名册》,以及《国际投资争端仲裁员行为守则》(以下简称《行为守则》),国际仲裁界媒体《环球仲裁评论》认为这两份文件的发布体现出北仲"已经为投资争议解决做好准备"。[32]《行为守则》旨在解决国际投资仲裁遇到的"前所未有的合法性危机"。[33] 该守则包括了专业资质、独立性与公正性、披露、廉洁、保密以及勤勉与高效等方面的规定。《行为守则》第 4 条是关于仲裁员独立性与公正性的规定,要求仲裁员不因任何私利、外界压力而影响仲裁案件审理的公正性,以及始终平等对待当事人,避免作出可能给当事人造成不公平印象的行为。与之相关的,是第 3 条关于履行要求的规定,要求仲裁员应尽量避免同时在多起涉及相同当事人,或相同国际投资协定,或相同事实的仲裁案件中担任仲裁员、代理人、顾问、仲裁庭或法庭指定的专家、专家证人等。

(一)强调独立性、公正性的重要性,符合国际仲裁规则的趋势

《行为守则》第 4 条在原则层面规定了仲裁员保持独立性和公正性的要求,强调仲裁员理应保持独立性和公正性。《行为守则》第 4 条可以从以下几个方面解读:一是在内心动态方面,要求仲裁员不因任何私利、外界压力而影响仲裁案件审理的公正性。二是在外在表现形式上,要求仲裁员始终平等对待当事人,避免作出可能给当事人造成不公平印象的行为。即使这两个方面均属于仲裁员公正性和独立性要求的应有之义,但仲裁员一旦被质疑,如仲裁员是否受到外界压力影响、是否不平等对待当事人等问题的判断,终将落入仲裁机构或仲裁庭的动态裁量范围,蕴含大量的价值判断,使得结果具有不确定性。相比之下,第 4 条第 3 款的规定——仲裁员不得在本会的仲裁案件和申请撤销或不予执行本会仲裁裁决的案件中担任代理人——则因其只包含事

---

[32] Beijing centre gears up for investment disputes,载 Global Arbitration Review 官网,https://globalarbitrationreview.com/article/beijing-centre-gears-investment-disputes,最后访问时间:2022 年 8 月 10 日。

[33] 《北京仲裁委员会/北京国际仲裁中心〈国际投资争端仲裁员名册〉〈国际投资争端仲裁员行为守则〉正式发布》,载北京仲裁委员会官网,http://www.bjac.org.cn/news/view?id=4095,最后访问时间:2022 年 8 月 10 日。

实评价而不包含价值评价而更加具有确定性和可预测性，这也是解读《行为守则》第 4 条的第三个方面。

（二）披露义务范围和审查标准的规定

1. 法定披露义务范围不宜包含反复指定情况

《行为守则》第 5 条给仲裁员施加了披露反复指定情况的义务，但同时限缩了反复指定的范围，即限缩在"近五年内涉及当事人的其他案件"，与《利益冲突指南》规定的三年期限相比，增加了两年，这或许是考虑到国际投资仲裁审理时间通常比国际商事仲裁要长，即使《利益冲突指南》并没有明确排除其在国际投资仲裁案件中的可适用性以及国际投资仲裁庭也频繁引用《利益冲突指南》的规定。然而，本文认为，给仲裁员施加这一义务并不妥当，主要原因有以下三点：

一是国际投资仲裁的透明度改革已经使得很多信息公开可获取。国际投资仲裁的公开度和透明度是近些年热烈讨论的话题，国际社会也在推进国际投资向透明度改革，且目前已经取得了良好的进展，即是说，仲裁员在过去五年中担任什么案件的仲裁庭成员，属于公开的信息，当事人可以轻而易举地找到这些资料。

二是当事人理应得知反复指定的详细情况。国际投资仲裁中双方当事人大多数均有出色的国际律所代理，其代理人更是深谙仲裁之道的律师，对仲裁界的人物、仲裁员的风格、审理案件理应胸有成竹，正如学者所指出的那样，仲裁实践中，当事人对仲裁员信息的调查一直存在，某些做法已经得到仲裁机构的认可，[34]因此，要求仲裁员披露的信息或许本身就已经为当事人所知悉。

三是过多的信息披露义务影响仲裁案件的实际推进和仲裁员自身的利益。[35]马占军认为，仲裁员披露事由的范围应被限定在当事人有正当怀疑理由的范围内，正当理由应该是明确而直接的。[36]加上如前所述，反复指定本身并不构成质疑仲裁员公正性和独立性的直接且明确的事由，因此，要求仲裁员披露自身被反复指定的情形，扩大了仲裁员披露义务范围，加重了仲裁员的

---

[34] 谭立：《商事仲裁程序问题的经济分析》，武汉大学 2015 年博士论文。

[35] 谭立：《商事仲裁程序问题的经济分析》，武汉大学 2015 年博士论文。

[36] 马占军：《国际商事仲裁员披露义务规则研究》，载《法学论坛》2011 年第 4 期。

工作负担，不符合仲裁经济效益原则。

故而，要求仲裁员披露反复指定这一信息不符合仲裁的经济原则，宜把这一信息披露要求从法定披露转为申请披露或选择性主动披露，即在当事人认为有需要且经申请的情况下，才能要求仲裁员行使披露义务，或者赋予仲裁员选择权，在当事人没有申请的情况下，仲裁员认为有必要的，也可以予以主动披露。

2. 采纳"合理怀疑"标准认定反复指定对仲裁员公正性和独立性的影响

《行为守则》第 5 条规定，"仲裁员在接受指定或选定时，应书面披露可能导致对其公正性与独立性产生合理怀疑的任何事实或情形"。在这里，《行为守则》所采取的是"合理怀疑"标准，而没有采纳《ICSID 仲裁规则》的"明显缺乏"标准。可以认为，这一规定是妥当的。因为国际投资仲裁相比于商事仲裁而言，对仲裁员公正性和独立性应当提出更高的要求，因而，当事人质疑仲裁员的公正独立品质时，应当采取合理及较低的标准和门槛，确保仲裁员的公正与独立，以便投资争议的解决令人满意。

（三）提醒当事人注意反复指定情况，充分尊重当事人意思自治原则

《行为守则》第 3 条第 4 款规定，"仲裁员应避免同时在多起涉及相同当事人、相同国际投资协定或相同事实的仲裁案件中担任仲裁员、代理人、顾问、仲裁庭或法庭指定的专家、专家证人等"。实际上，这一款在要求仲裁员避免反复指定的情况发生。这一款值得注意的地方是《行为守则》第 3 条第 4 款属于建议性规定，而非强制性规定。从措辞上看，该款的措辞为"应避免"，而不是采用"不得""禁止"等强制性的否定性用语；从程序设计上看，并没有与之相匹配的措施保障反复指定情况的出现，即纵使某仲裁员确实被反复指定，也并不存在相关的措施否认其担任仲裁员的资格。可以认为，《行为守则》第 3 条第 4 款的建议性规定是妥当的，一方面反映了北仲对国际投资仲裁前沿问题的关切，另一方面，北仲没有通过极端的方法应对这一问题，而是对仲裁员和当事人给予温和的建议，把选择权交回到仲裁员和当事人之间，充分尊重了仲裁意思自治原则。

结　语

《国际投资争端仲裁员行为守则》中有关仲裁员公正性与独立性的规定，一方面符合当下对国际投资争议仲裁员的要求，另一方面依旧存在可圈可点之处。确保仲裁员的公正性与独立性是仲裁界一以贯之的追求，国际社会日益密切的经贸交往、对法治的追求均对公正独立第三方提出更高的期待，在保证仲裁灵活高效的前提下，通过合理的制度设定及标准适用，确保仲裁员的公正与独立，是仲裁制度必须重视的问题。

从"自治"归于"他治"的空中楼阁

——论当事人共同选定仲裁员制度中的意思自治

陈令祚[*]

- **摘　要**

　　仲裁员决定着仲裁的质量，当事人选定仲裁员是其在仲裁程序中享有的重要权利。然而，我国《仲裁法》以及仲裁机构的仲裁规则对于该权利都作出了一定的限制。不仅在制度上，在实践中也鲜有双方当事人能够成功地选定首席仲裁员或独任仲裁员。取而代之，仲裁机构指定仲裁员作为当今各仲裁机构规则中普遍存在的兜底方案，则成为仲裁员产生的主要方式。这就从选定仲裁员事项上的"自治"转向了"他治"。本文从该问题入手，梳理当事人共同选定仲裁员制度的历史发展和价值取向，着眼于当事人选定仲裁员的意思自治原则对于仲裁的重要意义，收集中国和世界主流仲裁机构对于该制度的实践情况，并对于目前存在的问题提出可能的解决方案。

- **关键词**

　　仲裁员　首席仲裁员　独任仲裁员　仲裁庭组成　意思自治

　　Abstract: The arbitrator determines the quality of the arbitration,

---

[*] 陈令祚，中国人民大学法学院法律硕士，现供职于上海市方达（北京）律师事务所。

and the party's choice of arbitrator is an important right in the arbitration proceedings. However, the Arbitration Law of PRC and arbitration rules of arbitration institutions impose certain restrictions on this right. Not only institutionally, but also in practice, few parties have succeeded in appointing a presiding arbitrator or a sole arbitrator. Instead, the appointment of arbitrators by the arbitration institution, which is the prevalent underwriting scheme in the rules of today's arbitration institutions, has become the primary method of arbitrator appointment. This has shifted from "self governance" to "other governance" in the matter of appointing arbitrators. This article begins with a review on the historical development of joint appointment of arbitrator, gathers practical facts of the mechanism in mainstream domestic and international arbitration institutions, focuses on the importance of the principle of party autonomy in appointing arbitrators, and propose possible solutions to current problems.

Key Words: arbitrator, presiding arbitrator, sole arbitrator, composition of the arbitral tribunal, party autonomy

第1章 当事人共同选定仲裁员制度的一些基本问题

本章对当事人共同选定仲裁员制度的一些基本问题进行阐述。具体而言：首先，考虑到仲裁及其相关术语在本文的表述中可能存在一些歧义，因此对"仲裁员""仲裁员的选定""意思自治"三个概念进行界定，厘清本文的讨论范围；其次，结合仲裁制度的历史发展，总结当事人选定仲裁员制度的历史渊源和现今发展；最后，结合仲裁正义和效率的双重价值，对当事人选定仲裁员制度本身的价值取向进行简要分析。

1.1 概念界定

1.1.1 仲裁员

在商事仲裁中，"仲裁员"一词本身就有着不确定的含义。
我国《仲裁法》第11条规定"仲裁委员会应当具备下列条件：……（四）有聘任的仲裁员"；第13条第2款规定"仲裁员应当符合下列条件之一……"，第3

款又规定"仲裁委员会按照不同专业设仲裁员名册"。以上语境中，无论是耳熟能详的"三八两高"门槛[1]，还是名册制的要求，其中"仲裁员"一词均象征着一种资格、一种可能性。这意味着，即使一个自然人符合了"三八两高"的条件，又确实地被列入了某家仲裁机构的仲裁员名册，也只是"可能"参加到某一案件的审理活动中去。

《仲裁法》第四章第二节中出现的"仲裁员"一词，则与前段所列有所不同。例如，第32条规定，"当事人没有在仲裁规则规定的期限内约定仲裁庭的组成方式或者选定仲裁员的，由仲裁委员会主任指定"；第37条规定，"仲裁员因回避或者其他原因不能履行职责的，应当依照本法规定重新选定或者指定仲裁员"。可以观察到，此处的仲裁员均与"仲裁庭"相关，是指在某一案件中实际参与审理活动的一位或多位仲裁员。即，在此处，该等自然人以"仲裁员"这一身份出现。

对比上述关于"仲裁员"的两重概念，两者既有区别也存在联系。在我国《仲裁法》的基础上，仲裁员"资格"是成为仲裁员"身份"的前提和基础，仲裁员"身份"是拥有仲裁员"资格"的自然人经过一定的选择程序后，在一定时间内享有特定权利、履行特定义务的状态；具有仲裁员资格并不必然代表该自然人实际地参与某一案件的审理，但组成仲裁庭的具有仲裁员身份的人，一定具有仲裁员资格。本文探讨的仲裁员"选任""选定"等，均主要研究的是上述第二种定义，即符合仲裁员任职资格的人获得某一案件中仲裁员身份的过程，而非自然人获得仲裁员资格的过程。下述"仲裁员"一词，如无特殊标注，均指以上"仲裁员"的第二种定义。

1.1.2 仲裁员的选定

在谈及第1.1.1部分中提到的第二种定义，即"身份"范畴的仲裁员的选定时，我国的学术文章"选任"[2]"选择"[3]"任命"[4]三词均有出现，而《仲裁

---

[1] 参见《仲裁法》第13条第2款。

[2] 赖震平：《我国商事仲裁制度的阙如——以临时仲裁在上海自贸区的试构建为视角》，载《河北法学》2015年第2期。

[3] 马占军：《首席（独任）仲裁员产生规则论》，载《河北法学》2015年第5期。

[4] 丁夏：《仲裁员制度的比较与反思——以〈上海自贸区仲裁规则〉的人本化为视角》，载《法学论坛》2015年第2期。

法》以及诸如《中国国际经济贸易仲裁委员会规则》（以下简称《贸仲规则》，凡本文所引仲裁规则，如无特别说明，均指最新版本的规则）、《北京仲裁委员会规则》（以下简称《北仲规则》）等国内主流仲裁机构的规则文本均使用了"选定"一词[5]。

考虑到当事人与仲裁员之间的法律关系包含合同关系（详见本文第4章），而有合同的地方就有意思自治，因此"选定仲裁员中的意思自治"在主体维度存在歧义，因为此处的意思自治可能存在于双方当事人之间，也可能存在于一方或多方当事人与仲裁员之间。作为澄清，本文将仅讨论基于当事人合同（仲裁协议）的意思自治，而不讨论仲裁员被选定时的意思自治。

仲裁庭一般由三名或一名仲裁员组成（为行文方便之需要，仲裁庭人数为三名和一名的仲裁程序以下统一简称为普通程序和简易程序，即使在某些国家或某些仲裁机构其名称并非如此）。在简易程序中，仲裁庭只包含一名独任仲裁员，而在普通程序中，仲裁庭的构成则稍微复杂一些。由于本文讨论的问题为中国这一项法域下的仲裁实践，此处便以我国《仲裁法》对仲裁庭的组成的规定为例加以讨论。

《仲裁法》第31条第1款有意区分了普通程序中当事人"各自选定或者各自委托仲裁委员会主任指定"的仲裁员和"由当事人共同选定或者共同委托仲裁委员会主任指定"的仲裁员，并明确规定由后一种方式产生的一位仲裁员为首席仲裁员。相应地，虽然《仲裁法》中无此表述，与首席对应的、通过双方当事人各自产生的仲裁员一般被称为"边裁"。在一般的情形下，边裁的确定仅需双方当事人中一方的意思表示，因此本文讨论的当事人间的意思自治主要集中在普通程序中的首席仲裁员和简易程序中的独任仲裁员的产生上。在首席仲裁员和独任仲裁员的选择中，双方当事人即使各自有心仪的人选且发出了明确的意思表示，仍需对方的同意方可选定。

当然，我们不能忽略近年来仲裁实践的热点问题多主体仲裁，因为一方超

---

[5] 在本文中，以下不区分仲裁员的"选定""选择"，但区分"选定"（当事人角度）和"指定"（仲裁机构角度）。另外值得一提的是，虽然在国内的文献中就选定的用词不甚统一，但在外文文献中，当事人选定仲裁员的动作基本均被表述为"appoint（appointment）"，而"selection"仅在比较有限的文献中出现。

过一个当事人的仲裁案件确实可能产生仲裁员选定事项上意思自治的问题。[6]在一方当事人众多（大部分情况下为被申请人一方）的普通仲裁程序中，这一方当事人可能在内部存在利益冲突，从而无法对于边裁的选定达成一致。这一情形也包含"若规定时间内未能选出则由仲裁委员会指定"的模型，因此理论上也属于本文讨论的范围，但由于在实践中多主体仲裁的实践方兴未艾，从立法、规则到实践均不具备太多样本，因此以下暂不专门讨论。

综上，本文所讨论的仲裁员的选定或选择，是指双方当事人在法律和仲裁规则所规定的程序下，通过合意或借由仲裁委员会的补充性程序，选择其参与的仲裁的首席仲裁员或独任仲裁员，或一方当事人多主体之间在法律和仲裁规则规定的程序下，通过合意或借由仲裁委员会的补充性程序，选择其参与的普通仲裁程序的一方边裁，直至该等仲裁员最终确定的过程。

1.1.3 意思自治

意思自治原则又称"自愿原则"，意思自治的内涵包括"可以按照自己的或者按照彼此的共同意愿自主地行事，不受外在因素的干预，尤其是不受公权力的干预"[7]。在民法的领域内，这一表述概括了绝大部分法律行为主观层面的状态，是一个覆盖面较广的概念，但在本文讨论的当事人选定仲裁员的语境下，"意思自治"则更侧重于后一种内涵，即"按照彼此的共同意愿自主地行事"。

在仲裁活动中，部分事项属于当事人一方的意思便能决定的事项，例如边

---

[6] 例如上海市方达律师事务所在其专题栏目《仲裁三人谈》第13期提到，在日渐频繁的多主体仲裁中，不仅存在着申请人与被申请人之间的矛盾，一方（往往是被申请人）内部也存在着一定的利益冲突，而在申请人提交仲裁申请后才开始的仲裁程序中，被申请人有时并无充分的时间选定边裁，即使积极行权也可能无疾而终。更有极端的情况，即申请人（公司）故意将其内部高管作为被申请人一并提交仲裁，而该高管事实上与公司并无利益纠纷，以其作为被申请人只是为了妨碍被申请人作为一个整体在合适的时间内选定边裁。对此，不同仲裁机构对于边裁最终产生方式的安排各有不同。第一种方案规定，若一方主体无法在规定期限内选定边裁，则由仲裁机构直接指定全部三名仲裁员，在国内，贸仲便采用了该等做法。该方法杜绝了申请人恶意妨碍被申请人选定仲裁员的问题，但仲裁机构在此情况下直接剥夺双方合意选定首席仲裁员的权利（而此时双方并非没有可能就首席仲裁员的选定达成合意）是否妥当尚有疑问。另一种做法则仍采取与单一主体相同的处理方式，由仲裁委员会指定未能在规定时间内选定的边裁，北仲是国内采取该做法的代表。该方法保留了双方共同选择首席仲裁员的权利，但对于恶意申请难以防止，从而存在无法达到实质公平的风险。

[7] 王利明主编：《民法（第七版）》，中国人民大学出版社2018年版，第26页。

裁的选择就无须参考另一方或多方当事人的意见，不违反法律或仲裁规则的规定即可生效。但是，"意思自治"出现的更多场合，指的是双方的意思自治，即各方当事人按照共同的意愿决定某些事项，这些事项上的合意，既可产生于争议出现之前，例如合同仲裁条款对于仲裁机构、仲裁地、准据法的约定，也可产生于争议出现之后，例如本文讨论的首席仲裁员或独任仲裁员的选定。本文特此申明，以下所讨论的"意思自治"，特指双方或各方当事人按照共同的意愿（而不是一方自己的意愿）行事的状态。

本文聚焦的仲裁中对意思自治的实质性限制，笔者曾寻找过法律对意思自治的限制相关的研究，但是归纳来看，来自法律的限制均是在民事法律行为的效力层面，即违反法律规定或未达到法定生效要件的民事法律行为可能被认定为存在效力瑕疵，从而出现无效、可撤销等非完全的状态。但在本文提出的问题中，并非当事人的约定存在效力上的问题，而是当事人根本无法就选定仲裁员的问题实现意思自治，从而失去了自主决定的权利，这与法律对意思自治的限制属于完全不同的情况，因此本综述便不将该类限制加以讨论。

1.2 当事人共同选定仲裁员制度的历史渊源和当今发展

1.2.1 当事人共同选定仲裁员制度在全球的产生和发展

作为平行于诉讼的争议解决方式，仲裁拥有悠久的历史，其诞生远早于国家审判。有学者认为，古以色列联合王国国王所罗门是当今可以追溯到的最早的仲裁员，且其就两位妇女争夺小孩的案件中所采用的程序与当今的仲裁程序非常相似。[8] 在一些记载中，在公元前6世纪，古希腊城邦国家之间已开始采用仲裁的方式解决争议。克利夫兰-马歇尔法学院教授埃摩森（Frank D. Emerson）撰文表示，仲裁这一解纷机制在国家间争议和民事争议中都已经得到广泛应用[9]，在公元前600年左右，雅典和墨伽拉就萨拉米斯岛的归属产生争议，而本纠纷被提交至五名作为仲裁员的斯巴达人处，后者将案涉岛屿

---

[8] Elkouri, F., E. Elkouri, M. Volz, E. Goggin. *How Arbitration Works: Elkouri and Elkouri Fifth Edition*. BNA Books, 1989. 本案为两妇女就婴儿的归属产生争议，所罗门假意称先用宝剑将婴儿砍成两部分，一人一半，随后指出表示出不忍的妇女为孩子的亲生母亲，不在意孩子死活的妇女则不是。

[9] Emerson, Frank D., *History of Arbiration Practice and Law*. Cleveland State Law Review, 1970, p. 156.

裁定给了雅典。另外，作为一个非正式的参考，据南宁仲裁委员会撰文介绍，"古希腊广为流传的神话故事是帕黎斯就三个女神中最美丽的一位作出了裁断。古罗马共和国时期在公元前454年至公元前452年之间颁布制定了《十二铜表法》[10]，这部法典中就有多处专门对仲裁的规定"。[11]

11世纪左右，随着商业的发展，地中海沿岸、意大利各城邦国家之间出现了专用于调整商事关系的商人习惯法，而其中就包括仲裁制度。可考证的最早的仲裁法案是英国议会于1697年通过的，其首次正式地承认了仲裁制度[12]。

19世纪后期，法国、德国、瑞典、日本等国家纷纷在法律体系中正式确立仲裁制度，仲裁机构逐渐开始出现在仲裁的舞台上。1892年设立的英国伦敦国际仲裁院、1902年设立的瑞典斯德哥尔摩商会仲裁院、1911年设立的瑞士苏黎世商会仲裁院相继问世，仲裁的形式进入了机构仲裁和临时仲裁并举的新时期。

当事人共同选定仲裁员制度的产生与仲裁本身在时间上基本是一致的。事实上，有学者认为，仲裁的最初诞生本就是双方当事人共同寻找有声望的、双方都能服气的长者来对问题表态。[13]如在上段提到的婴儿仲裁案中，两位妇女在产生争议的时候，便自主地寻找双方都能信服的所罗门国王进行裁判，而所罗门的裁决也事实上生效并确认了双方的权利义务。在川岛武宜的《现代化与法》中，曾举过一个例子——河竹默阿弥的有名歌舞伎狂言《三人吉三廓初买》里的"庚申冢之场"一幕，两名恶人为一笔赃款大打出手，此时一名叫"高名"的和尚出现，两人便将争议交由他解决，最终甚至在和尚的主持下义结金兰。[14]这个例子便是日本语境下对上述情境的一个文学性复原。

在所罗门或者斯巴达人接受他人的委托而审理当事人之间的争议时，抑或

---

[10] 如第二表"审理"中规定："如因重病或因争讼涉及外邦人，可另定开庭日期。如因此使法官、仲裁员或双方当事人有任何不便，开庭日期必须推迟"。在此处，仲裁员和法官被放在了并列的位置，从而意味着仲裁和法院诉讼是两种平行的争议解决方式。

[11] 南宁仲裁委员会：《仲裁的起源》，载南宁仲裁委员会官网，http://www.legaldaily.com.cn/Arbitration/content/2021-04/16/content_8483816.htm，最后访问时间：2022年6月18日。

[12] 黄进、徐前权、宋连斌：《仲裁法学》，中国政法大学出版社1997年版，第9页。

[13] Michael John Mustill, *Arbitration*: History and Background, 6 Journal of International Arbitration, 1989, p. 43.

[14] ［日］川岛武宜：《现代化与法》，申政武等译，中国政法大学出版社1994年版，第182页。

是公元前480年科林斯（Corinth）人和科希拉（Corcyra）人就卢卡斯（Leucas，地名）的所属向地米斯托克利（Themistocles）提起仲裁[15]时，《十二铜表法》都还没有颁布，仲裁作为一个法律概念只存在于人们的实践中，而无具体的法律渊源。正因为仲裁的实践早于"仲裁"一词被初次定义[16]，所以诸多学者对于"仲裁"的界定也是由其早期的实践出发，从而将其理解为一种当事人可以自主安排程序性事项的解纷机制。当"意思自治"直接地融入"仲裁"的内涵之中，其自然成为与仲裁不可分割的价值追求。

19世纪之前，由于没有仲裁机构被组建，本就不存在机构仲裁和临时仲裁的划分。在仲裁机构如雨后春笋般成立的近一百年，仲裁逐渐呈现机构仲裁和临时仲裁二分天下的格局。对于临时仲裁而言，争议双方当事人对于争议解决程序有着相当高的自主性，从仲裁员、仲裁地、准据法到仲裁方方面面的各种程序，均有着自由安排的空间；对于机构仲裁，为保持仲裁意思自治的核心地位，当事人对于上述事项的自我安排仍得到尊重，但是仲裁的程序一般受制于某一仲裁机构的规则（绝大部分情况下为提交仲裁的仲裁机构的规则），仲裁机构为仲裁程序的规范性进行了背书。专就选择仲裁员的问题来看，临时仲裁中当事人选定仲裁员几乎没有任何限制（特别是名单的限制），而在机构仲裁中，考虑到合意选定仲裁员所带来的效率层面的成本，当事人选定仲裁员的自治将会受到一定的限制。

1.2.2 当事人共同选定仲裁员制度在中国的产生和发展

一般认为，古代中国常常处于厌讼社会的状态，但也有相反的论断。[17]但无论如何，各种观点都不否认人们将争议提交家族的长者处理，并相信后者有能力和权威解决该等纠纷。但是，单纯的商事纠纷并非如邻里之间有着共同的"长者"，因此作为争议双方共同信服的仲裁员的，往往是本身就带有审判职能的国家官员（而该提交争议至权威机构的行为，也恰如其分地被称为"告官"），历史有名的裁判者包拯、狄仁杰等，皆在此列。邓瑞平、孙志煜认

---

[15] 本案亦载于Emerson教授的 History of Arbitration Practice and Law，如前文所引。

[16] 毕竟如上所述，仲裁的萌芽诞生于古希腊罗马时期，商人习惯法中的仲裁诞生于11世纪，而现代的仲裁制度为国家所确立直到19世纪后期才发生。因此，当现代意义上的"仲裁"在法条中出现时，仲裁已经在实践中应用许久了。

[17] 范愉：《诉讼社会与无讼社会的辨析和启示》，载《法学家》2013年第1期。

为，仲裁并非一个主流的解纷机制，甚至在早期的中国，仲裁和调解并没有严格的区分。[18]纵观中国历史，《周礼·地官》中所提到的调人、秦汉时期的啬夫，乃至唐宋元时期的里正、坊正、社长，均从某种程度上兼具着仲裁员和调解员的职能。[19]就当事人选定仲裁员制度而言，由于仲裁制度本身就"若隐若现"，对仲裁员的选择就难以谈起——不过，就街坊邻里的简单民事纠纷而言，将纠纷提交至长者不啻一种自由选择的形式。

到了明清两代，中国部分地区出现资本主义萌芽，作为商人间组织的行会也随之出现。有英国学者认为，这些自带正式章程的商人协会，已经属于一种仲裁机构。[20]随着时代推移，商会的解纷功能逐渐发展完善，经历了一个"由小到大、由非正规到正规"[21]的过程。商会的纠纷解决机制并未被法律所规定，但是商人们自发地构建了这样的新的秩序，并自发地执行，这本就是对意思自治的一种反映，这种意思自治，当然也体现在仲裁员选择的层面上。从逻辑上来看，与现代仲裁制度的仲裁诉讼互相排斥不同，如果当事人对于仲裁员的安排不满意，完全可以另行提交诉讼；从行会诞生的背景来看，在商会诞生前，商事纠纷的解决耗时耗力，"法官不谙商情，不仅拖延时日，而且裁判结果常常是非不明，难昭公允，经年累月，法院积案颇多，影响民生甚巨，致使商民怨声载道"[22]，可见其诞生之初便承载着为商人们自主解决纠纷提供平台的功能，如果居间的仲裁员同法官一样"不谙商情"，那么商人们自然也不会愿意选择商会解决纠纷，而这与仲裁这一解纷方式的专业性也是一致的。

《仲裁法》的颁布和生效意味着中国现代商事仲裁制度的确立，当事人选定仲裁员制度首次在国家法律中被确立起来。但是，由于新中国长期实行的行政仲裁已经有着深远的影响，政府在仲裁中的影响力甚至可以占主导地位。

---

[18] 邓瑞平、孙志煜：《论国际商事仲裁的历史演进》，载《暨南学报》2009年第6期。

[19] 常怡：《中国调解制度》，重庆出版社1990年版，第3—4页。

[20] ［英］S. 斯普林克尔：《清代法制导论——从社会学角度加以分析》，张守东译，中国政法大学出版社2000年版，第117页。文中对商会仲裁的描述"调解委员会，有关当事人及证人在一座寺庙见面。在那儿，引发这场纠纷的货物，摆在委员会面前，各方都简短作了证。听了证人发言，经短暂商议之后，委员会作出裁决。双方接受这一终局裁决，站了起来，向委员会鞠躬，彼此相互鞠躬，……倘若告官，……会带来诸多不便"的确与现代仲裁非常类似。

[21] 郑成林：《近代中国商事仲裁制度演变的历史轨迹》，载《中州学刊》2002年第6期。

[22] 任云兰：《论近代中国商会的商事仲裁功能》，载《中国经济史研究》1995年第4期。

直至现在，不仅民众对仲裁有着广泛的误解，甚多法官也误以为仲裁机构与法院或政府机关有着隶属的关系。[23]这种误解不仅是理解上的偏差，甚至有可能让非专业的当事人陷入不知、不敢或不能按照自己的意思选定仲裁员的泥沼。今天，仲裁行政化的问题正在逐渐改善，仲裁也得以逐步回归本位，当事人共同选定仲裁员制度不仅被各仲裁机构依法沿用，其在实践中的应用也受到理论界和实务界的关照。在《仲裁法》面临修改的背景下，当事人共同选定仲裁员制度在法律层面得到进一步完善和发展。

第2章 意思自治在当事人共同选定仲裁员制度中的意义

即使是最极端的保守主义者，也不能否认仲裁过程中大量存在的意思自治的元素。正如前文所述的，在仲裁机构、仲裁地、仲裁员、准据法、仲裁规则等各方面，当事人都有意思自治的余地。本部分将深入地关注意思自治在仲裁中的意义，即在结合当事人选定仲裁员制度的同时，试论为何在仲裁活动中应当尊重当事人的意思自治，乃至意思自治为何被众多学者称为"核心"。

2.1 意思自治在当事人选择仲裁员程序中的核心地位

2.1.1 作为仲裁基本原则的意思自治

意思自治作为仲裁的基本原则，在仲裁这种争议解决方式中居于核心位置，存在多方面的因素。但一一看来，意思自治的重要性都离不开仲裁制度的历史发展。

首先，仲裁的诞生始于当事人对更高层次意思自治的追求。仲裁诞生于民间，仲裁人实际上接受了双方当事人交与他的权利，而在仲裁开始之时，双方当事人也都有接受仲裁结果约束的意思表示（至于民间的"仲裁"没有法律意义上的执行力，则是另一层面的问题），正因为这些特点，意思自治成为仲裁中应有之义。董连和仲裁员也指出，"仲裁起源于意思自治并在意思自治原则的推动下逐步完善；意思自治原则是仲裁制度的根本原则，也是仲裁与诉讼相区别的特有原则……意思自治是仲裁制度的理论基础，是仲裁制度产生的直接原因"。[24]邓瑞平等在研究仲裁制度在中外的发展历程后也总结出，无

---

[23] 刘丹冰：《试论中国商事仲裁法律制度演进中的政府作用与修正》，载《广东社会科学》2014年第1期。

[24] 董连和：《论我国仲裁制度中的意思自治原则》，载《清华大学学报》2006年第3期。

论中外，仲裁的早期发展都离不开"自治"的主题，"它强调的不是秩序，而是赋予双方当事人权能以解决争议的自由"[25]。张铁铁在《我国法律制度对商事仲裁性质的误解》一文中就指出，"仲裁制度的根本性质在于它是一种基于当事人私权利基础之上建立的争端解决机制"。

其次，意思自治是仲裁作为一种不同于诉讼的解纷制度与诉讼和谐共生的生命力来源。20世纪70年代后期，接近正义的第三次运动主张"以ADR程序来弥补传统诉讼程序在当事人接近正义方面的不足"[26]，正是在这一阶段，弗兰克·桑德教授提出了"多扇门法院"，即制度化的ADR（被法院控制的ADR）的概念。但值得注意的是，ADR虽在客观上，对于争议解决的理论和实践都起到了重大的作用，但是"ADR"本身的"alternative"一词，就表明了多种争议解决方式之间的主从关系。诚然，由于各国、各文化下社会的发展，在法院解决纠纷已经成为世界上大部分国家的人民容易想到的解纷方式，但诉讼和在定义上属于"ADR"的仲裁（即使是机构仲裁）本应是平行的，仅仅是在意思自治的方面有着根本的区别，即当其他条件全都一致的时候，通过其中意思自治的程度仍可以分辨两者。诉讼和仲裁的关系正如自行车和摩托车——两者均为两轮的代步工具，其根本差异便是动力来源，若是出现了"没有引擎"的摩托车，其和自行车在本质上也没什么两样了。由于分析当前制度的问题，不可能脱离当前的实际，因此在承认机构仲裁才是有效的仲裁形式的前提下，让仲裁机构尽可能地独立于行政机关，区别于法院，当事人的意思自治是其中最需要把握的核心区别。正如林一所言，"'自治性'则是全面契合'意思自治原则'的本意的……这种权威的权力来源于当事人的授信，各种权利义务责任在自治秩序内部消化"[27]。在诉讼中，权威的权力来源于国家暴力机器的属性，而仲裁作为同样具有强制力的解纷机制，其根本区别于诉讼的，便是依赖当事人的自主安排。如果在仲裁中，当事人的意思自治不能保障，仲裁和诉讼的界限就会逐渐模糊，那么这一制度存在的意义便随之烟消云散了。因此，在机构仲裁向行政机关乃至法院趋同的背景下，强调

---

[25] 邓瑞平、孙志煜：《论国际商事仲裁的历史演进》，载《暨南学报》2009年第6期。

[26] [澳]娜嘉·亚历山大：《全球调解趋势：乘上第三次浪潮》，王福华等译，中国法制出版社2011年版，第4—5页。

[27] 林一：《国际商事仲裁中的意思自治原则》，法律出版社2018年版，第13页。

当事人意思自治是使得仲裁与其他机制泾渭分明的手段,也是仲裁得以与诉讼和谐共生的活力源泉。

2.1.2 意思自治在仲裁员选定环节的特殊性

仲裁员在仲裁程序中也起着举足轻重的作用,正如法谚所言,"仲裁的质量取决于仲裁员的质量"。伦敦玛丽女王大学的仲裁调查报告显示,多达39%的受访者认为选择仲裁员是仲裁最有价值的特点。[28]

2.1.2.1 当事人与仲裁员之间的复杂法律关系

仲裁员与当事人之间有着双重的法律关系:一方面,仲裁员的选择在仲裁的意思自治范围之内,是当事人意思自治的结果;另一方面,仲裁员组成的仲裁庭作出裁决后,对当事人又有公法意义上的约束力。这种对当事人影响深远的法律关系,导致仲裁员的选择格外地重要。

理论界对于当事人和仲裁员之间的法律关系定性,主要有合同说、准合同说、特殊法律关系说等。在国际范围,比较传统和被广为接受的理论是合同说。早在19世纪,英国就有判例,认为仲裁员和双方当事人之间成立合同关系,在实体问题上对立的双方当事人在合同中共为一方。[29]《德国仲裁法》第1030节甚至直接规定,仲裁员合同是通过仲裁当事人与仲裁员之间的要约与承诺形成的。笔者认为,在中国的语境下,双方当事人与仲裁员之间成立合同关系也是比较合理的判断。根据我国《民法典》第469条第1款(合同的形式)、第471条(合同订立的方式)规定,合同的形式不拘泥于书面,而当事人也可通过不同的方式订立合同。在双方当事人共同选定仲裁员的程序中,当事人选定仲裁员的意思表示即为要约,仲裁员作出同意担任仲裁员的意思表示时,即为承诺。对于选择仲裁员的合同,在当事人和仲裁员之间事实上成立要约和承诺后,合同即告成立(不出意外也同时生效),并无特殊的生效要件。仲裁员与当事人之间成立了非书面形式的合同,合同内容在仲裁活动的大量实践中得到确定。至于当事人与仲裁员之间成立何种合同关系,王苹归纳为委托合同说、雇佣合同说、承揽合同说、特殊合同说等不同理论,在

---

[28] School of International Arbitration at Queen Mary University of London, White & Case LLP. International Arbitration Survey: The Evolution of International Arbitration [R]. 2018: 8.

[29] Crampton & Holt v. Ridley & Co. (1887) 20 Q. B. D. 48.

此不再展开。[30]

在承认当事人和仲裁员之间成立合同关系的同时，也不能忽视仲裁员作出的裁决可能会有公法上的效力，这与民事合同无执行力构成了根本的区别。《仲裁法》第 62 条赋予了仲裁裁决执行力，而该条中提到的"民事诉讼法的有关规定"，在《民事诉讼法》中体现为第 248 条第 1 款的"对依法设立的仲裁机构的裁决，一方当事人不履行的，对方当事人可以向有管辖权的人民法院申请执行。受申请的人民法院应当执行"。在笔者看来，本条的内涵至少有三点：第一，在一定条件下，仲裁裁决可得到国家强制力的保障得以强制执行；第二，能够到法院申请执行的仲裁裁决，必须是依法设立的仲裁机构的裁决，即机构仲裁的裁决而非临时仲裁的裁决，这一点已在前文中讨论过；第三，仲裁机构自身并没有执行机构，无法由自身直接执行所作出的裁决，须借由法院的力量。综上三点所述，仲裁裁决与普通的合同相比，有明显特殊的公法效力。因此，不少学者也认为双方亦构成某种特殊的法律关系。[31]

综上，如果说意思自治是仲裁制度的核心，那么笔者认为选定仲裁员环节的意思自治便是意思自治的核心。

2.1.2.2 首席仲裁员／独任仲裁员在仲裁中的关键地位

进一步地，首席仲裁员或独任仲裁员在仲裁庭中又占据更加关键的地位。法律和仲裁规则赋予他们的权限使得他们的意见举足轻重，因此在仲裁员的选择中，本文重点观察的首席仲裁员和独任仲裁员的选定又更具重要性。

首席仲裁员和边裁虽然都是普通程序的三人仲裁庭的组成人员，但他们仍有较大区别：第一，在程序上，边裁的产生无须双方的合意，除出现仲裁员廉洁性问题等特殊情况，实践中边裁的确定一般可以通过一方当事人单一的意思表示来实现[32]；第二，在审理过程中，虽然仲裁员的公正性是仲裁这一解纷方式需要保证的首要对象之一，但作为一方当事人选出的仲裁员，许多边裁难免产生倾向性，甚至在开庭中相互争论，代为行使律师的职权，而相比之

---

[30] 王苹:《仲裁员与当事人法律关系探讨》，载《辽宁商务职业学院学报》2004 年第 2 期。

[31] 范铭超:《仲裁员与仲裁当事人法律关系模型的困境及其解决》，载《北方法学》2014 年第 6 期。

[32] 随着仲裁实践的发展，这一论断可能会面对越来越大的质疑，如在包含两个或更多申请人或被申请人的仲裁中，一方（往往是被申请人方）的多个当事人可能无法达成合意，而此时在实践中这一方选择边裁的权利就不得不让渡给仲裁机构。

下,首席仲裁员则不具有或少有类似的偏向性;第三,在权责范围方面,首席仲裁员不仅主导整个仲裁程序的推进,一般还需独自承担撰写裁决书的工作,工作量远大于边裁。[33] 上述的第三点尤为重要,因为我国《仲裁法》第53条明确指出,"仲裁庭不能形成多数意见时,裁决应当按照首席仲裁员的意见作出"。除非两边裁的意见一致而与首席不一致,在其他所有情况下,裁决的作出均取决于首席仲裁员的意见,而这基本覆盖了所有的案件。同时,首席仲裁员需撰写裁决书,裁决书自作出之日起便发生法律效力,因此这份决定当事人双方具体权利义务的法律文件,也是由首席仲裁员主导的。在独任仲裁员的情况下,情况更是如此。

因此,在仲裁意思自治的前提下,首席仲裁员或独任仲裁员对于案件的影响又是仲裁员中最大的,因此以意思自治作为核心优势和吸引力的仲裁,赋予当事人选择首席仲裁员或独任仲裁员的权利方可最大化地让当事人的意思自治作用于当事人自身,使其自主选择具有意义。

2.2 当事人选择仲裁员意思自治对当事人和仲裁制度的意义

2.2.1 对当事人的意义

本文语境下的意思自治是仲裁当事人的意思自治,因此从当事人权利的保护维度出发是一个常规且合理的思维路径。事实上,也的确有学者认为仲裁中的意思自治有利于保护当事人的权益。

一方面,当事人通过自己的意思选定仲裁员,对于纠纷的解决、达到"胜负皆服"的结果,有着积极的作用。相反,若首席仲裁员或独任仲裁员是由仲裁机构指定,难免"有行政委派之嫌,很难令当事人满意","主任指定的首席仲裁员未能充分体现当事人的意愿,难以取得当事人的信任,且难以从一开始树立起首席仲裁员应有的公信和权威"[34]。

另一方面,如果说"胜负皆服"仅是争议解决的理想状态,而裁决的确定力和执行力无论当事人态度如何都可以通过法律的方式来维护,那么通过意思自治选定仲裁员事实上能够保护当事人的权利,则是一个不可忽略的裨益。

早在1994年,国内就已经有学者意识到仲裁员选定的意思自治问题,并

---

[33] 从权责一致的角度来看,首席仲裁员也拥有着更大的"权力",如《仲裁法》第53条规定,"仲裁庭不能形成多数意见时,裁决应当按照首席仲裁员的意见作出"。

[34] 李登华:《论仲裁庭首席仲裁员的确定》,载《武汉仲裁》2011年第1期。

加以阐述。对比诉讼，由于当事人提起仲裁的权利来源于性质为合同的仲裁协议，而非来源于国家授权，因此当事人意思自治在仲裁这种制度得到的支持力度应当更大。作为这一特点的结论，"仲裁员主要是对当事人和国际商事交易负责，而不是对任何主权国家或国内法负责"[35]。郑远民教授这一番见解，便并非从仲裁固有的形态出发，而是认为仲裁裁决应当对当事人负责，亦即维护当事人的权益。

德国著名仲裁员 Karl-Heinz Böckstiegel 在《当事人意思自治与案件管理：来自一位仲裁员的几点经验与建议》一文中提到，在仲裁领域，广义的意思自治表示，"当事人可以自主决定仲裁程序的方方面面，仅受强制性法律的某些约束"[36]，此处的方方面面，自然包括选定仲裁员的自治。而对于当事人而言，似乎可以推断出 Böckstiegel 的立论基础便是仲裁程序中的意思自治有利于当事人权利的保护，因为"商界人士都强烈希望根据各自的需求和利益来塑造他们之间的商业关系，并自由选择属于他们自己的纠纷解决机制"[37]。在这段论述中，Böckstiegel 先生不仅具体解释了仲裁中的意思自治得以体现维护当事人权利的缘由，还认为意思自治在仲裁中的"根本性"来源于宪法中的契约自由权利。

窃以为在实践中对当事人的意思自治维度加以限制是家长主义立法思维的表现。一方面，仲裁员名册之外的以及不符合"三八两高"法定条件的，可能"欠缺专业性""有徇私之危险"的自然人作出的裁决不被信任；另一方面，在当事人有限的选择空间内，效率价值的地位又被提高，因为国家仅赋予了仲裁机构指定仲裁规则的机会，而基于效率的考量，仲裁规则的内容又显现出当事人选定仲裁员权利的淡化以及机构对于该权利的"入侵"。这样一来，当事人有时并非在自主地"选择"仲裁员，而是被仲裁机构体系化的程序推动，甚至迫使着在形式上参与了"选择"的过程。将决定仲裁程序的权利交回到当事人手中，既是对当事人作为成熟的（民）商事主体自我维权能力的肯定，也是仲裁制度走向成熟的必由之路。而在全球商业行为日益增多、

---

[35] 郑远民：《论意思自治原则与国际商事仲裁制度的完善和发展》，载《社会科学家》1994年第3期，第89—94页。

[36] ［德］Karl-Heinz Böckstiegel：《当事人意思自治与案件管理：来自一位仲裁员的几点经验与建议》，傅攀峰译，载《北京仲裁》2014年第4期。

[37] 同前注。

商事主体的行为愈加发达的情况下，当事人更在意、也的确有能力比仲裁机构和国家更好地维护自己的利益。因此，当事人共同选定仲裁员制度中的意思自治，有利于当事人的权利保护。

2.2.2 对仲裁制度的意义

尽管在世界范围内，仲裁的起源形态是临时仲裁的形态，但由于《仲裁法》的硬性规定，我国即使存在临时仲裁，也存量极少，未在国内仲裁界占据足够的分量。而对于机构仲裁，有研究者一针见血地认为，"我国设立仲裁制度的目的是在司法系统无力解决商事争端的情况下，为社会中突然大量产生的商事纠纷提供替代性的解决方案……仲裁被视为一种体现公权力的'准司法'制度"[38]。而就仲裁员选任问题，也有国外学者指出，无论国内仲裁还是国际仲裁，仲裁庭的组成常依靠指定机构的指定而非当事人直接协商选定。[39]

事实上，直至今日，我国的仲裁机构也以类似于事业单位的性质存在着，与《仲裁法》第14条"仲裁委员会独立于行政机关，与行政机关没有隶属关系"以及独立于法院的应然状态仍有一定区别。学界普遍地认为，仲裁机构与行政机关走得太近，会导致其在当事人（尤其是外国当事人）心中的中立性程度和可信任程度降低。[40]

肖芳在2005年就已提出，中国的仲裁机构质量互相差距很大，有追赶并有望达到世界水平的，亦有尚处于非常基础的发展阶段的。因此，主观地认为仲裁机构会把维护当事人的利益放在工作的核心位置，必然是过于理想化而不切实际的。因此，需要在立法上对于仲裁机构多加规范，推动和促使仲裁机构蓬勃发展。[41]

具体到本文研究的话题，即仲裁员的产生上来看，当事人选择仲裁员本就是仲裁更具自治性的特征，也是仲裁之所以对当事人具有吸引力的诸多原因之一，若该等权利无法落地，那么当事人（尤其是简易仲裁程序中的当事人）

---

[38] 张铁铁：《我国法律制度对商事仲裁性质的误解》，载《北方法学》2020年第4期。

[39] Fouchard etc., *Fouchard Gaillard Goldman on International Commercial Arbitration*, Aspen Publishers, Inc., New York, 2003, p. 445.

[40] 刘丹冰：《试论中国商事仲裁法律制度演进中的政府作用与修正》，载《广东社会科学》2014年第1期。

[41] 肖芳：《论仲裁庭组成的有关问题》，载《仲裁研究》2005年第2期。

只能等待一个未知的仲裁员对自己所涉的案件作出裁决，这和在诉讼中无法挑选法官的情形在本质上并没有太大差别。有时，机构指派的仲裁员是双方当事人均不想选择的仲裁员，这样的结果显然完全走向了"自治"的另一边，而当程序推进到组庭阶段时，当事人事实上也没有退一步作出选择的余地。仲裁员选任的意思自治与仲裁本身的意思自治拥有高度的一致性，因此保护当事人自主选择仲裁员的权利，也赋予了仲裁作为重要的解纷方式的生命力。

第3章 当事人共同选定仲裁员制度中的意思自治在制度与实践中的问题

本章将讨论当事人共同选定仲裁员制度在制度和实践中存在的问题——归根结底，是实践中的问题。本段采取了比较法研究的方式，选取了在全球负有盛名的五家仲裁机构：国际商会仲裁院（以下简称ICC）、香港国际仲裁中心（以下简称HKIAC）、新加坡国际仲裁中心（以下简称SIAC）、伦敦国际仲裁院（以下简称LCIA）、斯德哥尔摩商会仲裁院（以下简称SCC）[42]，以其为例，通过梳理其所在地的仲裁法律、其仲裁规则和仲裁实践，阐述我国仲裁中当事人选定仲裁员制度的问题。

3.1 我国法律对当事人选定仲裁员意思自治的制度保障甚少

3.1.1 仲裁员的选定在中国仲裁法律中的体现

与1889年就已经制定出第一部仲裁法、1892年就已建立伦敦仲裁院的英国相比，我国的仲裁法直到一百年后的1994年才颁布生效，仲裁这一制度在我国并不拥有一段悠久的历史，也尚未随着时代的推移、案件的累积，自主地发展到一个非常成熟的阶段。目前，我国与仲裁法律体系中对仲裁员作出规定的主要包括《仲裁法》第二章中的仲裁机构对仲裁员的聘任和监督，第四章中的

---

[42] 本文参照了英国伦敦玛丽女王大学（Queen Mary University of London）和美国伟凯律师事务所（White & Case）共同发布的《2021年国际仲裁调查报告》（*2021 International Arbitration Survey*），其中评选了全球最受欢迎的仲裁机构，参见http://www.moj.gov.cn/pub/sfbgw/fzgz/fzgzggflfwx/fzgzggflfw/202105/t20210525_411158.html，以及https://www.163.com/dy/article/G9GPHC950514AN1F.html，最后访问时间：2023年3月11日。按照得票顺序，国际商会仲裁院、香港国际仲裁中心、新加坡国际仲裁中心、伦敦国际仲裁院、中国国际经济贸易仲裁委员会、国际投资争端解决中心、斯德哥尔摩商会仲裁院分列前七位。考虑到贸仲将在国内仲裁机构部分详述，ICSID专门解决国际投资仲裁，因予以暂时排除，本文重点研究的五家仲裁机构分别为ICC、HKIAC、SIAC、LCIA和SCC。

仲裁员的组成、开庭和裁决中对仲裁员的程序性要求、第五章中的撤销仲裁裁决的事由,第七章中的涉外仲裁的仲裁员聘任,以及最高人民法院在诸如《最高人民法院关于现职法官不得担任仲裁员的通知》《最高人民法院研究室关于人民法院其他工作人员能否担任仲裁员的答复》《最高人民法院关于人民法院办理仲裁裁决执行案件若干问题的规定》《最高人民法院关于审理仲裁司法审查案件若干问题的规定》第 18 条(仲裁员廉洁性问题)等文件中的零星规定。

此外,值得一提的是,1954 年由政务院颁布的《中央人民政府政务院关于在中国国际贸易促进委员会内设立对外贸易仲裁委员会的决定》仍在生效中,其中对仲裁员的有关规定与《仲裁法》中"仲裁庭的组成"一节较为相近(但考虑到《仲裁法》第 14 条对于仲裁机构的定性,该规定在本文中暂不考虑)。

在我国香港地区,仲裁员选定的法律规定则较为翔实。在香港进行的仲裁受《香港仲裁条例》(2011 年)调整。该条例独以《联合国国际贸易法委员会国际商事仲裁示范法》(以下简称《示范法》)为基础,改变了先前版本以 UNCITRAL 示范法为基础和英国 1950 年仲裁法为基础的二分格局。

《香港仲裁条例》第 23 条、第 24 条详述了当事人选择仲裁员的规定。首先,香港沿用了 UNCITRAL 的立法体例,允许当事人选定任意数量的仲裁员来解决争议,而无奇数偶数之区分。仅当双方当事人未就仲裁员的人数达成一致时,才根据法定默认为一人或三人。进一步地,选定仲裁员的程序可由当事人约定,未达成此约定的,如《示范法》所述,在三人仲裁庭中,由双方当事人选出的边裁选出首席仲裁员(事实上,《示范法》似乎并未明示第三名仲裁员为首席仲裁员),若一方当事人在收到另一方的选定仲裁员请求后 30 日仍未能选定边裁,或两名边裁在被选定后 30 日仍未能选定首席仲裁员,则"经一方当事人请求",由法院或其他机构加以指定;在独任仲裁员的仲裁中,当事人未就仲裁员选定达成协议的,经一方当事人请求,由第 6 条规定的法院或其他机构加以指定。[43]

在上述各情形中,仅在当事人未约定仲裁员选定程序,且仲裁员人数为奇数但超过三人时,第三方机构(HKIAC)会直接介入仲裁员选定程序,指定尚缺位的一名或多名仲裁员。在其他各情形中,即使当事人未能选定首席

---

[43]《香港仲裁条例》第 24 条在引用《示范法》的基础上,增添了约定的仲裁员人数为偶数、仲裁员人数为奇数但超过三人时的情形。

或独任仲裁员,也是"经一方当事人请求",法院或仲裁机构才得以介入。仅此半句已在很大程度上尊重了选定仲裁员作为意思自治范畴之一的本质,表明即使选定程序出现僵局,仲裁员的最终确定也很大程度上取决于当事人的意愿。

3.1.2 我国仲裁立法在当事人选定仲裁员制度方面存在的问题

我国的仲裁法律体系中虽然对仲裁员提及不少,但对于仲裁庭的组成、仲裁员的产生方式(尤其是首席仲裁员和独任仲裁员)并未做过多规定。因此,就仲裁员选定这一事项在仲裁活动中的实践,往往由仲裁机构补充制订更详细的规则,或由仲裁机构经考量后决定。与此对比,无论是我国香港地区,还是前文提及的法国、新加坡、英国和瑞典,在一定程度上体现了对当事人选定仲裁员意思自治的制度保护。

由此看来,我国立法在当事人选定仲裁员的事项上仍有可为之处。加强对当事人选定仲裁员意思自治的制度保障,不必然意味着《仲裁法》的修改需要强行添加仲裁员选定的相关规定,而通过行政法规、规章等下位法的调整,仍然可以在客观上缓解法律缺位的问题。举例而言,以《最高人民法院关于为自由贸易试验区建设提供司法保障的意见》为指导的《横琴自由贸易试验区临时仲裁规则》便在特定地区为临时仲裁开了绿灯,客观上增加了当事人选定仲裁员的范围,有利于当事人通过意思自治选定仲裁员。

3.2 我国仲裁机构规则对仲裁员选定规范翔实但收效甚微

3.2.1 仲裁员的选定在中国主流仲裁机构规则中的体现

在中国国内,中国国际经济贸易仲裁委员会(以下简称贸仲)和北京仲裁委员会/北京国际仲裁中心(以下简称北仲)是在全球拥有相当影响力的两家仲裁机构。在仲裁规则的演变、仲裁制度的革新方面,贸仲和北仲也走在同行前列,代表着中国仲裁的最高水平。因此,本部分仅选取贸仲和北仲的仲裁规则加以讨论。

《贸仲规则》(2015年版)第25条至第28条规定了仲裁庭组成相关制度。依照我国《仲裁法》的规定,贸仲和其他所有国内仲裁机构一样,编制了仲裁员名册。我国在此前的相当一段时间内实行的都是"强制名册制",当事人不得在仲裁员名册之外选定仲裁员。贸仲是国内首家突破这一限制的仲裁机构,目前当事人可在贸仲的仲裁员名册之外选定仲裁员,但是以此法选定的仲裁员须经仲裁委员会确认。在普通程序中,当事人可自行选定或委托仲委员会主任选定首席仲裁员，当事人未能选定的，由仲裁委员会主任指定。值得一提的是，贸仲将可作为当事人选定首席仲裁员（并增加选中同一仲裁员的概率）的"名单法"直接纳入了仲裁规则，这一做法在其他主流的仲裁机构规则中都并未提到。贸仲的独任仲裁员与首席仲裁员的产生方式完全相同，在仲裁规则的编制上，其直接引述了后者作为程序规定。与许多国际仲裁机构规则的设计不同，贸仲的仲裁员选定并不区分"提名"与"任命"。

《北仲规则》（2022年版）第20条统一规定了普通程序（三名仲裁员）中有关仲裁庭组成的各种问题。第55条为简易程序的组庭方式，该条中明确说明简易程序的独任仲裁员选择可以参照第20条第4款，即参照普通程序的仲裁员选定规定。与贸仲类似，北仲规则也明确在名册中选定仲裁员并非必需，但选择名册外的仲裁员需要经由仲裁委员会主任确认。在首席仲裁员的选定方面，当事人可自行选定或共同委托仲裁委员会主任指定，也可通过分别提供名单，或在仲裁委员会的协助下在后者提供的缩小名单中继续选择，以增加达成一致的概率。在当事人未能就仲裁员选择达成一致的情况下，仲裁委员会可决定由已选出的边裁共同选定首席仲裁员。仍然无法选出的，首席仲裁员由仲裁委员会指定。

3.2.2 当事人选定仲裁员的意思自治在中国主流仲裁机构实践中的体现

据笔者在多家国内主流仲裁机构的网站上统计，北仲是目前唯一一家将仲裁员的产生方式作为一项指标详细地记入年度总结的。另外，上海国际仲裁中心也列出了境外仲裁员参与案件的产生情况，但样本较小，且在何种程序产生也不甚清晰。[44] 北仲的统计为本文的定量研究提供了宝贵的数据支撑，同时作为国内最专业、最负盛名的仲裁机构之一，北仲的数据也在一定程度上代表着中国仲裁的领先水平。但即使如此，北仲在当事人共同选定仲裁员事项上的数据也难以令人满意。

《北京仲裁委员会/北京国际仲裁中心2021年工作总结》中指出，双方共同选定首席仲裁员的案件为15件、选定独任仲裁员的案件为13件，共计28件，

---

[44] 在上海国际仲裁中心官网的统计中，2022年共有37人次的外籍仲裁员参与案件审理，其中11人次由当事人选定，26人次由仲裁委员会主任指定。参见 https://www.shiac.org/pc/SHIAC?moduleCode=annual_report&securityId=bkohgHz_o5JBWca_XrDg0w，最后访问时间：2023年2月25日。

而在该年度，由北仲主任指定的首席仲裁员有 1300 人次、独任仲裁员有 5285 人次。如此计算，在普通程序中，各方当事人通过合意选定首席仲裁员的比例为 15/1315，即大约 1.14%；在简易程序中，各方当事人通过合意选定独任仲裁员的比例为 13/5298，即大约 0.25%。综合所有案件来看，各方当事人通过合意选定仲裁员的比例为 28/6613，即大约 0.42%。

2020 年度，双方共同选定首席仲裁员的案件为 9 件，选定独任仲裁员的案件为 16 件，共计 25 件——对比该年度 5617 件的总受案量、5274 件的总结案量，乃至 3188 件的裁决结案量（事实上，即使以调解、撤案结案，也并非意味案件尚未进入组庭阶段，因此，有仲裁员产生的案件一定大于 3188 件），当事人合意选定仲裁员的案件同样仅占所有案件的比例不到 1%。在 2019 年度，北仲的受案量较 2020 年要多，当事人选定仲裁员的案例也更多，但大体上成功选任案件所占比例保持一致。国内其他几家仲裁机构的年报或工作总结中尚未列明当事人选任仲裁员的数量，但是据笔者了解，在贸仲仲裁案件中，当事人共同选定仲裁员的成功率也远远未达到一半的比例。

HKIAC 的 2020 年和 2021 年年度报告也统计了当事人选定仲裁员情况的数据。根据 2021 年年报，HKIAC 在当年总共的 203 件仲裁案件中指定仲裁员 142 人次，对当事人或边裁选定的仲裁员 164 人次进行确认。2020 年，HKIAC 在 183 件仲裁案件中指定仲裁员 149 人次，对当事人或边裁选定的仲裁员 135 人次进行确认。HKIAC 并未公布更详细的数据，因此其中多少为当事人或边裁选定的独任仲裁员或首席仲裁员难以知晓。但是我们仍可以根据已有的数据进行简单的估算：以 2021 年为例，假定 203 件仲裁案件均为独任庭和三人庭，共计 306 名仲裁员，那么根据鸡兔同笼原理，可知有 51 或 52 件为三人庭（此处取 52）、151 件为独任庭。那么，即使全部当事人均积极地行使了选定边裁的权利，产生了 104 名边裁，仍有 60 名独任或首席仲裁员为当事人或边裁选定，占全部案件的 29.6%。事实上，实际的比例远比这个数据要高，因为可想而知，并非所有边裁均为当事人选定。

3.2.3 当事人选定仲裁员的意思自治在外国主流仲裁机构实践中的体现

本节将以作为研究对象的仲裁机构所公开的年度报告为基础，用数字直观地展示外国主流仲裁机构当事人成功选定独任仲裁员或首席仲裁员的比例，从而进行定量的研究，通过对比展示出中国仲裁实践中在当事人选定仲裁员的意思自治上能够改进的空间和方向。

3.2.3.1 ICC

经笔者检索，ICC 官网上并没有提供近几年的年报，能够免费直接获得的仅有 2017 年争议解决统计数据。[45] 在这份报告中，详尽地介绍了以下数据：

	独任仲裁员	三人庭边裁	首席仲裁员
当事人提名	63	777	23
边裁提名	N/A	N/A	239
仲裁院指定	172	63	145
其他机构指定	0	0	2
总计	235	840	409

如上表，在 2017 年 ICC 进行仲裁的案件的所有的独任仲裁员中，有约 26.8% 为当事人提名（并由 ICC 确认）；在所有的首席仲裁员中，有 5.6% 为当事人提名、57.9% 为边裁提名。

尽管近年来的数据缺失，但是 ICC 素来在受到当事人喜爱的仲裁机构中名列前茅，而根据国际商会仲裁院主席 Claudia Salomon 女士在一次 2022 年的演讲中所提及，近年来 ICC 当事人直接通过合议提名，或通过边裁联合提名仲裁员的比例高达约 75%，这也与 2017 年的数据可以互相印证。总之，ICC 规则虽然未对当事人选定仲裁员提供什么积极的帮助，但在实施的过程中仍然得以保障当事人直接或间接地选定仲裁员。

3.2.3.2 SIAC

本部分参考了 SIAC 的 2021 年年度报告。[46]

在该年报中，SIAC 在两处提及仲裁员选定的数据，但两部分数据稍有出入：在报告第 22 页，提及共指定仲裁员 179 人次（其中包括 144 名独任仲裁员和 35 名三人庭中的仲裁员），当事人或边裁共提名仲裁员 192 人次。在第 23 页，SIAC 共指定仲裁员 198 人次，当事人及边裁共提名产生了仲裁员 213 人次（其中当事人提名 160 人次，边裁提名首席仲裁员 53 人次），共计 411

---

[45] 参见 https://iccwbo.org/wp-content/uploads/sites/3/2018/07/2017-icc-dispute-resolution-statistics.pdf，最后访问时间：2023 年 2 月 25 日。

[46] 参见 https://siac.org.sg/wp-content/uploads/2022/06/SIAC-AR2021-FinalFA.pdf，最后访问时间：2023 年 2 月 25 日。

人次（因为该统计是基于仲裁员的国籍进行的，而一些具有多重国籍的仲裁员被重复计算了）。

由于 SIAC 的仲裁员选定情况和案件总量统计情况系采用不同标准（因为根据年报，2021 年 SIAC 处理的案件量超过 400 件，而仲裁员一共只出现了 371 人次），因此无法估算当事人选定首席或独任仲裁员的比例。但简单比较 2021 年 HKIAC 的当事人、边裁选定仲裁员人数和机构指定仲裁员人数之比例，会发现两者数据十分接近（指定人数在 HKIAC 占 46.4%，在 SIAC 占 48.2%），虽然这一比例并无实际的意义（因为当事人、边裁选定仲裁员人数中包含当事人选定的边裁，所以当事人选定首席或独任仲裁员实际的比例极大地取决于独任庭和三人庭的比例）。

3.2.3.3　LCIA

本部分参考了 LCIA 的 2021 年年度报告。[47]

报告显示，在 2021 年所有产生的 449 人次、298 名不同的仲裁员中（包括组庭后变更仲裁员的情形），有 44% 为当事人提名，42% 由 LCIA 指定，14% 为边裁提名。由于 LCIA 给出了独任庭和三人庭的案件数比例（48∶52），该部分的计算较为容易：由于最终的结论是比例而非具体数据，不妨假定 LCIA 在 2021 年共审理案件 100 件，共 204 名仲裁员，那么当事人提名、LCIA 指定和边裁提名的仲裁员人数便分别是 90 人、86 人、28 人，且此处的 28 人均为首席仲裁员。所以剩余的 176 人为 48 名独任仲裁员加上 104 名边裁，再加上 24 名首席仲裁员。即使按照最极端的情况，即所有的 90 位当事人选定的仲裁员均覆盖在边裁之中，那么非由 LCIA 指定首席仲裁员（在此假定中数量为 28）或独任仲裁员（在此假定中数量为 0）在所有案件中所占的比例也达到了 28%，事实上这个数字一定会更大。

3.2.3.4　SCC

本部分参考了 SCC 发布在官网上的 2022 年统计数据。[48]

与 LCIA 类似，SCC 公开了由当事人选定、由 SCC 指定和由边裁指定的首席仲裁员的数据，其人数分别为 127 人、50 人、10 人，当事人选定的仲裁员人数甚至超过 SCC 指定和边裁指定的人数之和的两倍。即使按照最极端的

---

[47]　参见 https://www.lcia.org/LCIA/reports.aspx##，最后访问时间：2023 年 2 月 25 日。

[48]　参见 https://sccarbitrationinstitute.se/en/about-scc/scc-statistics，最后访问时间：2023 年 2 月 25 日。

情况,即仅有7件简易案件,剩余60件为普通程序案件,使得所有选定的仲裁员均尽可能系边裁,那么当事人选定首席仲裁员或独任仲裁员的比例也达到了11.7%,当事人和边裁选定首席仲裁员或独任仲裁员的比例达到了25.4%。

3.2.4 我国仲裁实践在当事人选定仲裁员制度方面存在的问题

意思自治是仲裁的基础。"意思自治之于国际商事仲裁的根基性和价值,如同其之于民法(私法),几近公理。"[49]不仅仲裁机构和仲裁员的权力完全来源于当事人之间的仲裁条款,仲裁机构、仲裁地、仲裁员等对于仲裁程序有着根本性意义的元素,当事人依据法律规定也有着非常充分的选择权。但是,在我国的仲裁实践中,共同选择仲裁员的制度却沦为空中楼阁,当事人在事实上并未得以充分行使该权利。本节中,将基于上节北仲提供的数据,对当事人共同选定仲裁员制度在中国仲裁实践中存在的问题进行叙述。

最明显和直接的问题,就是在中国的仲裁法律体系(包括和仲裁机构规则构建的仲裁机构体系)下,当事人选定仲裁员的权利难以真正地由自己行使,包括《北仲规则》在内的诸多仲裁规则中就当事人选定仲裁员事项作出的先进规定,就如同一座空中楼阁,难以落地。而在一次理想的仲裁程序中,当事人理应有权预定仲裁员的产生方式,以及(除非另有约定,将选定仲裁员的权利委托于任意第三方)有权通过双方的真实意思表达,最终协商确定仲裁员的人选。在实践中,诚然恶意阻滞仲裁庭组成的当事人普遍存在,但是这一现象的根本问题并非出在仲裁员选择之时,而在签订合同时已经出现。当事人在签订合同时若能够更加翔实地安排仲裁员选定的相关事宜,在矛盾诞生后扯皮的现象就会相应地减少一些——而签订完备而有保障的合同,对于以真实意思签订合同的商事主体而言,是有着正面的利益的,因此当事人有动力在仲裁条款中更翔实地规划仲裁员选定事宜。

笔者在北仲工作期间,便注意到了仲裁员的选任问题。由于在大部分情况下,双方当事人只能通过"碰运气"的方式与对方达成合意(即双方提交的选定仲裁员的函上各自所填写的是同一位首席仲裁员或独任仲裁员),实现共任仲裁员的难度极高,成功的案例也少之又少,甚至因此有律师专门致电仲裁委员会声明放弃选定(独任)仲裁员的权利。但是,在提出该问题时,笔者也只能凭借回忆指出"绝大部分的仲裁案件中,当事人都不能共同选定仲

---

[49] 林一:《国际商事仲裁中的意思自治原则》,法律出版社2018年版,第13页。

裁员",而不能罗列具体的数据。类似地,在过往的学者研究中,由于数据的缺失,对仲裁员的选定和指定相关问题的讨论往往以感性的认识为基础,但近年来,随着一些仲裁机构的年报范围愈加广泛、内容愈加详细,也使得基于数据的理性成为可能。然而在看到数据的时候,令人难以想象同时又感到遗憾的是,尽管国内仲裁机构在当事人选定仲裁员的仲裁规则的制定上已经十分先进,但实践中这些规定实际上还并未发挥应有的作用。

如果说当事人直接通过约定选定首席仲裁员或独任仲裁员是一种直接的意思自治,由双方当事人选出的边裁至少在某种程度上被当事人认为是符合自身利益的,其对于首席仲裁员作出的选定也可称为一种"间接"的意思自治。但是在国内,不仅当事人直接选定仲裁员的案例少之又少,由于边裁选主裁的制度未包含于《仲裁法》中,其在仲裁机构的实践中更是凤毛麟角,几乎可以忽略不计。如此一来,我国的当事人所面临的首席或独任仲裁员,绝大部分均是仲裁机构直接指定的,那么该等仲裁员为双方所不满意的概率,就大大增加了。进一步,仲裁规则规定仲裁机构(主任)指定仲裁员,却没有规定指定仲裁员时应符合的条件,也没有对仲裁机构对当事人提出异议的决定权的限制[50],这无疑也将当事人的权利置于一种不确定之中。

诚然,考虑到《北仲规则》为2022年新修订,且当事人—边裁—主任的三步选定程序系该版本规则最新添加,但同样世界领先(甚至直至现在都仍然领先)的"名单法"则早在2015年版规则中就已经包括,而这样先进的规则并未在实践中展现明显的效果。

更令人担心的是,即使在目前非常有限的当事人能够就选定仲裁员事项达成一致的案件中,也并非全为解决纠纷所用。武汉仲裁委员会委员李登华指出,"我们发现,一方当事人认为满意的人选,另一方往往不满意……由当事人共同选定首席仲裁员的概率非常低,真的是微乎其微,屈指可数"。[51]

对比前述国际主流仲裁机构中当事人选定或通过边裁选定仲裁员的比例,这样的差距的确令人深思。考虑到北仲和贸仲均属国内具有国际影响力的重要仲裁机构,有理由推测在其他仲裁机构中,也均存在同样的问题,且当事人共同选定仲裁员的比例可能更小。"当事人共同选定一名首席仲裁

---

[50] 乔欣:《仲裁权研究》,法律出版社2000年版,第45页。

[51] 李登华:《论仲裁庭首席仲裁员的确定》,载《武汉仲裁》2011年第1期。

员或独任仲裁员裁决案件的可能性几乎等于零"[52]，便是对现状的一种真实刻画。

需要说明的是，指出"当事人无法通过合意选定仲裁员"的事实并非对现状的指责，毕竟各仲裁机构的仲裁规则均系根据《仲裁法》制定，且仲裁机构也大多规定，当事人选择该机构为仲裁机构时，自动使用该机构的仲裁规则，因此仲裁委员会依照规则指定仲裁员也在法律的容许范围之中。换句话说，当事人选择该仲裁规则管辖自己参与的案件时，事实上默许了仲裁机构（负责人）在一定条件下代为行使选定仲裁员的权利。从外观上看，当事人对选任仲裁员权利的放弃的确符合"意思自治"的构成要件，但是，合规并非意味着现状处于理想状态。朱玥在论证开放名册制的优越性时指出，"虽然仲裁总是一种相对的意思自治，但是意思自治的相对程度越高越能反映仲裁的契约性本质"[53]。笔者深以为然，相似地，同在合规的前提下，意思自治的程度可能不同，而意思自治的程度本应是体现仲裁本质的重要指标，在可能的情况下应当尽量地尊重。因此，由仲裁委员会指定仲裁员并非仲裁活动最终的应然状态，仍有提升的空间。

3.3 小结

经过对国内外仲裁机构规则及其在当事人选定仲裁员程序中的实践情况的梳理，我们可以发现：

在仲裁规则方面，仲裁庭的组成方式往往包括当事人选定、边裁选定、仲裁机构指定方式。我国领先的仲裁机构贸仲和北仲的仲裁规则体现了以当事人为本的服务理念，在仲裁员选定的制度设计上尽可能地考虑了当事人的意思自治，当事人对仲裁庭构成的意思表示处于优位。事实上，贸仲和北仲在当事人共同选定仲裁员制度的设计上已勾勒出较为完善的框架，不仅有各种情况下该如何处理的详细引导，还有建议性的补充说明，在制度上从许多方面来说都比国际领先的数家仲裁机构完备。

在仲裁实践方面，国际领先的仲裁机构均有大量仲裁员由当事人选出，也有相当一部分首席仲裁员系由当事人选出的边裁选出。在国内，边裁选首席

---

[52] 王治英、任以顺：《我国仲裁员制度的缺陷及运行失范之矫正》，载《青岛科技大学学报》2010年第4期。

[53] 朱玥：《自治与效率：仲裁员开放名册制实施路径研究》，载《西部法学评论》2020年第3期。

仲裁员的制度几乎无踪影，而当事人直接选定首席或独任仲裁员的案例所占比例极小，在这一方面与 ICC 等国际仲裁机构差异甚大。

当事人选定仲裁员的制度难以落实，是实践中长期普遍存在的一个问题。尽管仲裁委员会指定仲裁员的行为合法合规，从某种程度上来说也是当事人放任的后果，符合当事人对于权利的处分，但这一现实离当事人通过意思自治决定处理纠纷的仲裁员的理想状态仍有差距。仅当各方当事人能够通过自己的意思，在大部分情况下达成一致，主动地选定各方都能满意的仲裁员（而非被动地接受指定），选定仲裁员的意思自治才能说完全得到了落地。

第 4 章　保护当事人选择仲裁员的意思自治的建议和对策

在国内过往的研究中，已经有一些学者对于当事人选定仲裁员的程序提出过改进方案。例如，有的学者提出应以"名单法"限制仲裁机构的权力[54]；有的学者提出当事人第一次无法共同选定时可在选仲期内循环进行多次该等操作以增加达成一致的可能性[55]，有的学者归纳出"三种方式""两上两下"[56]的方法指定仲裁员也与前者一致；有的学者则主张对名册制进行改革以给予当事人更多的自主权。[57] 上述解决方案在当时乃至现在都属于非常有创见的方案，但是笔者认为并非都能实际对我国仲裁员选任的困境起到作用。以名单法为例，2004 年《北仲规则》（以下简称《北仲规则 2004》）第 18 条第 2 款就已经在规则中通过"名单法"的方式协助当事人选定仲裁员了。从制度层面，《北仲规则 2004》的规定已经相当成熟，与诸多国际仲裁机构的规定相似，且也一直沿用

---

[54]　马永双、赵金龙：《仲裁员制度的现状与改进》，载《河北法学》2005 年第 8 期；谢静：《浅析仲裁员选任之程序构建》，载《重庆科技学院学报》2009 年第 1 期；周丽：《当前仲裁员制度的不足与完善》，载《人民论坛》2016 年第 17 期；王宣：《我国仲裁员制度之问题与完善——基于意思自治原则的分析》，载《商事仲裁》2016 年第 1 期。

[55]　王治英、任以顺：《我国仲裁员制度的缺陷及运行失范之矫正》，载《青岛科技大学学报》2010 年第 4 期。

[56]　"三种方式"包括当事人直接协商选定、当事人间接列出名单选定、当事人委托各自所选的仲裁员协商推荐后共同选定；"两上两下"即通过"民主—集中—再民主—再集中"的流程确定仲裁员人选。参见杨艳芬：《仲裁员聘任与选定过程中的若干问题探析》，载《天水行政学院学报》2011 年第 3 期。

[57]　李留松：《浅析仲裁员的选任制度——从当事人意思自治角度》，载《法制与经济》2006 年第 21 期；凌冰尧：《我国仲裁员任职制度的合理性分析与完善建议》，载《国际商务研究》2020 年第 6 期。

至今，但根据 2020 年的统计数据，显然这样的规则并未对现状起到改良作用。以下，笔者将提出一些当下尚未实践，但可行性较高的方案，以期当事人选定仲裁员的制度真正地"落地"。

4.1 对于立法：加强对新制度的法律保障

在中国，20 世纪 90 年代诞生的仲裁制度仍处于发展初期，仲裁领域的立法体系还较为不全面，对于仲裁事项中的许多细节，法律尚未作出明确的规定。仲裁作为一个朝气蓬勃的新制度，亟待走向科学化、现代化、体系化，同时仲裁作为一个国际化的解纷机制，与国际接轨是其必然的内在要求。

4.1.1 进一步推广临时仲裁的试点和应用

与本文的绝大部分内容不同，学术界对于临时仲裁的讨论几乎从未停止过。在 2017 年《横琴自由贸易试验区临时仲裁规则》（以下简称《横琴规则》）生效后，更是如此。事实上，除了《临时仲裁应当缓行》一文提出我国推及临时仲裁存在时机不成熟，会对机构仲裁造成冲击，且涉及诚信问题，也并不比机构仲裁灵活、快捷等[58]原因，绝大部分学者都站在了支持临时仲裁的那一面。

从必要性来看，推广临时仲裁，有以下积极作用，而其中第三点特别地呼应了当事人选定仲裁员的意思自治：

首先，虽然中国的仲裁发展仍处于初期，但这并不代表着"时机尚不成熟"。如前文所述，仲裁的概念从民间诞生之时起，便是以临时仲裁的形式存在的，因此说哪个国家或地区没有孕育临时仲裁的土壤，这显然站不住脚。临时仲裁在我国虽然没有法律地位，但并不代表没有法律实践。恰恰相反，临时仲裁不仅存在，而且已经在实践中取得了一定的成功。[59]

其次，如有学者指出，临时仲裁的缺位可能导致我国与其他国家在《纽约公约》等多边、双边国际条约下义务不对等的情况。[60] 依据条约，中国有义务承认和执行其他承认临时仲裁效力的国家所作出的临时仲裁，而在中国作出的临时仲裁却会由于违反仲裁地法律的原因而无法得到承认与执行。

再次，如有学者指出，不承认临时仲裁，不利于我国发展国际经济贸易。

---

[58] 刘茂亮：《临时仲裁应当缓行》，载《北京仲裁》2005 年第 1 期。
[59] 康明：《临时仲裁的成功实践及其思考》，载《仲裁与法律》2001 年第 3 期。
[60] 陈磊：《自贸区临时仲裁的制度基础与完善路径》，载《南京社会科学》2020 年第 8 期；黄思怡：《论在我国建立临时仲裁制度的重要性》，载《兰州学刊》2012 年第 1 期。

在我国只承认机构仲裁的背景下，仍与行政机关有着千丝万缕联系的仲裁机构带有"半官方"的性质，从而使外方当事人产生不信任感，而完善我国的外商投资环境，临时仲裁制度也是因素之一。[61][62]

最后，回到当事人选定仲裁员的意思自治上，临时仲裁是最能体现当事人在仲裁员选择这一事项上的意思自治的制度。在仲裁员的选择上当事人无须被名单所囿，更无须在短暂的期限截止后就不得不将选定仲裁员的权利交给仲裁机构，因而极大地保护了当事人的意思自治，尊重了仲裁这一解纷方式的根本特征。之所以在仲裁员选定的主题下提及临时仲裁，正是因为临时仲裁对于仲裁庭（仲裁员）的安排充分体现了当事人的意思——无论是委托仲裁机构代为选定当事人（此处虽然选定仲裁员的主体仍为仲裁机构，但系当事人有意为之，因此并非不得已而沦为的"他治"），还是当事人自己选定仲裁员，在仲裁庭组成的阶段，当事人享有着高度的意思自治。同时，由于临时仲裁要求当事人自行安排仲裁员的选择事宜，也间接上有利于当事人在签订合同时更加细致，考虑得更加周到，从而实现自己维护自己的权利。

从可行性上来看，一方面全球范围内临时仲裁的实践屡见不鲜，目前也并无"因为当事人选择了临时仲裁，所以仲裁员难以确定、仲裁程序因此停滞不前"的研究结论或实践困难；另一方面中国的仲裁随着领先仲裁机构的发展，也逐渐与国际接轨，临时仲裁难以推广的困难有一部分也不复存在，随着《横琴规则》的推出，进行更大范围、更加长期的试点也并非天方夜谭。

基于以上理由，我国在《横琴规则》落实后，一方面可以主动地跟进临时仲裁制度在珠海横琴自贸区的应用情况，及时总结正反两面的结果，以为临时仲裁的全面部署积累经验；另一方面可以在国内其他自贸区进一步加强临时仲裁制度的应用，以拓展临时仲裁适用的广度，从而在各地仲裁实践的异同中总结出一套普适于全国的正式规则。

---

[61] 王岩、宋连斌：《试论临时仲裁及其在我国的现状》，载《北京仲裁》2005年第1期。

[62] 但亦存在不同观点，如高特兄弟律师事务所法国合伙人威廉·劳伦斯·克雷格先生在《跨国公司和政府间的争议》中便指出缺乏临时仲裁并不会阻碍外国投资进入中国："就我个人而言，更倾向于机构仲裁，尤其是像国际商会这样的国际仲裁机构的仲裁。当然根据联合国国际贸易法委员会的仲裁规则进行临时仲裁的情况也很普遍，但我并不认为缺乏临时仲裁会形成外资进入中国的大障碍。"转引自刘晓红、周祺：《我国建立临时仲裁利弊分析和时机选择》，载《南京社会科学》2012年第9期。

4.1.2 在立法上支持对名册制的开放性改造

名册制，即《仲裁法》第13条第2款所称的"仲裁委员会按照不同专业设仲裁员名册"，对当事人选定仲裁员的权利进行了第一层的限制，即可选仲裁员的范围应当是仲裁员名册上的有限位业内专家。在名册制下进一步细分，又有强制名册制和开放名册制，前者即当事人只能从仲裁机构提供的仲裁员名册中选择仲裁员，后者则允许当事人在仲裁员名册之外选择仲裁员，不过也需要经过一定的程序。强制名册制对于当事人自主地选定仲裁员造成了一定的阻碍。由于当下我国尚还不承认临时仲裁，而在机构仲裁中当事人又依法必须在仲裁员名册中选择仲裁员，这在法律层面就限制了当事人选定仲裁员的范围。因此，解决这一问题，应当考虑打破或者弱化法律对选仲权利的限制，即如汪祖兴所言，"仲裁员名册的开放性改造"[63]。

从教义学的角度来看，《仲裁法》并未建立非强制名册制不可的名册制度。全法仅两条提到了仲裁员名册，即第13条第3款（名册的设置）和第25条第1款（名册的送达）。而就法律未规定的部分，"以权利来描绘自由，则自由就是扣除禁令余下的所有行为可能性的权利，是一种扣减权而非加计权。'法无禁止皆自由'足以凸显自由为'扣减权'的无所不包的特性，从而营造最大的自治空间"。[64]因此，在法律未作出明确的禁止性规定的情况下，采取开放名册制不违反法律。

事实上，以《贸仲规则》为代表的若干国内仲裁机构的规则已经突破了强制名册制。《贸仲规则》第26条第2款非常清晰地表明仲裁员名册并非仲裁员选定的范围，为推荐而非强制。在实践中，也并没有因为仲裁员超出名册规定而导致仲裁裁决被撤销或不予执行的先例。但是，《仲裁法》仍未对开放名册制进行任何规定，实践中通过适用开放名册制从而选择仲裁员名册以外的仲裁员的案例也非常有限，开放名册制仍属于一个亟待通过实践开发的留白地带。[65]

---

[63] 汪祖兴：《当事人共任仲裁员不能之救济实践及完善》，载《中国法学》2012年第5期。

[64] 易军：《"法不禁止皆自由"的私法精义》，载《中国社会科学》2014年第4期。

[65] 朱玥在《自治与效率：仲裁员开放名册制实施路径研究》一文中提出了诸多富有创见的观点，但其引用的"选定的仲裁员名册内从而导致裁决被撤销"的（2016）津72民特29号案，事实上裁决并未被撤销。笔者进行补充检索后，也并未发现由于选定的仲裁员未登记于仲裁员名册而导致裁决被撤销的先例。

对于仲裁员名册制度的应用采取开放态度，截至目前运转良好。在仲裁法修改的契机下，可对仲裁员名册制度进行一定的完善，在保障仲裁作为准司法制度的专业性的同时兼顾当事人意思自治的最大化，以更加明确的制度保障开放名册制的推广和使用——而《贸仲规则》对仲裁员强制名册制的突破正是一个不错的参考。

4.2 对于仲裁机构：推动仲裁员选任制度创新

仲裁机构是仲裁活动的主战场，各仲裁机构的仲裁规则在《仲裁法》的原则性规定下，近年来也经历了多次的自我更新。仲裁员制度是否能得到改善，虽然与法律的规定息息相关，但仲裁机构在其中起着最重要的作用。仲裁机构对仲裁员制度进行革新，可以为当事人无法共同选定的现状带来最直接的冲击。

4.2.1 创设仲裁员选定的新模式

选定仲裁员，简单地说就是在符合当事人的意思的前提下，在仲裁机构的仲裁员名册或其他方式确认的仲裁员名单中选定一个审理案件最为合适的人选，而此处的"合适"不仅考虑到仲裁员的专业知识，也考虑当事人的意愿、仲裁员的繁忙程度、仲裁员的独立性等各方面。从这个剥离出的非常简单的模型来看，一定有无数种方式将此处的一个人选出，因为法律并没有对选出仲裁员的程序作出任何禁止性规定。

然而在实践中，仲裁员的选定几乎均使用相同的模式。以北仲为例，常规的做法是在收到申请人的仲裁申请后，将选定仲裁员的函分别寄给申请人和被申请人两方，双方分别填写边裁的人选后（简易程序的函则无此项），再填写期望选择的首席仲裁员（或独任仲裁员），当且仅当双方提交的函上所写的首席或独任仲裁员为同一人时，才得以通过意思自治选定仲裁员。虽然《北仲规则》事实上也包括了"名单法"，但在绝大部分案件中，在对效率的考量下（事实上，意思自治在多大程度上为效率让步系价值取向问题，本文暂不详加讨论），并不会进行额外的选定程序。在其他仲裁机构中，也鲜有丰富多彩的仲裁员选择机制。所以，与其在实践之前断言其有消极影响，不妨进行一些仲裁员选择方式的创新，从吸取国外的选定程序做起——以下将以"两名边裁选主裁"的经典方式为例讨论。

对于普通仲裁程序来说，两名边裁选任首席仲裁员的规则已不是新鲜的制度安排。《联合国国际贸易法委员会国际商事仲裁示范法》第 11 条第 3 款 A

项即规定,"在仲裁员为三名的仲裁中,当事每一方均应指定一名仲裁员,这样指定的两名仲裁员应指定第三名仲裁员",以此作为当事人未能在规定时间内完成共同选任的第一层救济,其下一层才是仲裁机构指定。如果说仲裁机构(主任)直接指定过于直接和粗暴,边裁共任的制度至少在某种程度上间接反映了当事人的意愿(尽管仲裁员应当保持中立性,但是当事人选任该边裁至少说明其对该边裁的信任程度要大于名册上的其他仲裁员)。边裁共同选首席仲裁员的制度,也完全可以成为当事人直接共任和仲裁机构指定之间的缓冲地带,成为各仲裁机构常规的仲裁员选定方式。

笔者注意到,在许多仲裁机构的官网上,都附有仲裁条款的模板文本。在创设了仲裁员选定的一些新规则后,仲裁机构大可将该等安排编入其提供的模板之中。事实上,北仲的官网上已经提供了一套较为翔实的示范文本,其中也包含仲裁员选定的部分[66],如下所引,该示范条款使得当事人在提交仲裁前就已经选定了某一特定仲裁员,虽然北仲为仲裁员无法接受选定提供的兜底条款仍为"则由北京仲裁委员会主任指定独任/首席仲裁员",但当事人当然可以自行另作约定,作为服务机构的仲裁机构也可以在此提供更多样的条款供选择。

上述方案仅为"创设仲裁员选定的新模式"的区区一例,在仲裁机构执业多年的专家和领导,对于仲裁实践中的问题的把握自然较笔者深刻得多,创设新模式的思路也应比笔者开阔得多。因此,笔者在此仅为抛砖引玉地提出可能作出改进的一例,而本节的重点在于呼吁仲裁机构积极尝试,摒弃与仲裁之"性格"所不相符的保守思想,为仲裁制度和实践的发展助力。

4.2.2 增设当事人了解仲裁员的渠道

由于如前所述,当事人和仲裁员成立一种合同关系,那么双方当事人选任仲裁员之前,若对仲裁员已经有一定的了解(尤其是面对面的了解),可能更有利于仲裁员的确定,而非凭借极少的公开信息"碰运气"。

据笔者所知,在大部分的仲裁案件中,当事人本人并不会介入仲裁员的选择。作为争议解决专家的律师往往由于职业的圈子,会更容易与仲裁员相

---

[66] "【特定人员】双方一致同意,选择_____(某人)担任本案独任/首席仲裁员。如该仲裁员拒绝或者无法接受双方选定或在规定期限内无法联络或未作出回应的,则由北京仲裁委员会主任指定独任/首席仲裁员。"参见 https://www.bjac.org.cn/page/zc/zctk.html。

识或对仲裁员有一定的了解。但即使如此，律师在了解仲裁员的时候也会花费大量的时间调查各仲裁员的背景资料，检索仲裁员作为学者的学术观点、作为律师的执业经历，以及作为法官时的裁判思路，而律师的时间就是当事人的支出，理论上当事人需要对律师进行该等调研所花费的时间负责。而且，在花费大量时间和精力后，对于仲裁员的了解可能也并不充分。

因此，一些学者已经开始提出解决方案，试图解决当事人对仲裁员信息了解不全面的问题。在笔者所查阅到的文献中，有学者首先提出了当事人面试仲裁员的制度设计。[67]从必然性和必要性的角度来看，可能在年受案量数千的仲裁机构很难真正落实。虽然该设计可能存在低效的弊端，且时间协调的困难也增加了仲裁机构（实际是仲裁秘书）的工作负担，但是这不失为一种极具参考价值的提议。

根据这一思路，仲裁机构确实可以为当事人提供与仲裁员"面对面"的机会——提供的仲裁员信息可以不仅仅是一本载有仲裁员姓名和专长的冷冰冰的名册，而可以是在仲裁机构官网上为每位仲裁员专设的个人主页，每位仲裁员通过视频录制的方式在主页上面对面地向来访者介绍自己的身份、成就、研究领域、专长，以及所作出的部分裁决的分析思路。该途径在技术上完全可以实现，而且各位仲裁员也只需录制一次视频，并在仲裁委员会或同事的协助下进行主页设计，无须在每个案件中都单独花费时间进行更新。

总结与反思

自仲裁诞生之日起，意思自治的价值便深深地融合在这一制度当中。注重仲裁中的意思自治，尊重当事人对于仲裁员等各方面的选择，是有效化解纠纷、保护当事人权利的重要方式。在公正和效率的双重价值取向的影响下，当事人共同选定仲裁员制度发展成为今天的模式，在选定范围和选定期限的限制内，尽可能地保护当事人对于仲裁庭组成的自决权。

当事人共同选定仲裁员制度普遍地存在于各国立法和各大仲裁机构的规则当中。中国的仲裁机构北仲和贸仲已经发展出了相当完备的仲裁员产生规则，且在规则中较为浓墨重彩地体现了当事人选择仲裁员的意思自治。然而，

---

[67] 杜焕芳、李贤森：《仲裁员选任困境与解决路径——仲裁员与当事人法律关系的视角》，载《武大国际法评论》2020年第2期。

在中国的仲裁实践中，当事人成功通过约定选出首席仲裁员或独任仲裁员的比例微乎其微，几乎所有的案件都须借助仲裁规则中的仲裁委员会指定方法决定该仲裁员的人选，这表明在绝大部分案件中，当事人都没有很好地行使选定仲裁员的权利。

但是，当事人选择仲裁员的意思自治具有非常重要的意义，其应当在实践中受到更高的重视。一方面，意思自治本身就是仲裁的基本原则，而仲裁员（尤其是首席仲裁员和独任仲裁员）又是仲裁中最重要的组成部分之一；另一方面，当事人选择仲裁员的意思自治不仅有利于增强当事人对纠纷解决结果的信任感，有利于维护当事人的权利，还在推进纠纷解决机制多元化，推进中国仲裁事业与国际接轨乃至达到世界领先水平的背景下，使仲裁作为平行于诉讼的解纷机制，保持其独立的运行特色。

针对提出的问题和该问题的关键性，我国有必要抓住仲裁法修改的契机，并开展仲裁机构的内部改革，为当事人提供更为丰富的仲裁员产生方式和程序，给予当事人深入了解每一位仲裁员的机会。

从裁决到协商:我国国内 ISDS 机制的新趋势
——兼议外商投资投诉制度

刘子婧[*]

● 摘 要

  我国国内投资者—国家争端解决(ISDS)机制显露出从裁决模式到协商模式的转变趋势。一方面,以合法性与合理性裁决为主的行政复议制度在新一代国际投资协约中较少被提及,此前则经常被作为默认的当地救济机制;另一方面,以协商和调解为主要特征的外商投资投诉制度获得了全国性的确立和推广。ISDS 改革窗口期提供的时代机遇、亚洲长期重视社会和谐的文化取向和建设多元纠纷解决机制的国家目标共同解释了这一转变产生的原因。该趋势暗示,在跨国投资纠纷解决中,我国的国家注意力正逐渐转向争端预防与解决机制,并借助外商投资投诉制度开辟一条自下而上的政策生成路径。我国实践或许能够为当前 ISDS 改革讨论提供新的启发。

● 关键词

  ISDS 外商投资投诉制度 行政复议 当地救济

  Abstract:China's domestic investor-state dispute settlement (ISDS) mechanism reveals a transition trend from an adjudication

---

[*] 刘子婧,浙江大学光华法学院博士研究生。

model to a negotiation one. On the one hand, administrative review, a quasi-judicial mechanism to adjudicate the legality and rationality of administrative actions, is rarely mentioned in the new generation of international investment treaties. Previously, it served as a default local remedy before international arbitration. On the other hand, the foreign investment complaint mechanism with the features of consultation and mediation has been established and promoted nationwide. There are multiple motivations of the trend, including the historic opportunity provided by the ISDS reform, the Asian culture advocating harmony, and China's national goal to establish a diversified dispute resolution mechanism. It implies that China's national attention is gradually shifting to dispute prevention and management and using the foreign investment complaint mechanism to build a bottom-up policy generation path. China's practice may provide new inspiration for the current discussion of ISDS reform.

Key Words: ISDS, foreign investment complaint mechanism, administrative review, local remedy

1. Introduction

In recent years, alternative dispute resolution (ADR) has become a hot topic of discussion in investor-state dispute settlement, with more and more scholars repeatedly referring to conciliation and mediation in the design of future ISDS.[1] However, only some of them notice that host states are already gradually adjusting their domestic ISDS mechanism in a more

---

[1] See Catherine Kessedjian et al., *Mediation in Future Investor-State Dispute Settlement*, 14 Journal of International Dispute Settlement 192, 192-212 (2023); Romesh et al., *Conciliation and Mediation in Investor-State Dispute Settlement Provisions: A Quantitative and Qualitative Analysis*, 38 ICSID Review 201, 201-237 (2023); Ignacio de la Rasilla, *'The Greatest Victory'? Challenges and Opportunities for Mediation in Investor-State Dispute Settlement*, 38 ICSID Review 169, 169-200 (2023).

collaborative way to settle international investment disputes with mutual consensus instead of unilateral decisions. China, for example, is paying more attention to consensual dispute resolution mechanisms rather than an adjudicative one in international investment dispute settlement against the ongoing ISDS legitimacy crisis. Three signs indicate that change is happening: firstly, the number of administrative review provisions is dropping in recent international investment agreements treaty drafting. Previously, it was the default local remedy mechanism. The number of lawsuits brought by foreign investors against local government has also declined. Secondly, China is advocating the stipulation of cooling-off period provisions in investment treaties, which require a mandatory period for negotiation. Thirdly, a foreign investment complaint-handling mechanism was established nationwide by China's latest legislation with the feature of negotiation, mediation, and complaint handling.

Therefore, this article argues that there is an emerging trend in China's domestic ISDS mechanism from an adjudicative model to a negotiated one. It means that the previous local remedies, such as administrative review and administrative litigation, still need to be abandoned. Instead, a more collaborative dispute settlement mechanism is now emerging to make up for the deficiencies of the old one and has attracted more of the state's attention. A study on the new trend of China's domestic ISDS provides an excellent window to observe host States' reactions to the ISDS crisis and its reform. First, China's case is typical. China is one of the world's most prominent destinations for foreign direct investment (FDI).[2] Furthermore, it turned from a net capital-

---

[2] China, having surpassed the United States in 2020, signed 146 Bilateral Investment Treaties (BITs) with other countries. Among those BITs, 19 were signed but are not in force, and 19 were terminated. Therefore, there are 107 BITs that China is a party to currently in force. The relevant statistics and list of Chinese BITs are available at https://investmentpolicy.unctad.org/international-investment-agreements/countries/42/china (accessed April 8, 2022).

importing country to a capital-importing and exporting country in 2016.[3] More interestingly, as the world's largest FDI destination, it remains almost immune from ISA as a respondent.[4] Second, against the background of ISDS reform, China's experience helps to explain its attitude and position in the current reform and may provide insights into future reform.

This article proceeds as follows. It first illustrates the adjudicative model in China's domestic ISDS and how it has faded recently. The administrative review mechanism will be taken as a significant example. Then, it demonstrates the emerging negotiation model represented by the newly established foreign investment complaint handling mechanism. Its merits, defects, and feature improvements are also discussed. Last, it canvasses several possible motivations for the new trend and its implications for future ISDS reform.

2. Adjudication—the use of administrative review as a domestic ISDS option

Although ISA has become the most frequently used ISDS option at the global level, [5] local remedies remain a sensible option for investors as they offer cost-

---

[3] In 2016, Chinese outbound FDI reached a record high of USD 196.15 billion, accounting for 13.5% of global foreign investment, and first surpassed the amount of its inbound FDI (USD 126 billion). For the statistics of Chinese outbound FDI in 2016, see MOFCOM, "Chinese Outbound FDI Bulletin", http://www.mofcom.gov.cn/article/tongjiziliao/dgzz/201803/20180302722851.shtml (accessed April 8, 2022). For Chinese inbound FDI in 2016, see Commercial Data Centre, "Monthly Report about Chinese Inbound FDI," http://data.mofcom.gov.cn/lywz/inmr.shtml (accessed April 8, 2022).

[4] For greater certainty, the immunity here does not mean no case was brought against China. Instead, it means few investment cases were brought against China compared with the quantity of its inbound FDI. Only seven investment arbitration cases in which China served as a defendant from 2010 to 2021 and no investment arbitration was brought to China before 2010. See Maniao Chi and Qing Ren, *Annual Observation on Investment Arbitration in China*, 116 Beijing Arbitration, 48-51 (2021). For the list of the cases, see UNCTAD, "Cases as Respondent State (China)", https://investmentpolicy.unctad.org/investment-dispute-settlement/country/42/china/investor (accessed April 8, 2022).

[5] UNCTAD, "Investor-State Dispute Settlement Cases Pass the 1000 Mark: Cases and Outcomes in 2019", https://unctad.org/system/files/official-document/diaepcbinf2020d6.pdf (accessed April 8, 2022).

saving, efficient, and enforceable solutions.[6] The administrative review is another option for local remedies in investor-state disputes aside from litigation in a national court. In China, the administrative review previously served as a default local remedy option. However, the number of administrative review provisions has decreased these years in China's treaty drafting.

2.1 Administrative review as a local remedy

In China, administrative review refers to the mechanism that provides a remedy for a natural person, legal person, or any other organization whose right has been infringed by the act of the government or its departments, including the act conducted by its public servant, which is attributable to the government. It is stipulated in the Administrative Review Law of the People's Republic of China. A competent authority will review the administrative act after receiving the administrative review application from the applicant and then determine the legality and proportionality of the disputed administrative act within 60 days.[7] For example, in the dispute between Hong Kong Carilai company (applicant) and Beijing Municipal Bureau of Commerce (respondent) in 2001, the respondent made an administrative decision to cancel the applicant's shareholder status of a Sino-Hong Kong joint venture for the reason that applicant failed to invest capital within an appropriate period. The applicant then submitted an administrative review application to the Ministry of Commerce of China (MOFCOM), which reviewed the administrative decision, held that the basis was non-existent, and canceled the disputed administrative decision.[8]

One of the core functions of administrative review is to implement

---

[6] Manjiao Chi, *Privileging Domestic Remedies in International Investment Dispute Settlement*, 107 ASIL Proceedings 26, 27-28 (2013).

[7] Generally, the "competent authority" in administrative review refers to justice department of the corresponding People's Government. See article 24 of the Administrative Review Law (2023 Amendment).

[8] Although MOFCOM canceled the wrongful administrative decision through the administrative review procedure in 2022, the dispute between the applicant and respondent was settled when it went through a court trial twice in 2015. See Zhongle Zhan, *The Legal Disputes of Foreign-funded Enterprises*, 10 China Development Observation, 51, 51-52 (2005) (original in Chinese) (translation by author).

supervision and self-governance within the administrative system.[9] In other words, administrative review is a supervision system to correct mistakes made by administrative organs.[10] Another notable function of administrative review is the relief function, which colors administrative review with a quasi-judicial feature.[11] Those functions are well illustrated in the Carilai case, in which the MOFCOM, the superior authority of Beijing Bureau of Commerce, is responsible for adjudicating the legality and proportionality of the disputed administrative act, correct the administrative decisions made by the respondent (if there is any), and protect the lawful right of foreign investor.

Administrative Review provisions are standard in China's BITs. In principle, Chinese BITs are divided into three or four generations, and the period for each generation is defined differently by various scholars. For instance, Congyang Cai has divided Chinese BITs into three generations in terms of the main features of each generation;[12] Yuwen Li and Cheng Bian have divided them into three generations in terms of the scope of consent to ISA;[13] Qingjiang Kong and Kaiyuan Chen have divided them into four generations marked by four versions

---

[9] See Article 1 of the Administrative Review Law of China.

[10] See Jinyu Yang, *Explanation on the Administrative Review Law of the People's Republic of China (Draft)*, delivered at the fifth Session of the Standing Committee of the Ninth National People's Congress on October 27, 1998 (original in Chinese) (translation by author). Available at http://www.npc.gov.cn/zgrdw/npc/zfjc/xzfyfzfjc/2013-10/11/content_1809238.htm?msclkid=050f8702b57d11ec8b38a49f3ceadf13 (accessed April 8, 2022).

[11] See Li Wang, *On the Function of Administrative Reconsideration: Aim to Breakthrough the Effectiveness Dilemma* 178-179 (Beijing: Social Science Academic Press 2012) (original in Chinese) (translation by author).

[12] The three generations divided by Congyang Cai are the Conservation Paradigm (1982-1998), the Liberal Paradigm (1998-2005), and the Balanced Paradigm (2006-). See Congyang Cai, *China-EU Negotiation and the Future of Investment Treaty Regime: a Grand Bilateral Bargain with Multilateral Implications*, 12 JIEL, 457, 461-462 (2009).

[13] The three generations divided by Yuwen Li and Cheng Bian are the first generation (1982-1999), the second generation (1997-2011), and the third generation (2007-). See Yuwen Li, Cheng Bian, *China's Stance on Investor-State Dispute Settlement: Evolution, Challenges, and Reform Options*, 67 Netherlands International Law Review, 503, 505 (2020).

of China's Model BITs.[14] This paper divides China's BITs into four generations, which are: first-generation BIT (1982-9), second-generation (1990-7), third-generation (1998-2009), and fourth-generation (after 2010).[15] The early generations of China's BITs were relatively conservative, which permitted international arbitration only for the 'amount of compensation for expropriation'.[16] The third and fourth generations of China's BITs reflect a liberalizing BIT regime in China, and most of these BITs provide full access to ICSID jurisdiction.[17]

Along with the expansion of investor-dispute provisions in the new generations of China's BITs, administrative review provisions increasingly appear as pre-arbitration requirements either in the arbitration clauses of BITs or in their Protocols or Appendixes. Almost all third-generation BITs contain clear stipulations that the investor must first have availed of the domestic administrative review procedures before resorting to international arbitration.[18] For example, the China-Uganda BIT allows foreign investors to submit the dispute to ICSID 'provided that the Contracting Party involved may require the investor concerned to go through the domestic administrative review procedures specified by the laws

---

[14] Four generations divided by Qingjiang Kong and Kaiyuan Chen are: first-generation BIT (1982-9), second-generation (1990-7), third-generation (1998-2009), and fourth-generation (after 2010). See Qingjiang Kong and Kaiyuan Chen, *ISDS Reform is the Context of China's IIAs*, 10 ICSID Review, 1, 12 (2022). Four versions of China's Model BITs have been published: the Model BITs of 1984, 1989, and 1997 and the Model BIT 2010 (Draft).

[15] The period of the first three generations is also adopted by Norah Gallagher and Wenhua Shan. See Norah Gallagher and Wenhua Shan, *Chinese Investment Treaties: Policies and Practice* 35-45 (OUP, 2008).

[16] See ibid., 313. The restrictive wording of the scope of arbitration can be found in the following BITs: the Chinese BITS with Albania (1993), Bolivia (1992), Bulgaria (1989), Cambodia (1996), Chile (1994), Croatia (1993), Cuba (1995), Egypt (1994), Estonia (1993), Ethiopia (1998), France (1984), Georgia (1993), Greece (1992), Hungary (1991), Iceland (1994), Italy (1985), Jamaica (1994), Lao People's Democratic Republic (1993), Lebanon (1996), Lithuania (1993), Mongolia (1991), Poland (1988), Slovenia (1993), Turkey (1990), the UK (1986), Uruguay (1993), and Vietnam (1992).

[17] See ibid, 41-42. A table of the liberalized BIT is available in Table 1.2 of the book on page 42.

[18] See ibid, 321.

and regulations of that Contracting Party before the submission to the ICSID'.[19] Similar statements also appear in Protocols or Appendixes of China's BITs.[20]

2.2 Reasons for advocating administrative review in previous domestic ISDS

Firstly, China has developed a complex and systematic mechanism of administrative review as an effective measure to resolve administrative disputes to provide relief to the applicant whose legal right was infringed by unlawful or unproportionate administrative action.[21] Thus, it is unsurprising that China applies the already existing domestic dispute resolution system to resolve international investment disputes.

Secondly, almost all of the investment disputes arose from the acts of local governments or the acts of its departments as well as public servants rather than national legislation or regulatory change. Therefore, the administrative review procedure, as a supervision mechanism, is feasible to resolve and curb the disputes before they escalate. Meanwhile, if investment disputes arise from national legislation, the administrative procedure won't be capable of resolving them. Because the competent authorities belong to the executive branches, which are not entitled to judge the decisions made by the legislative branches, currently, all of the investment arbitration brought against China today was

---

[19] See Art 8 (2) (b) Uganda BIT. See other similar examples where the proviso appears in the dispute resolution clause: Art 9 (3) Benin, Art 9 (3), Art 8 (2) Bosnia and Herzegovina, Art 9 (2) Brunei, Art 9 (3) Cambodia, Art 9 (3) Djibouti, Art 10 (4) Guyana, Art 10 (3) (b) Jordan, Art 9 (3) Democratic People's Republic of Korea, Art 9 (3) (b) Myanmar, Art 10 (2) (b) Trinidad and Tobago, and Art 153 (2) New Zealand FTA 2008.

[20] See Art 9 (1) of the Tunisia BIT protocol. Other BITs that include the proviso in an Appendix of the Protocol include Ad Art 8 Belgium and Luxembourg, Ad Art 9 Finland, Art 6 Germany, Ad Art 9 Latvia, Ad Art 10 the Netherlands, Ad Art 9 Portugal, and Ad Art 9 Spain.

[21] One typical example of unproportionate administrative action is that the penalty imposed by the administrative agencies is significantly disproportionate to the wrongful act of the applicant. For example, the tax paid by a foreign-funded enterprise was delayed for a couple of months while the tax authority imposed a heavy penalty on the enterprise.

triggered by local governments' actions.[22] For instance, in Ekran v. China, the People's Government of Hainan Province nullified the claimant's subsidiary rights to a leasehold land due to an alleged failure to develop the land as stipulated under local legislation.[23] In Ansung Housing v. China, a dispute arose between the Ansung Housing company and a district-level government based on their investment agreement on the construction of a golf and country club and luxury condominiums in Sheyang-Xian, Jiangsu province.[24] Therefore, unlike the investment arbitration claims launched against other host countries, which may be triggered by a national policy or regulatory change made by central governments, such as the series of cases brought against Spain due to the change of its royal decree about solar policy,[25] The cases against China were mainly caused by actions taken by local governments. Therefore, it's feasible to apply administrative review to supervise and correct the administrative acts of local governments by the higher level authority, and the relief provided by administrative review is more timely (within 60 days) compared with the lengthy judicial procedure as well as ISA, to some extent.

Lastly, one of the significant functions of administrative review in ISDS is to serve as a precondition of ISA, enabling China to curb, manage, and resolve domestic investment disputes. Specifically, China is motivated to embrace more liberalized investor-dispute provisions in its BITs to protect its increasing

---

[22] Till today, there are seven international investment arbitrations against China. Six of them are disclosed and accessible on the website of the UNCTAD Investment Policy Hub. Available at https://investmentpolicy.unctad.org/investment-dispute-settlement/country/42/china/investor (accessed on April 8, 2022). One of them is undisclosed on the website, but its information is found in a periodical essay named "Annual Observation on Investment Arbitration in China (2021)". See supra note 6, Chi and Ren, *Annual Observation* (2021), 50.

[23] See Ekran Berhad v. People's Republic of China (ICSID Case No. ARB/11/15).

[24] See Unsung Housing Co., Ltd. v. People's Republic of China (ICSID Case No. ARB/14/25).

[25] See Charanne v. Spain (SCC, 2016), Eiser v. Spain (ICSID, 2017), Masdar Solar v. Spain (ICSID, 2018), Foresight v. Spain (SCC, 2018), Stadtwerke v. Spain (ICSID, 2019), RWE Innogy v. Spain (ICSID, 2019) etc. The cases are available at https://investmentpolicy.unctad.org/investment-dispute-settlement/country/197/spain (accessed on April 8, 2022).

outbound investment. At the same time, it is hard for China to estimate the risk of being held liable as the respondent in ISA with its extensive consent to arbitration due to its limited experience. Therefore, the administrative review procedure helps China to balance its interests as a capital importer and a capital exporter.

2.3 A new trend of dropping administrative review in China's New BIT-making and its implication

Though the administrative review provision was widely used in the third generation of China's BITs as a precondition of ISA to balance the national interest as a major country of both investment-importing and investment-exporting, there is an emerging trend to drop the administrative review provision in China's new BIT-making.

An empirical study concerning the administrative review provisions in China's IIAs reveals that China has started to drop them in its IIAs.[26] It shows that the number of investment treaties concluded by China with a pre-ISA administrative review provision sharply decreased from 43 treaties (in the 2000s) to 6 treaties (in the 2010s).[27] The statistic reflects an emerging trend to drop pre-ISA administrative review provisions in the new generation (after 2010) of Chinese BITs. Notably, the 2015 China-Australia FTA and 2018 China-Singapore FTA do not include an administrative review provision as a pre-ISA requirement, despite both IIAs incorporating a broad ISA clause.[28] The administrative review is quickly losing attractiveness and significance in China's foreign investment governance, especially as a pre-ISA requirement, as it could be substituted by other ISDS options, such as consultation, complaint handling mechanism, and International Commercial Courts established by China.[29]

---

[26] See Manjiao Chi and Zongyao Li, *Administrative Review Provisions in Chinese Investment Treaties: 'Gilding the Lily?* 12 Journal of International Dispute Settlement 125, 142 (2020).142.

[27] See ibid, table 3 at page 142.

[28] See Article 9.12-9.14, 2015 China-Australia FTA; Art 26-28, Chapter 10, 2018 China-Singapore FTA.

[29] See supra note 26, Chi and Li, 145-148.

The inherent defects of administrative review may constitute a significant reason for the trend of dropping the provisions in recent BITs. First and foremost, In the administrative review procedure, the competent authority performing the administrative review is not the same agency as the governmental authority that committed the unlawful or unproportionate act, though it's the following higher-level authority that is directly responsible for the agency's misconduct. For example, in the Carilia case, the MOFCOM is the competent authority to review the act of Beijing Municipal Bureau of Commerce. The applicant was also able to submit its claim to the People's Government of Beijing since the commerce bureau is a department of the Beijing government. Those competent authorities to review the administrative decision of the Beijing Municipal Bureau of Commerce are its superior counterparts. However, the competent authorities and the respondent all belong to the executive branch and might be the same authority in the investor's eyes. Secondly, administrative needs more lacks finality and practical effectiveness because the decision can be submitted to a domestic court after administrative review. For example, in the Carilai case, Beijing Er Shang Group, another investor of a disputed Sino-Hong Kong joint company, brought administrative litigation to the court concerning the administrative review decision made by MOFCOM. The status of Hong Kong Carilai as an investor in the Sino-Hong Kong joint company was confirmed until the end of the second instance. Besides, statistics show that only a small portion of cases have been decided in favor of the applicant in the administrative review procedure of all kinds of administrative disputes.[30] For instance, according to recent statistics, out of 180,796 administrative review cases concluded in 2020, only 26,405 cases (14.6%) have ended in favor of the applicant.[31]

---

[30] See Ministry of Justice of China, "National Statistics of Administrative Review Cases and Administrative Litigations Cases in 2020", https://xzfy.moj.gov.cn/c/2021-05-27/489609.shtml (accessed on April 8, 2022)(original in Chinese)(translation by author).

[31] Another 22.22% of the administrative review cases in 2020 have been settled or otherwise terminated, some of which could have also ended in favor of the applicant. See ibid.

Another possible reason for dropping the administrative review provision is that the requirement, as a form of exhaustion of local remedies, is in contract with the liberation process of Chinese BITs and has lost its significance in the third generation of Chinese BITs. Historically, one of the major functions of these provisions was to serve as a pre-arbitration requirement. It is believed that those pre-arbitration administrative review provisions are stipulations of the exhaustion of local remedies in the third generation of Chinese BITs (1998-2009).[32] However, as China is increasingly liberalizing its ISA practice to facilitate its outbound investment, the exhaustion of local remedies is gradually replaced by other conditions for arbitration, such as pre-arbitration consultation, time limitation to arbitration, and the exclusion of national taxation from arbitrable matters.[33]

The trend to drop administrative review provisions in China's BITs-making indicates that the roles of administrative agencies as adjudicators are fading. By contrast, administrative agencies are increasingly playing the role of negotiators in investor-state dispute management.

There are several possible reasons for the fade of roles as adjudicators. First, although administrative agencies, as adjudicators in investment disputes, are capable of correcting the actions of their inferior counterparts and reducing the risk of being sued in international arbitration, the effect of such roles is limited since it cannot substantially preclude an investor from initiating either administrative litigation or international arbitration. Second, the time limitation of administrative review procedures is relatively strict (within 60 days), and it is hard for administrative review authorities to resolve complex disputes with the time limitation. By contrast, it is easy for investors to wait for 60 days and then launch international arbitration. In this sense, the pre-arbitration administrative

---

[32] See supra note 12, Li and Bian, *China's Stance*, at 515.

[33] Those conditions are observed in the dispute resolution provisions in China's Model BIT 2010 (Draft). For the text of provisions, see Xiantao Xi, *Discussions on China's Model BIT (Draft) (III)*, 2 Annual Journal of International Economic Law, 57, 59-61 (2012) (original in Chinese) (translation by author).

review serves as procedural conditions for arbitration rather than handling disputes substantively.

3. Negotiation—complaint handing mechanism as a new domestic ISDS approach

The administrative review mechanism is gradually losing its significance in adjudicating investor-state disputes in China. In contrast, the Mechanism of Coordinating and Handling the Complaints about Foreign Investment (compliant handling mechanism) is increasingly utilized to manage and de-escalate investor-state disputes. Unlike being adjudicators of disputes, the role played by complaint-handling agencies in the complaint-handling mechanism is more akin to that of negotiators who bring the disputing parties to the negotiation table and actively help them reach a settlement agreement.

3.1 Compliant handling mechanism as a new option for ISDS

The complaint mechanism refers to coordinating investment disputes between foreign investors and governmental agencies through ADR methods such as negotiation and conciliation by specific complaint-handling agencies. It has long been used to solve disputes between foreign investors and governmental agencies in China's provincial governments since 1989.[34] From 1989 to 2014, 16 regulations concerning the complaint mechanism were issued by provincial governments in Guangdong, Hebei, Zhejiang, Henan, etc.[35] The first central

---

[34] In 1989, the government of Shanghai enacted the first regulations about the Complaint Handling Mechanism of foreign investment disputes, the 'Complaint and Handling Measures of Foreign-invested Enterprises in Shanghai'. See Leibing Liu, *The Study on the Mechanism of Coordinating and Handling the Complaints About Foreign Investment—Taking the Foreign Investment Law (draft) as an example*, 8 (Master et al. University, 2018). The regulation was annulled in 2021 after the 'Foreign Investment Law (2020)' and the 'Work Measure for Complaints of Foreign-funded Enterprises (2020)' took effect. See People's Government of Shanghai, "Decision on the annulment of the 'Complaint and Handling measures of Foreign-invested Enterprises in Shanghai'", https://www.shanghai.gov.cn/nw12344/20210514/0e3761662cb34e7fa457ea2b03f8 6541.html (accessed on April 8, 2022).

[35] For the list of the regulations, see ibid, Liu, *The Study on the Mechanism*, table 1 on pages 9-10.

regulation about complaint mechanisms was enacted by the Ministry of Commerce in May 2006. However, it failed to establish a national-wide system due to its over-general provisions.[36] A complete system of complaint mechanisms was eventually established in March 2019 after the promulgation of China's Foreign Investment Law. Article 26 of this law explicitly stipulates that the state shall establish a complaint mechanism for foreign-invested enterprises to promptly deal with the problems reported by foreign enterprises.[37] A few months later, the Ministry of Commerce enacted the Work Measure for Complaints of Foreign-Funded Enterprises to supplement Article 26 of the Foreign Investment Law and to provide more detailed provisions concerning the operation of the complaint mechanism.[38]

The framework of the Complaint Mechanism is, generally, a two-tiered structure, including the National Center for Complaints of Foreign-funded Enterprises (NCCFE) set up by the Ministry of Commerce (MOFCOM) and local complaint handling agencies set up by local people's governments.[39] The scope of the admissible complaint includes any complaints involving an administrative action or any suggestions to improve investment-related policies and measures made by a foreign-funded enterprise or a foreign investor.[40] After accepting a complaint, the competent center or agency shall fully communicate with the complainant and the respondent, coordinate the handling of the complaint following relevant laws, and promote the proper resolution. The competent agency may organize a meeting between parties, and relevant experts may be

---

[36] See Zhang Demiao and Zhao Jianya, *The Practical Difficulties and Solutions of the Mechanism for Coordinating and Handling Foreign Complaints Given the Business Environment Under the Rule of Law*, 8 Chinese Legal Science, 48, 54 (2020).

[37] See Article 26 of the Foreign Investment Law of the People's Republic of China.

[38] See the Work Measure for Complaint of Foreign-funded Enterprises (2020). It was issued on 25 August 2020.

[39] See Article 6 and Article 7 of the Work Measure for Complaints of Foreign-funded Enterprises (2020).

[40] Ibid, Article 2, Article 6, and Article 7.

invited if needed.[41] A settlement agreement may be concluded between parties due to the complaint procedures, and the respondent will be held liable if it fails to perform the effective agreement. Besides, the competent authority could also submit recommendations to improve relevant policies according to the applicant's suggestion. The time limit for the complaint handing agency to complete the procedure is 60 working days.[42] There needs to be more national statistics about the complaint handling cases, though several municipal bureaus published the number of complaints they handled.[43] For example, Chongqing city has successfully handled 82 complaint cases submitted by foreign-funded enterprises concerning investment in 2020.[44] The details of those complaint-handling cases have yet to be disclosed. Apart from China, other countries also set up similar mechanisms to coordinate investment disputes. For example, Article 85 of Egypt Investment Law provides that "a ministerial committee entitled 'ministerial committee on investment dispute resolution' shall be established to look into the application, complaints or disputes ... arise among the investors and the State".[45]

Compared with the quasi-judicial administrative review procedure, the complaint handling process resembles ADR means such as conciliation, mediation, or negotiation. The functions of conciliation, mediation, and negotiation overlap inevitably, though they have different characteristics. Conciliation in the international context refers to "a method for the settlement of international disputes of any nature according to which a commission set up by the parties, either permanently or on an ad hoc basis to deal with a dispute, proceeds to the impartial examination of the dispute and attempts to define the

---

[41]　Ibid, Article 17.

[42]　Ibid, Article 19.

[43]　See supra note 4, Chi and Ren, *Annual Observation*（2021）, 39.

[44]　Chongqing Commerce Bureau, "Chongqing Utilized USD 10 Billion of Foreign Direct Investment and Ranked First in the Central and Western regions of China", website of Chongqing government, http://sww.cq.gov.cn/zymyq/ywxx/dtyw/202101/t20210128_8833072.html（April 8, 2022）（original in Chinese）（translation by author）.

[45]　See Article 85 of Egypt's Investment Law（2017）.

terms of a settlement susceptible of being accepted by them, or of affording the parties, with a view to its settlement, such aid as they may have requested".[46] The conciliation commission will examine the facts and law applicable to the case and then draft a confidential, non-binding recommendation to parties for a peaceful settlement. Similarly, mediation is a method for the peaceful settlement of international disputes involving the participation of a third party to help the parties to the dispute agree to a solution. At the same time, the mediator principally acts as an intermediary, ensuring that channels of communication between the parties remain open to reduce tensions and may.[47] Last, negotiation, as a means of settlement, emphasizes the discussion process between parties through their delegates or appointed negotiators to achieve a common understanding or agreement.[48]

The complaint-handling process shares some common points with the traditional State-level ADR approach but needs to fit neatly into all of them. The complaint handling agency shares some similarities with the third party involved in ADR. It hears the complaints, examines the dispute's merits, communicates with the disputing parties, and brings them back to the negotiating table. More importantly, it coordinates with the respondent and promotes the conclusion of a settlement agreement. The significant difference between the complaint handling agency and the third party participating in ADR is that the state establishes the agency before disputes arise, rather than being an independent third party jointly appointed by the disputing parties. Admittedly, the complaint handling system has drawbacks, such as a lack of independence or apparent lack of independence

---

[46] See Cot, Jean-Pierre, *Conciliation*, Max Planck Encyclopedias of International Law, https://opil.ouplaw.com/view/10.1093/law: epil/9780199231690/law-9780199231690-e20(April 8, 2022).

[47] See Orrego Vicuna, Francisco, *Mediation*, Max Planck Encyclopedias of International Law, https://opil.ouplaw.com/view/10.1093/law: epil/9780199231690/law-9780199231690-e61?rskey=t0ritN&result=1&prd=OPIL(April 8, 2022).

[48] See Kari Hakapää, *Negotiation*, the Max Planck Encyclopedias of International Law, https://opil.ouplaw.com/view/10.1093/law: epil/9780199231690/law-9780199231690-e67?rskey=YKUyEs&result=1&prd=OPIL(April 8, 2022).

from the investor's viewpoint, which will be demonstrated later. This paper argues that the NCCFE set by MOFCOM is a relatively independent organ from the governmental agencies or local governments.

The complaint-handling procedure is comparable to negotiation, and the complaint-handling agencies act as negotiators. The following cases can well illustrate the new trend in China's domestic ISDS. In Hela Schwarz GmbH v. People's Republic of China,[49] Investment disputes arose between Hela, a Sino-German food joint venture enterprise located in Jinan City, Shandong Province, and the government of Jinan City in China, which initiated an urban renewing program in September 2014 and expropriated Hela's food plant for urban renewing.[50] According to Article 9 of the China-German BIT (2003), Hela is entitled to submit the dispute to arbitration after a six-month cooling-off period,[51] The protocol of this BIT further provision three pre-conditions for an investor to initiate arbitration: (1) the investor has referred the issue to an administrative review procedure according to Chinese law, (2) the dispute still exists three months after review procedures, and (3) investor has withdrawn its claim to Chinese court if the issue has been brought to a Chinese Court.[52] In this case, Hela brought a lawsuit to the Intermediate People's Court of Jinan and appealed to the High Court of Shandong Province in 2016 but failed in both trials.[53] It then initiated an ICSID arbitration according to the China-German

---

[49] See Hela Schwarz GmbH v. People's Republic of China, ICSID Case No. ARB/17/19. For some basic information about the case, see UNCTAD, "Hela Schwarz GmbH v. People's Republic of China", https://investmentpolicy.unctad.org/investment-dispute-settlement/cases/805/hela-schwarz-v-china (April 8, 2022).

[50] See Tao Du, *Hela Schwarz v. China and the Concurrency of Litigation and Arbitration in ISDS*, 3 Economic and Trade Law Review, 130, 131 (2019)(original in Chinese)(translation by author).

[51] See Article 9 (2) of China-German BIT (2003). Available at https://investmentpolicy.unctad.org/international-investment-agreements/treaty-files/736/download (April 8, 2022).

[52] See Article 6 of the Protocol to the Agreement between the People's Republic of China and the Federal Republic of Germany on the Encouragement and Reciprocal Protection of Investments.

[53] See supra note 51, Tao Du, *Hela Schwarz v. China*, 131.

BIT (2003). China challenged the jurisdiction of ICSID because there is a concurrency between domestic judicial procedure and international arbitration. More importantly, Hela cannot withdraw the judicial case, which is the precondition of the stipulated arbitration. Therefore, the ICSID case is pending at present.[54] However, the scenario would change if the dispute arose in 2020 when China established a two-tiered national-wide foreign-funded enterprise complaint handling mechanism. The investor would be able to submit their complaint to the central complaint handling agency, which will then hear the case, coordinate the dispute between Hela and the People's Government of Jinan, and promote the disputing parties to reach a settlement agreement rather than determine on the legality and proportionality of the expropriation. Besides, in Ansung Housing v. China, the local government breached its investment contract with Ansung Housing. At the same time, the ICSID tribunal decided in favor of China because Ansung Housing exceeded the three-year time limitation to launch the ISA prescribed in Article 9 (7) of China-Korea BIT.[55] The result might have been different if a national complaint mechanism had been established at that time because negotiators in the complaint mechanism would not only consider legal issues in the disputes but also consider the fairness and influence of the disputes.

3.2 The merits and defects of the current complaint handling mechanism

The current foreign investment complaint mechanism has advantages and disadvantages and needs to be further improved.

(1) Merits. Compared with the administrative review, the complaint-handling mechanism has unique advantages, including preventing and de-escalating investor-state disputes, maintaining long-term relationships, and enforcing settlement agreements.

First, it is beneficial to prevent and de-escalate investor-state disputes. Compared with adjudication and arbitration, peaceful settlement means such as conciliation, mediation, and negotiation are less adversarial and result in

---

[54] See supra note 51, Hela Schwarz v. China.

[55] See Unsung Housing Co., Ltd. v. People's Republic of China (ICSID Case No. ARB/14/25).

a non-binding report/ proposal, which is helpful in not only resolving the dispute after it arose and preventing or de-escalating it beforehand. The scope of the complaint-handling mechanism demonstrates that it deals with specific administrative actions that infringe on foreign investors' legitimate rights and problematic regulatory policies issued by the government, which may trigger disputes in the future.[56] Legislators also stressed in the text of the regulation that one of the principal functions of this regime is to prevent disputes before they escalate.[57]

Second, it can assist parties in maintaining their long-term relationship. Compared with judicial or quasi-judicial approaches to dispute settlement, the complaint mechanism is beneficial to maintaining good relationships between investors and local governments. It optimizes the possibility of a win-win outcome, and neither party is stigmatized as having lost the dispute. Aside from its perceived lack of legitimacy, one of the criticisms of the current ISDS regime is that it increases the severance of the links between the host State and the investor, defeating the very purpose of investment promotion.[58] The criticism reads that "the nature of the relationship between the investor and the State involves a long-term engagement; hence, a dispute resolved by international arbitration and resulting in an award of damages will generally lead to a severance of this link ... arbitration is focused entirely on the payment of compensation and not on maintaining a working relationship between the parties". Particularly, host States in the Asian region attach importance to face-saving while losing in an international case makes them feel bad not only because of the compensation going to be paid but also because of the shame of losing face. As a result, it is

---

[56] See Article 6 of "Work Measure for Complaints of Foreign-Funded Enterprises" (2020).

[57] See Central People's Government of China, "Explanation about the Foreign Investment Law of the People's Republic of China (Draft)", http://www.gov.cn/xinwen/2019-03/09/content_5372190.htm (April 8, 2022). Also see ibid Article 6, which provides that "the NCCFE shall ... actively prevent the occurrence of complaints".

[58] UNCTAD, *Investor-State Dispute: Prevention and Alternatives to Arbitration*, in UNCTAD Series on International Investment Policies for Development, p.19 (2010).

hard for the complaint to maintain the relationship and continue to do business with the host States. By contrast, no one loses face for peacefully settling the dispute under the complaint mechanism.

Third, reaching an enforceable settlement agreement through the complaint mechanism is more accessible than traditional, non-adversarial, and voluntary ADR means. Compared with other widely-known ADR means, the complaint-handling mechanism imposes respondents an obligation to assist with the procedures.[59] By contrast, mediation or negotiation will only succeed if both parties are willing to apply the approach to the negotiating table. In other words, it is easier to bring the disputing parties to the negotiation table in a complaint-handling mechanism because respondents are obligated to cooperate with the negotiators, namely the complaint-handling agencies.

A survey by the International Dispute Resolution team at the National University of Singapore's Centre for International Law identifies the possible obstacles to settling investor-state disputes.[60] The survey shows that the most significant obstacles come from the States, including the desire to defer responsibility for decision-making to a third party, fear of public criticism or future prosecution for corruption, the existence of multiple stakeholders across all levels of government, etc.[61] Applying the complaint-handling mechanism in settling investor-state disputes may address the concern that states are usually reluctant to settle their disputes through ADR. On the one hand, instead of voluntary participation, the respondent should cooperate with the complaint-

---

[59] See Article 17 of Work Measure for Complaints of Foreign-Funded Enterprises (2020). It provides that "the complaint handling agency may obtain information from the respondent, and the respondent shall provide cooperation".

[60] See Centre of International Law of the National University of Singapore, "Report: Survey on Obstacles to Settlement of Investor-State Disputes (2018)", https://cil.nus.edu.sg/wp-content/uploads/2018/09/NUS-CIL-Working-Paper-1801-Report-Survey-on-Obstacles-to-Settlement-of-Investor-State-Disputes.pdf (April 8, 2022).

[61] See ibid, page 1-2.

handling agency, [62] This increases the chance of successfully settling disputes compared to other voluntary ADR means. On the other hand, the complaint mechanism remains optional rather than mandatory for foreign investors, who are free to decide whether to submit their complaint submissions. Besides, the complaint handling mechanism will allow investors to apply for administrative review or bring their disputes to court.[63]

For another thing, the procedure governing the complaint handling mechanism is as flexible as other ADR means. However, the resulting settlement agreement, if concluded by two parties, is binding to both complainants and the respondents. Furthermore, the respondent will be liable if it fails to perform it. Since mediation and conciliation do not produce a binding award, investors might worry that utilizing ADR wastes time and money if the result is non-binding. By contrast, the settlement agreement in the complaint handling mechanism is final and enforceable.[64] Therefore, the complaint-handling mechanism strengthens foreign investors' confidence in reaching a mutually beneficial, predictable, and enforceable settlement agreement. It reduces their concerns about wasting time and energy engaging in ADR procedures. Besides, since China has already ratified the United Nations Convention on International Settlement Agreements Resulting from Mediation ("Singapore Mediation Convention"), enforcing the settlement agreement overseas makes the complaint-handling mechanism more appealing to foreign investors.[65]

---

[62] See Article 17 of Work Measure For Complaint of Foreign-Funded Enterprise. It stipulates that "the complaint-handing agency may obtain information from the respondent, and the respondent shall provide cooperation."

[63] See Article 30 of the Regulation for Implementing the Foreign Investment Law of the People's Republic of China (2020).

[64] See Article 18 of Work Measure for Complaints of Foreign-Funded Enterprises (2020). It provides that "the settlement agreement shall be binding on both the complainant and the respondent".

[65] See Article 3 of the United Nations Convention on International Settlement Agreements Resulting from Mediation. It provides that: "Each Party to the Convention shall enforce a settlement agreement under its rules of procedure and the conditions laid down in this Convention."

(2) Defects. Even with this, the current newly established mechanism also has some defects, including the lack of independence and perception of bias, lack of detailed rules and guidelines, lack of expertise, and limited scope of settlement.

First and foremost, there needs to be more independence or at least a perception of bias in the compliant mechanism. The domestic court used to play an essential role in ISDS; nonetheless, the perception of bias and local protectionism make it a less favorable choice than ISA. The concerns about bias and local protectionism might emerge again regarding the complaint mechanism, particularly when the dispute is related to a public policy or regulation that affects a shared interest of the administrative system and even the whole State. Although the negotiators from the complaint handling agency do not necessarily share the same position as the respondent about the regulation or policy, the perception of bias from foreign investors is common and understandable. Such concern might become an obstacle for investors, making them hesitate to submit their complaints or hand their disputes to the competent agency.

The second one is the need for more detailed rules and guidelines. There is a lack of detailed rules and guidance for the complaint agency to follow when handling disputes between investors and local governments (or departments). It is true that, over the past decades, local governments have developed a series of local regulations concerning the complaint mechanism of foreign-funded enterprises. However, those regulations are fragmented and need to be revised after the enactment of China's Foreign Investment Law and the central regulation of the 'Work Measure for Complaint of Foreign-Funded Enterprises'. The central regulation stipulates the basic procedures and principles applicable to the complaint-handling mechanism, though detailed provisions and guidelines for the complaint-handling agencies are absent. For example, the law and central regulation are silent about the applicable rules to the disputes, the confidentiality of the decision, and the transparency of the complaint-handling procedure. Besides, the central regulation reads that "as required for handling a complaint, the complaint handling agency may solicit the opinions of relevant experts on professional issues", but says nothing about how the experts are selected, who will be the candidates, and whether parties are allowed to recommend experts.[66]

The third one is the need for the complaint-handling officer to have more expertise. Compared with a conciliation committee, which is usually constituted of a group of persons who are either experts in international law or the dispute's subject matter, the complaint handling agency is constituted of administrative officers or the leader of the government department, who are neither legal expertise nor are professional conciliators or mediators. One of the most prominent goals that led to the creation of ISA was to "depoliticize the dispute", removing the dispute from the realm of politics and diplomacy and shifting it into the realm of law.[67] In this sense, the ability to legalize disputes is significant in the ISDS context. However, the administrative officials might need to be more familiar with the legal issue or not think legally about the disputes. Even if the officer is familiar with China's domestic law relating to the dispute's subject matter, he or she might be unfamiliar with international investment law, including customary law rules, which are usually applied in ISA.

Besides, the success of conciliation or mediation heavily relies on the ability and wisdom of a skillful conciliator or mediator. For example, in the multiparty negotiation with more than 1000 delegates from more than 150 countries concerning the financial clauses in the United Nations Convention of Law of the Sea (UNCLOS), Chairman Tommy Koh, a skillful negotiator and an ambassador-at-large for Singapore, developed a strategy that helped the negotiation out of the zero-sum

---

[66] See Article 17.2 of the Work Measure for Complaints of Foreign-Funded Enterprises, issued on 25 August 2022.

[67] G. Kaufmann-Kohler, *Non-Disputing State Submissions in Investment Arbitration*, in L. Boisson de Chazournes, M.G. Kohen and J.E. Viñuales ed., *Diplomatic and Judicial Means of Dispute Settlement*, 307-26, (Martinus Nijhoff Publishers, 2012).

dilemma and led to the adoption by consensus of the text on the financial issues.[68] In the conciliation on the continental shelf area between Iceland and Jan Mayen, the chairman Elliot L. Richardson, who was an eminent lawyer and politician, also played an essential role in the success of the conciliation.[69] In short, the complaint handling agency's lack of expertise might result in difficulties for the two parties in reaching a mutually satisfactory agreement.

The last one is a limited scope of settlement. The scope of settlement under the complaint-handling mechanism should also be limited. Unlike that of company officials, the authorities of governmental officials to give their consent to settlement are limited, particularly regarding the settlement of compensation or other financial issues.[70] This defect is interrelated with the nature of the government's budget. Few governments have an allocated budgetary line within the government for investment treaty claims, awards, and settlement.[71] In China, local governments rarely have a particular budget for the settlement of investment disputes. Accordingly, a significant payment resulting from a settlement agreement requires that a relevant governmental agency (or local government) cut essential programs for the year, which is difficult to negotiate. More specifically, if China loses its case in ISA as a respondent, the treasury will pay the cost and compensation (if there is any). Suppose governmental agencies or local governments agree to settle disputes with investors through complaint-handling procedures. In that case,

---

[68] See Lance N. Antrim and James K. Sebenius, *Formal Individual Mediation, and the Negotiators' Dilemma: Tommy Koh at the Law of the Sea Conference*, in *Mediation in International Relations*, ed., Jacob Bercovitch and Jeffrey Z. Rubin 97 (St Martin's Press, 1992).

[69] Conciliation Commission on the Continental Shelf area between Iceland and Jan Mayen: Report and recommendations to the governments of Iceland and Norway, decision of June 1981, VOLUME XXVII pp.1–34.

[70] See Barton Legum, *The Difficulties of Conciliation in Investment Treaty Cases: A Comment on Professor Jack C. Coe's 'Toward A Complementary Use of Conciliation In Investor-State Dispute—A Preliminary Sketch'*, 21 Mealey's International Arbitration Report, 73 (2016).

[71] See *ibid*.

the monetary compensation (if there is any) will be paid by respondents from their annual budgets, which is hard to achieve.

Therefore, compared with international arbitration, the scope of settlement under the complaint mechanism is limited, especially for financial issues. However, it may be possible for the parties to settle their disputes without making any payment to the investor, such as modifying the terms of a concession agreement or permit, removing obstacles to the current investment, or offering other monetary benefits like tax incentives to cover the loss of investors.

3.3 The improvements of the complaint handling mechanism and the possibility of promoting it in ISDS

Considering the above-mentioned defects, several improvements should be applied to the complaint handling mechanism to make it a better choice in the domestic ISDS context and even a feasible option to be promoted regionally or internationally.

First of all, the complaint-handling agency should be financially independent of the local government and directly led by the central complaint-handling agency in the MOFCOM to enhance investors' confidence in the impartiality and independence of the agency. Second, more detailed guidance should be issued so that local complaint-handling agencies can follow it. Third, the complaint-handling agency can cooperate with a Chinese-based arbitration institution, such as China International Economic and Trade Arbitration Commission (CIETAC) or the Beijing Arbitration Centre (BAC), to constitute a roster of experts as candidates for the experts complaint-handling mechanism. Two parties should be allowed to appoint experts as advisors during the complaint-handling procedures. Last, the complaint-handling process should be confidential. However, confidentiality does not extend to the fact that a complaint-handling process is taking place or to the outcome of the complaint if significant public interest is involved in the settlement agreement unless permitted by laws or agreed explicitly by parties.

Moreover, there are several opportunities for China to promote its complaint mechanism regionally or even internationally:

The Belt and Road Initiative might provide the first excellent opportunity.

China's "One Belt, One Road" (OBOR) initiative is a development strategy put forward by President Xi Jinping and started by the Chinese government in 2013.[72] It refers to the New Silk Road Economic Belt, which links China with Europe through Central and Western Asia, and the 21st Century Maritime Silk Road, which connects China with Southeast Asian countries, Africa, and Europe.[73] The heart of the OBOR is to promote transnational infrastructure investment in the countries along the route. While the OBOR initiative witnessed colossal success and prosperity for the infrastructure investment, there needs to be more efficient universal dispute resolution mechanisms, particularly for investor-state disputes, in the OBOR regime currently.[74] Although China set up two China International Commercial Courts (CICC) in Xi'an and Shenzhen to deal with disputes involving the "Silk Economic Belt" and "Maritime Silk Road", respectively, the jurisdiction of the two courts is limited to commercial disputes.[75] The complaint mechanism can be applied as a valuable approach to resolve the investor-state disputes that arise from OBOR-related investments and fill the gap. While it might be argued that ISA can settle the investor-state disputes involving OBOR-related investment since most of the countries that participated in OBOR are contracting States of the ICSID Convention, [76] The paper submits that it is rare for those countries to consent to the jurisdiction

---

[72] For more detailed background about OBOR, see Lutz-Christian Wolff and Chao Xi ed., *Legal Dimension of China's Bel and Road Initiative*, 1-33 (Kluwer et al., 2016).

[73] See *ibid*, at 140.

[74] See Malik R. Dahlan, *Envisioning Foundations for the Law of the Belt and Road Initiative: Rule of Law and Dispute Resolution Challenges*, 62 Harvard International Law Journal 62, 2-21 (2020).

[75] China International Commercial Court, "A Brief Introduction of China International Commercial Court", in the CICC website, http://cicc.court.gov.cn/html/1/219/193/195/index.html (April 8, 2022).

[76] All the countries along the Belt and Road, except Palestine, Maldives, and Bhutan, are signatories to the ICSID Convention. One hundred five of the ICSID signatories have signed the OBOR cooperation document with China. See Yan He, Yinyin Liu, *Cooperation Between the Belt and Road Initiative and Multilateral Mechanism: Opportunities, Challenges and Win-Win Solution*, 195, (Hubei People's Press, 2020)(original in Chinese)(translation by author).

of ICSID tribunals in their BITs.[77] Besides, applying the ICSID Convention to the disputes involving the countries that participated in OBOR is limited by several requirements, such as fork-on-the-road provisions, exhaustion of local remedies, etc.

The cooling-off period provisions stipulated in BITs might provide another opportunity to utilize the complaint-handling mechanism. A cooling-off period provision requires disputing parties to use amicable means of dispute settlement for a specified period before initiating international arbitration. These amicable means may include negotiation, conciliation, and mediation but do not include local administrative or judicial remedies.[78] The cooling-off period provision is widely used in Chinese BITs throughout its BIT-making history. The overwhelming majority of the first-generation Chinese BITs include provisions that oblige disputing parties to seek an amicable settlement of disputes for six months as a pre-condition to resort to international arbitration.[79] Similar provisions are also found in the second, third, and fourth generations of Chinese BITs.[80] China's consistent BIT-making practice concerning the cooling-off period in China provides an opportunity to promote the complaint mechanism to foreign investors from the contracting parties who can resort to the complaint mechanism during the cooling-off period and fulfill the pre-ISA requirement of negotiation or conciliation.

Besides, China is not the only practitioner of the cooling-off period. A study estimates that some 90% of the treaties with ISDS provisions require

---

[77] The statistic shows that many BIT concluded by the OBOR cooperation countries exclude ICSID in their treaties. The statistics are available at https://icsid.worldbank.org/en/Pages/resources/Bilateral-Investment-Treaties-Database.aspx#a0 (April 8, 2022).

[78] See Martin Dietrich Brauch, *IISD Best Practices Series: Exhaustion of Local Remedies in International Investment Law*, International Institution for Substantive Development, 2-4 (2017).

[79] For instance, Art. 9.1 and 9.2 of China-Netherlands BIT (1985) and Article 9.2 of China-South Africa BIT (1997).

[80] For example, Article 9.2 of the China-India BIT (2006); Art. 9.3.1 of the China-Cuba BIT (2007), Article 12 of the China-Mexico BIT (2008), and Article 21 of the China-Canada BIT (2012).

that the investor respect a cooling-off period before bringing a claim.[81] For instance, treaties concluded by Mexico and the United States require the cooling-off period exclusively before international arbitration. Similar provisions are also contained in regional investment agreements. For example, the ASEAN Comprehensive Investment Agreement (ACIA) signed in 2009 by all ASEAN Member States requires that "in the event of a dispute between an investor and a member State ACIA parties must first seek a resolution of the dispute by consultation and negotiation through a written request delivered by the investor to the host State." [82] In some treaties and for some arbitral tribunals, the 'cooling-off' provision is a mere procedural condition precedent to arbitration with a prescribed time limit. However, if the complaint handling mechanism is utilized in the cooling-off period, it is more helpful to resolve the dispute substantively and fulfill the purpose of 'cooling-off' provisions. The widely used 'cooling-off' provisions in investment treaties make it easier to promote the complaint mechanism regional or even international.

4. Motivations of the new domestic ISDS trend and its inspiration

Considering the international, regional, and domestic backgrounds, we could better understand China's motivation to embrace a negotiation model in its domestic ISDS approaches.

4.1 Motivations to embrace a negotiation model in local ISDS mechanisms

(1) Criticism of ISDS' Legitimacy and Proposals for Reform

The last decade has witnessed a series of criticism from States, non-governmental organizations, and scholars of international investment law's (IIL's) rules and procedures, with much of the criticism centering on the legitimacy

---

[81] Pohl, J., K. Mashigo and A. Cohen, *Dispute Settlement Provisions in International Investment Agreements: A Large Sample Survey*, in *OECD Working Papers on International Investment*, 17 (OECD Publishing, 2012).

[82] Article 31 of the ASEAN Comprehensive Investment Agreement.

of IIL as well as the ISDS regime.[83] The United Nations Commission on International Trade Law (UNCITRAL) Working Group III on Investor-State Settlement Reform (WG III) identified three broad categories of criticism, including the concerns relating to the lack of consistency, coherence, predictability, and correctness of arbitral decisions,[84] concerns relating to arbitrators and decision-makers,[85] Furthermore, concerns relating to the cost and duration of ISDS cases.[86] Although the legitimacy of the ISDS regime has come under fire, States have yet to converge on which reforms to pursue among the three main proposals for ISDS reform, which are incremental reform, systematic reform, and paradigm shift reform, respectively.[87]

The ongoing crisis of ISDS is an essential motivation for two reasons. First, it spurs China to develop its dispute prevention mechanism to resolve investment disputes domestically and reduce the risk of being sued in ISA. To further manage investment disputes and reduce the potential risk, China has to resolve them substantively through its domestic ISDS means. However, the administrative review provisions usually serve merely as procedure requirements and cannot

---

[83] See Steven R. Ratner, *International Investment Law through the Lens of Global Justice*, 20 JIEL, 747, 747-775 (2017).

[84] United Nations Commission on International Trade Law (UNCITRAL) 'Report of Working Group III (Investor-State et al.) on the Work of its Thirty-Sixth Session (Vienna, 29 October-2 November 2018)' (hereafter UNCITRAL, '36th Session Report'). Concerns include: 1) divergent interpretations of substantive standards, divergent interpretations relating to jurisdiction and admissibility and procedural inconsistency (para. 39); 2) lack of a framework to address multiple proceedings (para. 53); and 3) limitations in the current mechanisms to address inconsistency and incorrectness of arbitral decisions (para. 63).

[85] Including: 1) lack or apparent lack of independence and impartiality (UNCITRAL, '36th Session Report' (n 1) para. 83); 2) limitations in existing challenge mechanisms (para. 90); 3) lack of diversity of decision makers (para. 98); and 4) qualifications of decision makers (para. 106).

[86] Including 1) lengthy and costly ISDS proceedings and the lack of a mechanism to address frivolous or unmeritorious cases (UNCITRAL, "36th Session Report" (n 1) paras. 122 and 123); 2) allocation of costs in ISDS (para. 127); and 3) concerns regarding the availability of security for cost in ISDS (para. 133).

[87] Anthea Roberts, *Incremental, Systemic, and Paradigmatic Reform of Investor-State Arbitration*, 112 AJIL, 410-432 (2018).

resolve disputes substantively. Therefore, the complaint handling mechanism is advocated to replay the former to manage investment disputes. Second, the ISDS crisis also gives China an excellent opportunity to join ISDS reform. It is easy to find that China advocates ADR measures and pre-arbitration consultation procedures in its submission to the ISDS reform.[88] Promoting the administrative agencies to change their roles from adjudicators to negotiators in ISDS aligns with China's position on ISDS reform.

(2) An Asian culture advocating social harmony

Another underlying motivation for the trend is Asian culture. Asian culture attaches great importance to social harmony and is influential to Asian countries and their choices to dispute settlement measures. Generally, Asian countries favor settling their disputes in a less adversarial, cooperative, and face-saving way. China was one of the first contracting parties to the Singapore Mediation Convention.[89] Observers contend that the speed with which the Chinese government signed the Singapore Mediation Convention is evidence that mediation "fits" with Chinese notions of restoring "harmony" in disputes.[90] Another example is the means of dispute resolution chosen by the Association of Southeast Asian Nations (ASEAN). It reached an agreement on dispute settlement under which ASEAN States are obliged to settle their disputes- arising

---

[88] See supra note 14, Kong and Chen, *ISDS Reform is the Context of China's IIAs*, 14. As for the proposal made by China, see China, *Possible Reform of Investor-State Dispute Settlement (ISDS) Submission from the Government of China*, note by the Secretariat of UNCITRAL, A/ CN. 9 / WG. III / WP. 177. It states, "China supports the inclusion of pre-arbitration consultation procedures, specifying that the investor and the central Government of the host country are the consultation principals and stipulating consultation as a compulsory obligation of both parties."

[89] See UNCITRAL "United Nations Convention on International Settlement Agreements Resulting from Mediation", https://uncitral.un.org/en/texts/mediation/conventions/international_settlement_agreements (April 8, 2022).

[90] See supra note 75, Dahlan, *Envisioning Foundations for the Law of the Belt and Road Initiative*, 9–10.

between each other through friendly negotiations.[91]

China's proposal for ISDS reform clearly stated that a more compelling investment conciliation mechanism should be actively explored in the context of ISDS reform, which emphasizes the value of harmony and can offer the host country and investors a high degree of flexibility and autonomy.[92] As evidenced by the speed with which China signed the Singapore Mediation Convention and the proposals made by China in ISDS reform, China embraces the notion of "harmony" and values ADR means. The concept of "harmony" in Asian culture can be further divided into three core themes: Confucianism, collective inclination, and prevalence of face concerns.[93] Collectivism emphasizes the interest of the group and the aversion to conflict, while face-saving concerns involve preserving respect, avoiding shame, and maintaining harmony and good relations.[94]

The new trend of China's domestic ISDS is interrelated and motivated by its harmony preference and conflict aversion. The complaint-handling mechanism becomes a better choice for China to manage its investment disputes than an administrative review because it helps maintain long-term relationships and save the face of administrative organs through its confidential procedures.

(3) National goal to establish a diversified dispute resolution mechanism

Last but not least, China's national goal to establish a diversified dispute resolution mechanism (DDRM) motivated the change in domestic ISDS. In 2014, the "Decision of the Communist Party of China (CPC) Central

---

[91] Treaty of Amity and Cooperation in Southeast Asia (TAC), 1st ASEAN Summit, Bali, Indonesia, 24 February 1976, Article 13. ASEAN is a regional economic integration agreement between ten member States: Indonesia, Malaysia, the Philippines, Singapore, Thailand, Brunei, Vietnam, Lao PDR, Myanmar, and Cambodia. See Loretta Malintoppi and Charis Tan ed, *Investment Protection in Southeast Asia*, 4, (Brill Nijhoff press, 2018).

[92] See supra note 89, China, *Possible Reform ISDS*, para 4.

[93] See Joel Lee and Teh Hwee, *An Asian Perspective on Mediation*, 42, (Singapore, Academy Publishing 2009).

[94] See ibid, 43–48.

Committee on Major Issues About Comprehensively Promoting the Rule of Law" points out that China shall "improve the mechanism for preventing and resolving social conflicts and disputes, and improve its diversified dispute resolution mechanisms for mediation, arbitration, administrative adjudication, administrative review, and litigation, which are interconnected and coordinated." [95]

The DDRM refers to the dispute resolution system composed of various, coexisting, and coordinating dispute resolution methods, procedures, or regimes (including litigation and non-litigation).[96] It emphasizes the coordination of litigation and non-litigation methods, the application of comprehensive methods to resolve disputes, and the utilization of multiple-level approaches to prevent and de-escalate disputes. China's ambition to promote the diversified dispute resolution mechanism is evidenced by the "Report on the Reform of Diversified Dispute Resolution Mechanism of Chinese Courts (2015-2020)" made by the Chinese Supreme People's Court in 2021, which summarized the progress made by China's Court system during the five years concerning the diversified dispute resolution mechanism, including the establishment of national-wide conciliation platform and the high usage of conciliation in civil cases (65.04% in 2020).[97] Further evidence is found in the "Opinions on the Establishment of the Belt and Road International Commercial Dispute Settlement Mechanism and Institutions" issued by China's State Council and CCP in 2018, which suggested establishing a DDRM to resolve the international commercial disputes arising from the Belt and

---

[95] See *Decision of the Communist Party of China (CPC) Central Committee on Major Issues About Comprehensively Promoting the Rule of Law*, the central government of China, Part 5, para 4, http://www.gov.cn/xinwen/2014-10/28/content_2771714_5.htm (April 8, 2022) (original in Chinese) (translation by author).

[96] See Yu Fan, *The Development and Enlightenment of Diversified Dispute Resolution Mechanism in Contemporary World*, 3 China Review of Administration of Justice, 48 (2017).

[97] See Supreme People's Court of Republic China, *Report on the Reform of Diversified Dispute Resolution Mechanism of Chinese Courts (2015-2020)*, https://www.court.gov.cn/zixun-xiangqing-287411.html (April 8, 2022) (original in Chinese) (translation of author).

Road Initiative.[98]

The newly established national-wide complaint handling mechanism is a product of the diversified dispute resolution initiative, which advocates conciliation rather than adjudication. More importantly, the core of DDRM is to resolve disputes substantively, and the trend from the adjudication model to the negotiation model promotes a substantive settlement of investment disputes.

In conclusion, the global, regional, and domestic backgrounds of the new trend are interrelated, which draws a complete picture of China's motivations.

4.2 Inspiration to the future ISDS reform

China's unique domestic experience can also provide the following inspiration for future ISDS reform.

(1) The emerging trend of host states' interest in DPMMs

The trend in domestic ISDS from an adjudication model to a negotiation one reflects the interest of host States to prevent investment disputes before they escalate rather than submit them to adjudicators, such as national judges or international arbitrators. More specifically, it reveals that host states increasingly emphasize dispute prevention and management mechanisms (DPMMs).

According to the definition provided by Roberto Echandi, dispute prevention policies refer to "any course of action adopted and pursued by one or more governments specifically aimed at preventing investor-state conflicts arising under IIAs from escalating into full-blown disputes under those agreements". The conflict management mechanisms refer to "concrete procedural mechanisms, established either by law or contract, to enable investors and host States to early manage investment-related conflicts and prevent dispute escalation".[99]

Compared with ISA, administrative review, and administrative litigation,

---

[98] See *Opinions on the Establishment of the Belt and Road International Commercial Dispute Settlement Mechanism and Institutions*, the website of the central government of China, http://www.gov.cn/zhengce/2018-06/27/content_5301657.htm (April 8, 2022).

[99] See R. Echandi, *Complementing Investor-State Dispute Resolution: A Conceptual Framework for Investor-State Conflict Management: Prospects in International Investment Law and Policy*, 295-6 (Cambridge et al., 2013).

which resolve disputes after they arise, the complaint handling mechanism is a conflict management mechanism that emphasizes the prevention and de-escalation of potential disputes. Thus, the new trend in domestic ISDS indicates that China is now paying more attention to DPMMs. Such a trend is also evidenced by the emerging DPMMs in other countries, such as Peru's Special Commission established under its State System of Coordination and Defense in International Investment Disputes,[100] Korea's investment ombudspersons,[101] Brazil's ombudsman,[102] Colombia's high-level inter-ministerial bodies to develop and coordinate measures to prevent and manage investment disputes,[103] And the complaint committee in Egypt.[104]

(2) A new approach to ISDS reform

As mentioned above, there is an increasing criticism of the drawbacks of ISA as a mechanism for settling foreign investment disputes. Among the three principal paths of ISDS reform identified by the WG Ⅲ and then summarised by scholars, another proposed path should be noted is the path to reforming the ISDS system by the use of methods of alternative dispute resolution as well as dispute prevention policies and conflict management mechanisms, which enable investors and governments to manage foreign investment conflicts before they escalate into disputes under international investment agreements.[105]

---

[100] Valderrama, Carlos Jose. *Peru—Best Practices for Confronting International Lawsuits Brought by Private Investors*, 33 ICSID Review 33, 103-24 (Winter 2018).

[101] See Shin, Hi-Taek. *An Ombudsman as One Avenue Facilitating ADR and Socio-Cultural Factors Affecting ADR in Investment Treaty Dispute Resolution*, In *Investor-State Disputes: Prevention and Alternative to Arbitration II*, edited by Susan Franck and Anna Joubin-Bret, 97-101 (New York: UN Conference on Trade and Development, 2011).

[102] See Brazil's Cooperation and Facilitation Investment Agreements (CFIA), Article 17-23.

[103] Constant, Silvia, *Investor-State Dispute Prevention Strategies: Selected Case Studies*, United States Agency for International Development (USAID), https://www.apec.org/docs/default-source/Groups/IEG/20130625_IEG-DisputePrevention.pdf?msclkid=ab6c8756ada311eca9f8f8058a0bf65e (April 8, 2022).

[104] See Egypt Investment Act of 2017, Article 1, Article 83, Article 84.

[105] See Rodrigo Polanco, *The Return of the Home State to Investor-State Dispute: Bringing Back Diplomatic Protection?*, 53 (Cambridge et al., 2020).

Therefore, China's experience in adjusting domestic ISDS might inspire ISDS reform. The incremental and systematic ISDS reform proposals focus either on the reform of the ISA procedure or the establishment of an investment court with an appellate mechanism, paying little attention to developing an effective, non-adversarial, preventive regime that fits the interests of the host States that want to attract foreign investors and prevention disputes as well. Hence, the shift of Chinese administrative agencies from adjudicators to negotiators in investor-state disputes could provide a new idea for the current ISDS reform and call for more attention to developing a viable dispute management regime rather than a mere dispute settlement.

Besides, dispute prevention policies and conflict management mechanisms have been applied and advocated in several countries such as Peru, Korea, etc., as introduced in the last sub-section. In Peru, a special commission was established by its royal decree and is constituted of members from the Ministry of Finance, Ministry of Foreign Affairs, Ministry of Justice, and private investment promotion commission. The functions of the special commission include gathering information on investment disputes, coordinating disputes involving multiple government departments, and disclosing contracts, protocols, and agreements with investment dispute resolution provisions.[106] In Korea, the investment ombudspersons are nominated by the Minister of Commerce Department and appointed by the Korean president to gather investment information, suggest investment promotion policies, and assist in coordinating complaints of foreign-funded enterprises.[107] The practices in investment dispute management in those countries can offer more experience to the new path of ISDS reform.

(3) A bottom-up approach to formulate investment policies

Last, the trend also implies that the Chinese government is embracing a more bottom-up approach to formulating and revising its policies on foreign

---

[106] See UNCITAD, *How to Prevent and Manage Investor-State Disputes: Lessons from Peru*, in *Investment Advisory Series B, Best Practices in Investment for Development*, 21-31 (2011).

[107] See supra note 102, Shin, *An Ombudsman as One Avenue Facilitating ADR*, 97-101.

investment. As a collaborator, the complaint handling agency not only deals with the complaints submitted by foreign investors but also hears investors' suggestions concerning China's investment environment and regulations. The complaint-handing mechanism provides a communication channel for investors to interact with regulators, making feature regulations more reasonable and the regulatory change more acceptable to investors. This might inspire other host States about how to balance the State's interest in regulation and investors' interest in a stable investment environment.

5. Conclusion

To conclude, this article argues that China's domestic ISDS mechanism is gradually shifting from an adjudication to a negotiation model. More specifically, the foreign investment complaint handling mechanism attracts more attention in solving investor investment disputes, while administrative review gradually loses its significance. Several motivations for the trend include the opportunity provided by ISDS reform, the Asian culture advocating harmony, and China's national goal to establish a diversified dispute resolution mechanism. It reveals China's instance of preventing and de-escalating investor-state disputes and reflects its national interests as a capital-importing and capital-exporting state. China's unique domestic experience also inspires future ISDS reform. It indicates an emerging trend of host states' interest in DPMMs and presents a feasible bottom-up approach to formulate investment policies.

诉仲间主管竞择的规制盲区及应对

——以《仲裁法（修订征求意见稿）》第 40 条后段为中心

张世超[*]

● 摘　要

诉裁间关系历来以司法对仲裁的横向监督为主线。这一视角虽投射出仲裁依附于司法的共生关系，却忽略了两者同为纠纷解决手段的并存竞争关系。市场经济条件下，仲裁与诉讼是可供当事人选择的解纷手段。但现行《仲裁法》"裁审自择"的审查模式给予当事人的选择权过大，隐伏着选择权滥用的风险。为拖延审理或谋求更优裁判结果，当事人可能在仲裁与诉讼间反复横跳，这不仅损害相对方利益、空耗司法资源，也实质架空了仲裁协议，从而引发主管竞择问题。既有规制手段通过个案裁量调控、审查模式改革和严格适用"抗辩驳回制"部分解决了当事人不正当的主管竞择。但既存制度漏洞赋予先行起诉的当事人先发优势，扭曲了仲裁协议履行的激励机制。为填补漏洞，应将《仲裁法（修订征求意见稿）》第 40 条后段放弃仲裁协议效力的主观范围扩及原被告双方，并将其客观范围限缩解释为"放弃就本案纠纷提请仲裁的权利"。

---

[*] 张世超，清华大学法学院 2021 级博士研究生，诉讼法专业（民事诉讼法）。

- 关键词

  仲裁协议默示放弃　管辖异议　管辖规避　主管竞择

Abstract: The relationship between litigation and arbitration has always been dominated by judicial supervision over arbitration. Although this perspective reflects the symbiotic relationship between arbitration and justice, it neglects the coexistence and competition of the two as means of dispute resolution. In a market economy, arbitration and litigation are available to the parties as means of dispute resolution.However, the review mode of "Litigate or not, Up to you" in the current Arbitration Law gives the parties too much option, which hides the risk of forum shopping.However, the loopholes of the existing system grant the first-mover advantage to the party who files a lawsuit first, distorting the incentive mechanism for the performance of the arbitration agreement. In order to fill the loopholes, the subjective scope of waiver of validity of the arbitration agreement in the latter paragraph of Article 40 of the Arbitration Law (Revised Draft for Comment) shall be expanded to include the plaintiff and the defendant, and the objective scope shall be narrowed down and interpreted as "waiver of the right to submit the dispute in this case to arbitration".

Key Words: implied waiver of arbitration agreement, objection to jurisdiction, avoidance of jurisdiction, forum shopping

引　言

　　诉讼与仲裁在我国均有着悠久的历史，[1]但现代商事仲裁在晚清和民国时期才从西方移植而来。1907年，成都商会建立起第一个名为"商事裁判所"

---

[1] 我国古代也使用"仲裁"一词，但其所指并非以私法为基础、半正式的纠纷解决中立体制，而是以双方满意为目标的解决方式。参见《仲裁在中国：法律与文化分析》，樊堃等译，法律出版社2016年版，第217—218页。

的民间商事仲裁机构。[2] 清政府忌惮商会借仲裁之名，行司法审判之实，不仅强令该机构更名为"商事公断处"，也同时规定公断处以息讼和解为主，两造不服仍得起诉。[3] 商事裁判所的更名事件如同一面棱镜，折射出审判权与仲裁权间微妙的张力关系；又似一句谶言，国内仲裁此后百年的发展无不周旋于"行政—司法"的两端。甚至可以说，一部仲裁发展史，半部是"去行政化"史，半部是"诉讼与仲裁""法院与仲裁委"的职权划分史。[4] 在这一叙事下，诉讼是认识仲裁的出发点。仲裁只是诉讼的民间简化版，依附于司法的强制执行力，亦受司法的干预和监督。[5] 相应地，司法对仲裁单向的监督与支持成为理解两者间关系的重要视角，甚至是唯一视角。随着市场经济的发展，纠纷解决的服务属性日渐显扬。诉讼不再是当事人争端解决的唯一渠道，而是"接近司法"（Access to Justice）的路径之一。[6] 以当事人的视角观之，诉讼与仲裁是可供当事人自由选择的不同解纷手段，[7] 是彼此竞争、互为替代的"竞

---

[2]《四川成都商会裁判所规则》，载《华商联合报》第17期，"海内外公牍"，第1页。转引自《仲裁在中国：法律与文化分析》，樊堃等译，法律出版社2016年版，第219页。

[3]《公断法草案》第21条，转引自《仲裁在中国：法律与文化分析》，樊堃等译，法律出版社2016年版，第220页。

[4] 对我国仲裁机构"去行政化"的发展的全景式观察，参见陈福勇：《未竟的转型：中国仲裁机构现状与发展趋势实证研究》，法律出版社2009年版。

[5] 传统观点认为仲裁是诉讼的原始形态，是诉讼发展的必经阶段。See 14 William Holdsworth, A History of English Law 187（A.L.Goodhart & H.G. Hanbury eds., 1964）. Quoted from Douglas Yarn, The Death of ADR: A Cautionary Tale of Isomorphism Through Institutionalization, 108 PENN ST. L. REV. 929, 938（2004）.
亨利·梅因爵士认为古代司法官吏模仿私人争执中人们的可能行为并在诉讼程序中作出裁断。言外之意，诉讼程序是对私人仲裁的继承与扬弃，仲裁是诉讼的非正式简化版本。参见[英]亨利·梅因：《古代法》，沈景一译，商务印书馆2009年版，第242页。

[6] See Ali Assareh, Forum Shopping and the Cost of Access to Justice-Cost and Certainty in International Commercial Litigation and Arbitration, 31 J.L. & COM. 1, 8（2012-2013）.

[7] 目前已有域外研究探讨诉讼与仲裁费率对当事人解纷选择的影响。See Ali Assareh, Forum Shopping and the Cost of Access to Justice-Cost and Certainty in International Commercial Litigation and Arbitration, 31 J.L. & COM. 1（2012-2013）.

品"。[8]当事人与解纷机构间的互动关系恰恰为诉讼与仲裁间"监督与被监督"的规制关系忽略。

多元并存的解纷体系带来了选择的自由，也滋生了选择的滥用，滥用的具体表现之一便是仲裁与诉讼衔接过程中隐伏的"主管竞择"问题。"主管竞择"脱胎于"管辖竞择"这一概念，后者是指一个以上的解纷机构均对争议有管辖权时，当事人选择对自己更为有利的机构解决争议，以此谋求更优的裁判结果或其他非正当程序、实体利益。这种现象常见于管辖选择过于宽泛时。[9]例如，多个国内法院享有平行管辖权或跨国纠纷中多个司法辖区的法院享有平行管辖权的情形。[10]诉讼与仲裁之间也可能存在类似问题，按照民事诉讼法的理论，将其称为"主管竞择"更为贴切。[11]

当事人的管辖竞择归根结底是私法自治的产物。[12]在意思自治的范畴内，当事人何时何地选择何种机构裁断其纠纷均无挂碍，司法亦不应介入干预。真正存在问题的是，管辖竞择的过程中当事人是否滥用选择权利，造成审理延宕、资源浪费，并损害他人利益和社会公共利益。因此，有必要通过立法或司法方案，帮助原被告双方更负责任地选择争议解决方式，促进双方诚实自主地履行仲裁协议。合理规制主管竞择正是本文的核心关切。

我国与主管竞择密切相关的法条是《仲裁法》第 26 条（《仲裁法（修订

---

[8] 实际上，我国已有学者注意到了诉讼与仲裁比肩而立的竞争关系。参见陈福勇：《未竟的转型：中国仲裁机构现状与发展趋势实证研究》，法律出版社 2009 年版，第 9 页。（"不仅不同的仲裁机构所承载的制度之间存在竞争，仲裁制度整体与诉讼、调解等制度之间也存在竞争。"）另见谭兵主编：《中国仲裁制度研究》，法律出版社 1995 年版，第 48 页。（"仲裁必将因其固有的缺陷而丧失与诉讼并肩存在的基础。"）

[9] Kevin M. Clermont & Theodore Eisenberg, Exorcising the Evil of Forum-Shopping，80 Cornell L. Rev. 1507, 1509 (1994–1995).

[10] 典型如美国的州法院与联邦法院之间就可能同时对纠纷享有管辖权。参见 Friedrich K Juenger, Forum Shopping & Domestic and International, 63 TUL. L Rv. 553 (1989)。

[11] 民事诉讼法理论中一般将仲裁协议对司法管辖权的排斥称为"主管权"。参见肖建国主编：《仲裁法学》，高等教育出版社 2021 年版，第 54 页。

[12] Bermann, George A. International Arbitration and Private International Law/. Pocketbooks of the Hague Academy of International Law. 2017.p.66.

征求意见稿）》第 40 条）。相关研究对此问题虽有触及，[13] 但侧重仲裁与诉讼衔接的研究较少，亦鲜少有研究触及诉裁竞争关系下当事人程序选择权的合理规制。[14] 在案多人少的整体背景下，当事人行为视角的引入不仅有助于深化对多元纠纷解决的理解，推动政策驱动的刚性分流向需求导向的合理引流转化，捋顺仲裁与诉讼的权责界限亦可避免替代性纠纷解决被降格为纾解案件压力的工具。本文虽定位于当事人主管竞择的规制，但对《仲裁法（修订征求意见稿）》第 40 条后段的教义学分析亦有助于明确司法裁判边界。以此为最终目的，本文将首先介绍主管竞择问题的中国缘起（第一章），结合司法案例展现主管竞择的实践样态（第二章）。在此基础上，本文将分析目前既有的应对策略（第三章）及相应的制度漏洞，最终给出填补漏洞的教义学方案（第四章）。

一、主管竞择问题的缘起

管辖竞择与《仲裁法》"裁审自择、法院优先"的司法审查原则密切相关。按照仲裁协议的独立性原则，订有仲裁条款的基础合同与仲裁条款分别构成彼此独立的两个合同。[15] 仲裁协议达成后，双方只能通过仲裁的方式解决协议项下纠纷。[16] 仲裁协议有效存在是仲裁庭管辖权的基础。当事人若质疑仲裁协议的存在或效力，仲裁庭的管辖权将处于待定状态，由此产生协议效力

---

[13] 国内相关研究不仅包括对《仲裁法》第 26 条所规定的默示放弃规则，也包含了进入仲裁程序后，放弃仲裁异议权的行为。参见秦绪才：《我国仲裁法第二十六条质疑》，载《中南财经大学学报》1999 年第 1 期；王琼妮、宋连斌：《从案例看我国仲裁法上放弃仲裁管辖权异议的效力》，载《北京仲裁》2006 年第 3 期；龙威狄：《国际商事仲裁协议的妨诉效力——以我国立法司法实践为中心》，载《政治与法律》2010 年第 10 期；高薇：《论仲裁异议权的放弃——德国法视角下的分析及相关司法实践》，载《甘肃政法学院学报》2010 年第 5 期；钟澄：《论当事人因在法院实体答辩而丧失仲裁权利》，载《仲裁研究（第 30 辑）》，法律出版社 2012 年版，第 1—8 页；朱科：《异议权默示放弃制度之完善》，载《人民司法（应用）》2018 年第 7 期。

[14] 诉讼与仲裁对接视角观察该条的研究数量较少，典型如肖建国、黎弘博：《仲裁协议默示放弃规则的重构——以〈仲裁法〉第 26 条后半部分为中心》，载《法律适用》2021 年第 8 期。

[15] 江伟、肖建国主编：《仲裁法（第三版）》，中国人民大学出版社 2016 年版，第 57 页。

[16] 乔欣：《仲裁法学（第二版）》，清华大学出版社 2015 年版，第 80 页。

自我审查的悖论。[17]传统理论认为就仲裁协议存在及有效性争议应受到司法管辖权的监督。[18]如果仲裁程序已经启动，却因管辖问题被诉讼程序打断，对以效率见长的仲裁而言无异于沉重一击。尤其在争端产生时，当事人可能会陷入"反应式贬低"（Reactive Devaluation）的认知偏见。[19]即便仲裁协议有效存在，鉴于双方当事人间的敌对关系，一方可能更倾向于否认或贬低事前签署的仲裁协议，认为协议不公或对自己不利。如此一来，无论协议有效与否，当事人都可能滥用异议权，惯性地提起管辖异议。这无异于在实体权利争议之外又开辟了程序权益争夺的"第二战场"。若默许此种"程序内耗"，仲裁高效便捷的优势也将蒙尘，显然不利于仲裁制度的良性发展。

有鉴于此，《联合国国际贸易法委员会示范法》第16条（《联合国国际贸易法委员会示范法（2010年修订版）》第23条）[20]确立了自裁管辖原则。根据该原则，仲裁庭被推定为有权对自己是否享有管辖权作出判定。[21]仲裁庭自裁管辖权原则（Kompetenz-Kompetenz）逐步在世界范围内广泛确立。但自裁管辖权原则并不意味着仲裁庭的管辖决定是终局的，也不代表完全排除法院确定仲裁管辖权的权力。联合国贸法会第一工作组在制定该规则时指出仲裁庭对自身管辖权作出的决定接受法院的司法审查。[22]自裁管辖权的核心在于限定法院干预仲裁管辖权的时间，尽量向后推延法院介入的时间，从而保障仲裁程序高效无中断地进行。[23]

---

[17] A/CN.9/207（14 MAY 1981），para. 58.["（仲裁协议的）这种独立性可能与仲裁庭就有关仲裁条款的存在或效力的异议有关，并促进仲裁庭就这些异议作出裁决。"]

[18] 江伟、肖建国主编：《仲裁法（第三版）》，中国人民大学出版社2016年版，第132页。

[19] 反应式贬低描述的是提议来源影响当事人对该提议之评价的现象。当事人可能会贬低从对手方收到的提议，即便相同的提议如果由中立方或盟友提出时是可以被接受的。Robert H. Mnookin et al., Beyond Winning: Negotiating to Create Value in Deals and Disputes，156（2000）. p. 165.

[20] 《联合国国际贸易法委员会示范法（2010年修订版）》第23条第1款：仲裁庭有权对其本身的管辖权，包括对仲裁协议的存在或效力的任何异议，作出裁定。为此目的，构成合同一部分的仲裁条款应被视为独立于合同其他条款的一项协议。仲裁庭作出合同无效的决定，不应自动导致仲裁条款的无效。

[21] [美]加里·B. 博恩：《国际仲裁：法律与实践》，白麟等译，商务印书馆2015年版，第70页。

[22] A/CN.9/216（23 MARCH 1982），para.82.

[23] See Albert Jan van den Berg, Commentary on the UNCITRAL Model Law on International Commercial Arbitration, Kluwer Law & Taxation Publishers（1990），p. 74.

我国在1988年《中国国际经济贸易仲裁委员会仲裁规则》第2条第3款曾采行此原则,该条赋予仲裁委员会就仲裁协议的有效性和仲裁案件的管辖权作出决定的权利。但我国1994年《仲裁法》是采用了"裁审自择"审查模式。该时期的文献资料显示,《仲裁法》对仲裁委员会的决定的司法审查并非事后监督,而是在仲裁的申请和受理阶段即行介入。法院和仲裁庭均可以对仲裁协议效力异议作出决定,且一定情形下法院享有优先权,最终由谁作出裁决由当事人自主选择。[24]并行审查的双轨模式意在充分尊重当事人意愿。早期介入仲裁协议效力的争议也有利于在开庭前解决此先决问题。[25]随后出台的《最高人民法院关于确认仲裁协议效力几个问题的批复》(以下简称《仲裁协议效力批复》)第3条、[26]《最高人民法院关于适用〈中华人民共和国仲裁法〉若干问题的解释》(以下简称《仲裁法解释》)第13条等延续了并行审查模式,并在此基础上进一步明确了法院审查的优先性——除非法院受理当事人确认仲裁协议效力的诉请前,仲裁庭已经对管辖权作出了决定,否则以法院管辖权为优先。[27]

二、主管竞择的实践现况

"裁审自择"的审查模式允许当事人在两种程序间作出"选择"。该模式赋予当事人选择权利的同时,也为当事人滥用诉讼程序、阻滞仲裁审理创造契机。一旦诉讼程序启动,法院即可介入争议并终止仲裁,客观上加剧了仲裁的程序迟滞,降低了仲裁效率。[28]如其所言,实践中的确出现了形态各异

---

[24] 江伟、李浩:《论人民法院与仲裁机构的新型关系——为〈仲裁法〉的颁行而作》,载《法学评论》1995年第4期。

[25] 江伟、李浩:《论人民法院与仲裁机构的新型关系——为〈仲裁法〉的颁行而作》,载《法学评论》1995年第4期。

[26] 《最高人民法院关于确认仲裁协议效力几个问题的批复》第3条:当事人对仲裁协议的效力有异议,一方当事人申请仲裁机构确认仲裁协议效力,另一方当事人请求人民法院确认仲裁协议无效,如果仲裁机构先于人民法院接受申请并已作出决定,人民法院不予受理;如果仲裁机构接受申请后尚未作出决定,人民法院应予受理,同时通知仲裁机构终止仲裁。

[27] 朱华芳、郭佑宁:《确认仲裁协议效力案件的实践观察与规则完善》,载《北京仲裁》2021年第1期。

[28] 池漫郊:《国际仲裁体制的若干问题及完善——基于中外仲裁规则的比较研究》,法律出版社2014年版,第101页。

的权利滥用方式，妨碍了解纷程序的顺畅进行。主管竞择的实践形态可粗略分为两类：一是规避仲裁主管，即双方虽订有仲裁协议，但一方为谋求程序利益或其他利益，隐瞒仲裁协议并提起诉讼；二是管辖投机，即先选择一种程序启动审理（通常是诉讼），审理中发现情势对己方不利，再撤诉或提出管辖异议。两种行为可能各自独立，也可能相伴相生，界限有时也不甚分明，但其规制重点仍有所侧重。

（一）管辖竞择的具体形态：仲裁主管规避

规避仲裁主管是指系争纠纷受仲裁协议效力所及，但当事人为追求特定程序或实体利益，故意创造或改变主管连接点，使系争纠纷在主体、客体范围方面溢出仲裁协议的覆盖范围。仲裁协议具有相对性，通常而言其效力仅及于协议签署方，而不及于第三人。[29]此外，仲裁协议事项需具备可仲裁性，法律规定不得仲裁的事项仅能提起诉讼。[30]根据诉讼法的处分原则，当事人对诉讼对象、请求内容、法律关系均有处分权利，可通过对主管连接点的弹性调整，间接选择纠纷解决机构。可能采取的方式如下：

一是增列或择列仲裁协议非签署方为诉讼主体。如仲裁协议签署方为 A 和 B，协议一方提起诉讼时将第三方 C 增列为共同被告或共同原告。这种情形为增列主体，是指在原本协议相对方的基础上增加非签署方为当事人；或 AB 中的一方起诉时仅将第三方 C 列为被告，将另一缔约方列为第三人。这种情形常见于彼此联系的关联合同纠纷中，典型如建设工程施工合同中发包人、承包人与实际施工人间的纠纷。[31]案例如下：

【案例1】[32]发包方 A 公司与承包方 B 公司签订《×市×路（一期）工程项目施工承包合同协议书》，B 公司将建设工程转包给 C 公司。后查明案涉工程的实际控制方为 D 公司，D 公司借用 B 公司的资质中标。B 公司与 C 公司间签有四份《建设工程施工专业分包合同》，每份合同均约定纠纷由武汉仲

---

[29] 肖建国主编：《仲裁法学》，高等教育出版社2021年版，第68页。

[30]《仲裁法》第2条、第3条；《仲裁法解释》第2条。

[31] 如（2020）京民终61号、（2018）内民终187号、（2016）粤民终468号、（2015）云高民一终字第227号。

[32] "朝阳建设集团有限公司、佛山市顺德北部中一路桥有限公司建设工程施工合同案"【（2020）粤民终466号】。

委员会管辖。因 B 公司拖欠建设工程款 1.3 亿余元，实际施工人 C 公司向法院起诉。但 C 公司与 B 公司间存在仲裁协议，其诉请的施工人工程款也为仲裁协议基础合同所覆盖。起诉时，C 公司将与其无直接合同关系，但可能承担补充责任的 A 公司拉入诉讼。法院最终认为本案应受仲裁协议管辖，驳回了原告起诉。

该案中原告起诉时将仲裁协议的非签署方 A 也拉入诉讼。尽管其本意未必是规避管辖，但其行为的确违背了 BC 间的仲裁协议约定。[33] 相较而言，若原告将仲裁协议非签署方列为被告，又未对其提出独立诉讼请求，此种情形更加典型。下述【案例 2】规避仲裁管辖的意图或许更为明显。

二是责任竞合时主张侵权责任以规避管辖。根据《民法典》第 186 条，因当事人一方的违约行为，损害对方人身权益、财产权益的，受损害方有权选择请求其承担违约责任或者侵权责任。依据该条的文义解释，"有权"意味着当事人在合同请求权与侵权请求权中拥有选择的权利，权利行使与否由当事人自主决定。[34] 仲裁解决平等主体间的纠纷，但争议事项必须满足可仲裁性的客体标准才能纳入仲裁的审理范围。《仲裁法》第 2 条将仲裁范围限定于平等主体间发生的合同纠纷和其他财产纠纷。但请求权竞合场景下的"侵权纠纷"与"其他财产纠纷"之范围只是部分重合，人身侵权纠纷不具有可仲裁性，[35] 涉及公共利益、公共道德、社会秩序的纠纷，国家也不允许当事人自由处分，[36] 若当事人在侵权和违约间选择了侵权纠纷，可能排除仲裁管辖，案件将由法院受理。纠纷属性对可仲裁性的影响若为当事人不当利用，亦可引发规避仲裁管辖的情况。

【案例 2】[37] 原告程某购入 A 公司为基金管理人、B 公司为基金托管人的某私募投资基金，并签署《基金合同》。该合同约定仲裁机构为上海仲裁委员会金融仲裁员。该基金设立后投向了 C 银行某分行托管了系列私募投资基金。

---

[33] 对本案而言，更加值得反思的问题或许是 A 对 C 可能存在法定赔偿责任的情况下，能否将仲裁协议的效力扩及于 A，从而将 A 拉入仲裁。

[34] 吴香香：《请求权基础：方法、体系与实例》，北京大学出版社 2021 年版，第 27 页。

[35] 《仲裁法》第 3 条第 1 款。

[36] 《仲裁法》第 3 条第 2 款、第 77 条。

[37] "程某其他合同纠纷案"【（2021）沪 74 民终 1054 号】。

后因基金运作过程中，ABC三公司未能审慎管理、存在重大过错，导致基金巨额亏损。故原告程某向ABC三公司提起侵权之诉。一审法院认为程某与AB公司间订有仲裁协议，故裁定不予受理。程某不服提起上诉，二审法院认为原告虽选择以侵权为由提起诉讼，但其提起的诉讼请求系赔偿基金投资款本息，涉案争议系与《基金合同》有关的争议，故原告与AB之间的纠纷解决应受仲裁条款约束。而程某对C银行并未提出独立的诉讼请求，有规避仲裁管辖的嫌疑，最终法院维持了原裁定。

最高人民法院在（2015）民四终字第5号案中认为，如侵权争议因违反合同义务而产生，违约责任和侵权责任有竞合关系，原告即使选择以侵权为由提出诉讼，仍应受合同仲裁条款约束，不应允许当事人通过事后选择诉讼来逃避仲裁条款的适用。即便原告提起诉讼时增列了未签订仲裁协议的其他被告，亦不影响有仲裁协议的原被告之间的纠纷适用仲裁协议。根据《仲裁法解释》第2条，当事人概括约定仲裁事项为合同争议的，基于合同成立、效力、变更、转让、履行、违约责任、解释、解除等产生的纠纷都可以认定为仲裁事项。侵权纠纷若因合同履行而产生，亦可落入该条的合同争议范畴之内。[38] 除此之外，对仲裁协议适用范围作宽泛解释也符合我国"支持鼓励仲裁"的政策导向，亦有助于和国际接轨。一般来说，标准化的仲裁协议会尽可能采用较为宽泛的表述，其目的在于扩张性地将特定合同中的全部争端包括在内，以高效解决纠纷。[39] 国际仲裁中，多数法院也会根据国内法确立的"支持仲裁"原则推定侵权主张受仲裁协议覆盖，当事人不能以此规避仲裁管辖。[40]

三是选择关联合同中未约定管辖条款的合同作为诉讼依据。随着经济的发展和改革的深化，交易模式的商业目的多元、牵涉利益主体众多、合同关系错综复杂。大量由多合同文本构成的民商事交易结构涌入诉讼，构成"合

---

[38] 江苏省高级人民法院民三庭：《江苏高院民三庭对〈最高人民法院关于适用仲裁法若干问题的解释〉的理解与适用意见》，载《北京仲裁》2007年第3期。

[39] ［美］加里·B.博恩：《国际仲裁：法律与实践》，白麟等译，商务印书馆2015年版，第117页，脚注3。

[40] ［美］加里·B.博恩：《国际仲裁：法律与实践》，白麟等译，商务印书馆2015年版，第120页。

同集群"。[41] 不同关联合同的具体权利义务内容可能略有差异，签署方也不尽相同，更重要的是，合同中管辖条款的内容也未必一致。尽管各个合同最终指向同一交易目的，彼此之间高度关联，但囿于相对性原则，基础合同中约定的仲裁协议仅能约束合同的实际签署人。非经仲裁协议主观范围扩张，无法约束其他交易相关方。管辖条款的不一致无疑为交易相关方择选主管机构提供了便利。当事人起诉时可避开甚至隐瞒订有仲裁协议的关联合同，而选择其他无仲裁协议的合同作为请求依据。可见，仲裁协议主观效力扩张问题映射到程序层面，也会牵涉仲裁主管规避。

【案例3】[42] 原告A公司与包括B公司在内的多名被告订有《联合拍摄协议》，后双方因投资纠纷产生争议，A公司起诉要求披露某电影在合作拍摄期间的财务信息并按分配规则支付20%的投资收益份额。但《联合拍摄协议》中未具体约定投资收益与分配规则。但被告方之一B公司与案外人C公司签署《××电影投资合作协议》《补充协议》约定了明确的投资收益分配方式。A公司曾与该案外人C公司签署《股权转让协议》并取得对该电影的投资收益权。此外，C公司曾就投资争议向B公司提起过仲裁并获得胜诉判决，A公司对此知情并于庭上对仲裁情况表示认可。本案两审法院均认为原告起诉所依据的《联合拍摄协议》仅约定了合作原则、电影基本要素等统筹影片拍摄的事项，并未涉及各签约方的投资份额、收益分配和亏损承担等与投资有实质性关联的内容。投资相关的内容分别约定在《××电影投资合作协议》《补充协议》及《股权转让协议》中。上述合同的缔约方虽并非完全一致，但均订有仲裁条款。故法院认为本案所涉纠纷不属于法院审理范围。

该案中，原告以未订有仲裁条款的《联合拍摄协议》起诉，请求的内容为投资收益分配。但投资收益分配方式以及相关方的权利义务规定在了订有仲裁条款的关联合同中。原告虽不是该关联合同的缔约方，但原告的投资权益受让自C公司（以入股的方式获得），A起诉时也已经知晓C公司曾就向本

---

[41] 吴智永、徐劲草：《论商事交易结构中合同集群的"穿透性审查"路径——以意思表示的体系化识别为视角》，载《法院改革与民商事审判问题研究——全国法院第29届学术讨论会获奖论文集（下）》，第921页。

[42] "上海番薯影业有限公司与北京影行天下文化传播有限公司等合同纠纷案"【（2020）京民终61号】。

案被告之一提起仲裁，请求对方支付相应投资收益。因此，本案符合《仲裁法解释》第9条的构成要件，A公司应受仲裁协议约束。在此情况下，A仍选择与本案纠纷关联不甚紧密的《联合拍摄协议》起诉，颇有挑选基础合同、规避仲裁主管的嫌疑。

（二）管辖竞择的具体形态：管辖投机行为

管辖投机行为是当事人滥用诉讼权利，任择管辖机构的另一表现。"管辖投机"是指，在系争纠纷受有效仲裁协议管辖的前提下，当事人并不当然遵守仲裁协议，而是按照其启动解纷程序时的具体利益诉求，在诉讼与仲裁间择选其一。若审理中发现情势对己方不利，再撤回诉讼或仲裁请求，提出主管异议或仲裁协议效力异议。当事人的管辖投机行为未必单纯为了获取更优的实体裁判结果，也可能是为了争取程序利益，[43]如便于保全，[44]或拖延时间。

管辖投机行为在实践中并不鲜见，但具体表现不尽相同。按争议内容，可将其进一步划分为：1）与仲裁协议效力问题相关的投机行为；2）与仲裁协议存在问题相关的投机行为。前者对应于《仲裁法》第20条（《仲裁法（修订征求意见稿）》第28条），后者对应于《仲裁法》第26条（《仲裁法（修订征求意见稿）》第40条）。

1. 与仲裁协议效力问题相关的"投机行为"

鉴于《仲裁法》第20条同时赋予了仲裁委员会和法院审查仲裁协议效力的权限，实践中，被申请人为妨碍仲裁审理，会先向仲裁机构申请确认仲裁协议效力。待仲裁机构作出决定后，再向法院重复提出确认仲裁协议效力申请。[45]尽管《仲裁法解释》第13条规定，仲裁机构作出决定后，当事人向法

---

[43] 如"贵州建工集团第一建筑工程有限责任公司、成都成通建筑材料有限公司因申请诉中财产保全损害责任纠纷案"【（2019）川01民终2956号】及与之关联的系列案件中，当事人就在订有仲裁协议的情况下提起诉讼并申请了诉中保全。此后又由于保全错误而引发财产保全损害赔偿纠纷。

[44] 我国仲裁财产保全制度存在一定缺陷，一是仲裁财产保全的审查权、裁决权和执行权由法院垄断，仲裁庭并不享有相关权利；二是与《民事诉讼法》的诉讼保全制度不协调，仲裁程序中仅有仲裁保全而缺乏仲裁受理前的财产保全安排。上述两项缺陷可能会影响当事人仲裁保全的效率。在有保全需求的情况下，诉讼相较于保全对当事人而言或许是更为稳妥的安排。参见汪祖兴：《中国仲裁制度的境遇及改革要略》，法律出版社2010年版，第232—234页。

[45] 徐京京、周晶敏：《再论〈仲裁法（修订）（征求意见稿）〉的重点问题》，载国枫律师事务所公众号2022年6月10日，https://mp.weixin.qq.com/s/hcr1MwzpWcrc18VYgZ6x2A。

院申请确认仲裁协议效力的，法院不予受理。但被申请人在请求时可能会隐瞒仲裁机构的受理情况，若仲裁申请人未及时提出异议，法院可能要等到开庭后才能全面了解实情。根据《仲裁协议效力批复》第 3 条，法院立案受理后会通知仲裁机构终止仲裁，进行中的仲裁程序因此而搁置。

现实中仲裁协议效力确认的受案情况在法院与仲裁委间很难做到实时同步，实践中经常发生当事人分别向法院及仲裁机构递交了申请，而且申请均被受理的情况。[46] 类似情况与制度间的信息壁垒不无关联。在法院优先审查的架构下，诉讼程序系属将导致仲裁审查程序终止。如此便将信息差转化为时间差，当事人可借此实现其拖延审理的不当目的。

2. 与仲裁协议存在相关的管辖投机行为

如前所述，管辖投机的形成原理是信息差与时间差的转化。这种转化也可能发生在《仲裁法》第 26 条（《仲裁法（修订征求意见稿）》第 40 条）的场景下。我国《民事诉讼法》实行"辩论原则"，法院对案件事实及证据的审查范围应限于当事人双方在辩论中提出的证据。[47] 国内外程序法理论中多将仲裁主管作为妨诉抗辩事项，非经当事人提出，法院无主动审查的必要。[48] 凡此种种意味着，如果当事人在起诉时不主动提出或刻意隐瞒仲裁协议存在的事实，法院在立案时也难以查明真实情况。上述客观限制为管辖投机创造了空间，当事人起诉时可改换诉请法律关系，隐藏仲裁协议，以此逃避仲裁主管。

【案例 4】[49] 原告 A 公司主张其曾于 2015 年、2016 年分别向被告 B 公司提

---

[46] 徐京京、周晶敏：《再论〈仲裁法（修订）(征求意见稿)〉的重点问题》，载国枫律师事务所公众号 2022 年 6 月 10 日，https://mp.weixin.qq.com/s/hcr1MwzpWcrc18VYgZ6x2A。

[47] 张卫平：《民事诉讼法（第五版）》，法律出版社 2019 年版，第 45 页。

[48] 杨秀清：《协议仲裁制度研究》，法律出版社 2006 年版，第 164—165 页；陈刚：《论我国民事诉讼抗辩制度的体系化建设》，载《中国法学》2014 年第 5 期；[日] 伊藤真：《民事诉讼法（第四版补订版）》，曹云吉译，北京大学出版社 2019 年版，第 118 页。

相反观点，高桥宏志认为仲裁协议抗辩并非本来意义的妨诉抗辩，因为被告即便提出异议，也不意味着他可以拒绝本案审理。法官通过合目的性裁量不会妨碍本案审理，这与严格意义上的妨诉抗辩有着很大差异。[日] 高桥宏志：《民事诉讼法重点讲义（导读版）》，张卫平、许可译，法律出版社 2021 年版，第 7—8 页。

[49] "安徽东方钙业有限公司与南京钢铁联合有限公司企业借贷纠纷案"【(2014) 苏商辖终字第 0091 号】。

供数额为 400 万元、100 万元、2600 万元的三笔借款，共计 3100 万元。B 公司一直未予偿还。另查明 2004 年，B 公司的三方股东即 A 公司、C 公司、D 有限公司签订《合资经营合同》约定，应将原股东 X 公司为 B 公司的 2600 万元银行贷款提供的担保替换为 A 公司。B 公司用现有的、有效的实物资产为 A 公司提供反担保，A 公司与 B 公司依法办理企业资产抵押手续。发生纠纷任何一方均应提交中国国际经济贸易仲裁委员会，按照申请仲裁时该会现行有效的仲裁规则进行仲裁。A 公司已向 B 公司支付了三笔款项，电汇凭证载明用途为"担保借款"。涉案三笔款项双方均没有签订借款合同及约定利息。涉案 2600 万元款项的担保合同因银行不同意变更担保人、B 公司未提供反担保而未实际履行。诉讼中，B 公司提出主管异议，主张 400 万元借款的诉请依据为 AB 间签订的《资金往来协议》，该协议订有仲裁条款。原告起诉时故意隐瞒双方签有协议并有仲裁约定的事实，是为了规避仲裁管辖。A 公司遂撤回了 400 万元借款的本息请求，仅主张 2700 万元及相应利息。对剩余借款，B 公司认为此两笔借款系因三方股东之间的合资经营合同纠纷而起，该合同已明确约定了纠纷提交中国国际经济贸易仲裁委员会仲裁，不属于人民法院的受案范围。但一审法院认为 B 公司未提供反担保，故无法认定 A 公司向 B 公司汇款是为履行涉案《合资经营合同》中所约定的担保责任，本案应按民间借贷纠纷确定管辖。B 公司不服提起上诉，二审法院维持裁定。

本案中，原告在借款发放前签署的《合资经营合同》载明了担保责任承担金额为 2600 万元，与借款金额一致，且电汇载明的借款用途为"担保借款"。上述间接事实足以表明借款纠纷系因《合资经营合同》而起，理应交由仲裁管辖。而 400 万元款项所依据的合同也订有仲裁条款。按理说，本案交由仲裁管辖并无异议。当事人以民间借贷法律关系提起诉讼，将多笔属于仲裁协议管辖范畴的借款打包处理，并在起诉时隐瞒借贷关系产生的基础合同。不论其隐瞒仲裁协议的动机如何，本案的确造成了"管辖逃逸"的客观效果。

三、主管竞择的既存规制措施

（一）主管规避的"个案判断标准"

在"支持仲裁"的政策引导下，法院对于刻意规避仲裁主管的行为多有所警觉。根据《民事诉讼法》第 127 条第 2 项、《仲裁法》第 5 条（《仲裁法（修订征求意见稿)》第 5 条）的规定，若立案阶段发现当事人间存在有效仲裁协议，法院通常会不予受理案件[50]或裁定驳回起诉。[51]但如前所述，为了让系争案件顺利为法院受理，当事人可能会改变诉讼对象和诉讼标的，尽量让系争纠纷溢出仲裁协议的管辖范围，人为制造法院主管连接点。此时，系争纠纷是否完整无虞地落入仲裁协议的规制范围就会产生争议。从司法裁判的情况来看，法院会采取二阶判断标准：第一步，判断诉讼标的的真正依据是否为订有仲裁协议的合同或诉讼标的能否为基础合同所吸收。若部分请求为仲裁协议覆盖，部分请求超出仲裁范围，则进行第二步——判断各诉讼请求之间是否存在实质关联，剥离仲裁协议项下的诉讼请求后，剩余请求能否独立审理。若否，则整体驳回起诉。若请求之间不存在逻辑上的先决关系，分别审理对案件结果无实质影响，法院可能部分地驳回起诉，继续审理余下请求。

  总体而言，通过创造连接点来规避仲裁主管，往往难逃法官的火眼金睛。即便案件牵涉主体复杂多样，法院也会沿循仲裁协议的覆盖范围裁剪、分割法律关系及诉讼请求。此处殊值反思的问题是，该做法是否符合纠纷解决的内在规律，是否背离了多元纠纷解决制度高效、快捷、一体化解纷的初衷。[52]将前述【案例 1】中部分纠纷交予仲裁，意味着当事人再向发包方请求承担补充责任时，需要等待仲裁案件审结。这对权利人而言也是无形的时间成本消耗，亦可能牵涉诉讼时效问题。对法院而言，切割彼此关联的诉讼请求也可能引发矛盾裁判风险。在当下"案多人少"、绩效考核压力较大的背景下，司法对仲裁的"力挺"或许更多源于法院当下面临的种种制度性

---

  [50]《民事诉讼法》第 127 条第 2 项规定，"依照法律规定，双方当事人达成书面仲裁协议申请仲裁、不得向人民法院起诉的，告知原告向仲裁机构申请仲裁"。杨秀清教授将仲裁协议的此种效力称为"禁诉效力"，与经被告抗辩方可驳回起诉的"妨诉效力"相对应。参见杨秀清：《协议仲裁制度研究》，法律出版社 2006 年版，第 75 页。

  [51] 在立案后发现不满足起诉条件/诉讼要件的，法院可裁定驳回起诉。参见王亚新、陈杭平等：《重点讲义民事诉讼法（第二版）》，高等教育出版社 2021 年版，第 48 页、第 270 页。

  [52] 类似问题在诉讼程序内部也颇为常见，如法院以另案处理裁判的方式拆分案涉法律关系或另案处理当事人的抗辩。参见马家曦：《民事诉讼另案处理的标准澄清与程序完善》，载《中外法学》2021年第 3 期；宋春龙、赵立慧：《民事诉讼抗辩另案处理的实践与反思》，载《政法学刊》2022 年第 1 期。不过，司法实践中同样存在与之相对立的另一种情形，即为贯彻一次性纠纷解决而扩充诉讼容量。参见任重：《民事纠纷一次性解决的限度》，载《政法论坛》2021 年第 3 期。

约束（Institutional Constraints）。[53] 纠纷回归仲裁的结果未必真正源于仲裁与法院间合理的职能划分，而可能是法院制度性约束下的附带结果。[54] 目前的这种操作方式是否真正有利于促进仲裁事业的发展，推动纠纷的妥善解决，有待进一步观察。

（二）"仲裁前置"模式的登场

改善主管竞择问题的另一重要举措是"裁审自择"模式的退场。此次《仲裁法（修订征求意见稿）》第 28 条实质性地改变了原有的平行审查格局，法院对仲裁协议效力的审查进一步后置。这也意味着"仲裁前置、仲裁优位"的审查模式将取代原有模式，成为今后的主流。

《仲裁法》第 20 条项下仲裁协议的"存在"与"效力"边界模糊。涉及仲裁协议主观范围扩张时，当事人间是否订有协议也与协议效力的主观范围紧密关联。法院是否对此享有主管权常常成为各方争执的焦点。[55] 一方面，《仲裁法（修订征求意见稿）》第 28 条进一步明确了主管异议的具体范畴。根据该条，仲裁庭审查的范围包括仲裁协议的有效性，协议是否存在，以及对仲裁案件的管辖权异议等情形。较之《仲裁法》第 20 条，该规定更为清晰准确。另一方面，《仲裁法（修订征求意见稿）》第 28 条大幅调整了仲裁协议效力及管辖争议的审查顺序，规定仲裁机构先行审查，当事人对仲裁机构的决定不服的，再向法院提出审查和复议。同时，人民法院的审查程序不影响仲裁程序的进行。若该条顺利通过，"裁审自择、法院优先"的平行模式将成为历史。

此外，上述变动也将导致《仲裁法》第 26 条（《仲裁法（修订征求意见稿）》第 40 条）的适用领域与现行法第 20 条进一步分化。新法时代，随着仲裁庭审查的前置与审查范围的扩大，《仲裁法（修订征求意见稿）》第 40 条前段将

---

[53] 法院的制度性约束（Institutional Constraints）是指法院和法官受到多种法律因素之外的外部约束，这些约束会限制法官何时能够使用法律，何时必须摒弃法律。参见 He, Xin. Divorce in China: Institutional Constraints and Gendered Outcomes, New York, USA: New York University Press, 2021. p. 29.

[54] 目前已有研究者注意到了此种现象。参见武振国：《论"仲裁协议存在"问题的可审查性》，载《仲裁与法律》第 144 辑。

[55] 武振国：《论"仲裁协议存在"问题的可审查性》，载《仲裁与法律》第 144 辑。

产生"被告异议自动触发法院驳回起诉"的实质效果。[56] 相较而言,该条后段的仲裁管辖默示放弃原则将占据更为重要的位置,该条的整体定位也将朝向"仲裁协议的放弃规则"延伸发展。[57] 但无论如何,若仲裁前置审查模式为立法所确认,并行审查引发的主管竞择、拖延审理现象将大为缓解。

(三)"抗辩驳回制"的筛选功能

我国另一协调仲裁管辖权与司法审判权关系的既存举措是仲裁协议审查的抗辩驳回模式。[58] 仲裁协议本身不是影响诉讼成立的起诉条件,而是判断案件能否进入实体审理的前提。[59] 诉讼功能在于判断纠纷是否适于以本案判决的形式解决。[60] 该项要件欠缺并不妨碍审理程序的启动。[61] 在诉讼要件的各种分类中,仲裁协议属于诉讼障碍要件,是否产生排除法院管辖的妨诉效果取决于被告是否提出该妨诉抗辩,法院不能依职权审查该项要件。[62] 若障

---

[56] 《仲裁法》第26条前段原本也负载一定的仲裁协议效力审查功能。根据该条及《最高人民法院关于适用〈中华人民共和国民事诉讼法〉的解释》(以下简称《民诉法解释》)第216条的规定,被告以有书面仲裁协议为由对受理民事案件提出异议的,人民法院应审查仲裁协议的效力。原告有仲裁协议而未予提出,被告以存在符合形式要求的仲裁协议为由提出异议,双方间的争议本身暗含了仲裁协议效力之争。而法院审查的内容同样是协议的效力,说明原被告间就仲裁协议存在的争议蔓延至效力问题并为后者吸收。按照《仲裁法(修订征求意见稿)》第28条,上述问题均应由仲裁庭处理。只要被告在首次开庭前提出异议,将自动产生驳回起诉,告知另行申请仲裁的效果。

[57] 《仲裁法(修订征求意见稿)》第40条原封保留了《仲裁法》第26条的规定。随之而来的问题是保留的价值何在?原本该条是《仲裁法》第20条的对应物,但新法出台后,法院实质上已经被剥夺了仲裁协议效力的直接审查权。如此一来,《仲裁法(修订征求意见稿)》第40条前段的重要性将有所下降,其适用重心自然要朝向后段偏移,聚焦于仲裁协议的放弃规则。否则就会与第28条相冲突。除此以外,由于仲裁协议效力审查统一收归仲裁庭所有,《民事诉讼法》第127条第2项、《民诉法解释》第215条但书、第216条等规则也应当联动修改,与新订《仲裁法》保持一致。

[58] 杨秀清:《协议仲裁制度研究》,法律出版社2006年版,第161页。

[59] [日]高桥宏志:《民事诉讼法重点讲义(导读版)》,张卫平、许可译,法律出版社2021年版,第3—4页。

[60] [日]伊藤真:《民事诉讼法(第四版补订版)》,曹云吉译,北京大学出版社2019年版,第119页。

[61] 张卫平:《起诉条件与实体判决要件》,载《法学研究》2004年第6期。

[62] [日]高桥宏志:《民事诉讼法重点讲义(导读版)》,张卫平、许可译,法律出版社2021年版,第7页。

碍条件解除，诉讼程序仍可继续进行。[63]

　　抗辩驳回制对主管竞择的规制并非压制性的，而是反应式的。法院是否介入完全取决于被告对原告起诉行为的反应。具言之，一方当事人就仲裁协议项下的事项向法院起诉后，若对方当事人以双方存在有效仲裁协议为由，向法院提出异议，法院将驳回原告起诉。相较于法院依职权审查仲裁协议的有无，该模式更加尊重双方当事人的私权处分。仲裁协议是双方合意达成的协议，若非存在约定或法定情形，任何一方均无单方解除或终止协议的权利。一方违背仲裁协议的约定向法院起诉，仅代表其单方放弃要求对方履行仲裁协议的权利，其行为并不影响相对方要求将纠纷提请仲裁的权利。[64]基于仲裁协议的上述构造，法院主管能否排除仲裁主管取决于相对方的意思。当事人一方隐匿协议、规避仲裁的行为也可通过赋予被告异议权的方式予以限制。但是，被告异议权的行使并非没有限制。即便双方受仲裁协议约束，若被告未在首次开庭前及时提出异议，案件进入实体审理阶段后，将产生失权的法律效果。[65]异议期间经过后，被告不得再以双方存在仲裁协议为由阻断诉讼审理，法院将取得完整的涉诉案件管辖权。之所以设置异议时限，一是避免司法资源浪费；二是避免给应诉方带来不必要的程序花费；三是避免纠纷解决的不当拖延。[66]究其本质，还是为了防止当事人恶意拖延程序或滥用管辖权异议。[67]换言之，异议权制度是一个双重保险，被告方异议权可制约原告对仲裁协议消极义务的违反，并敦促其积极配合履行仲裁的积极义务。[68]

---

[63] 陈刚：《论我国民事诉讼抗辩制度的体系化建设》，载《中国法学》2014年第5期。

[64] 杨秀清：《协议仲裁制度研究》，法律出版社2006年版，第161页。

[65] 肖建国、黎弘博：《仲裁协议默示放弃规则的重构——以〈仲裁法〉第26条后半部分为中心》，载《法律适用》2021年第8期。

[66] 龙威狄：《国际商事仲裁协议的妨诉效力——以我国立法司法实践为中心》，载《政治与法律》2010年第10期。

[67] 王琼妮、宋连斌：《从案例看我国仲裁法上放弃仲裁管辖权异议的效力》，载《北京仲裁》2006年第3期。

[68] [美]加里·B.博恩：《国际仲裁：法律与实践》，白麟等译，商务印书馆2015年版，第80页。

四、主管竞择规制盲区的教义学应对

捋顺仲裁主管权与司法审判权间的关系是合理有效规制主管竞择的关键。前述三项规制措施分别在不同向度上调整仲裁权与审判权的关系。个案判断标准系法院司法裁量介入,有利于个案认定的利益平衡;《仲裁法(修订征求意见稿)》废止了诉讼与仲裁的平行审查模式,贯彻"仲裁审查前置、司法审查后置"的原则,更利于诉讼向非诉的引流;抗辩驳回制通过原被告间程序权利的制衡,在尊重当事人意思自治的同时,也为法院的消极诉讼要件审查上了一道双保险,实现了风险负担由法院向当事人的重心转移。在三项机制的共同作用下,仲裁程序与诉讼程序间的衔接也将更为顺畅。即便如此,上述机制仍有未尽周延之处,主管竞择问题仍存在隐秘的规制盲区。

(一)主管竞择的规制盲区

民事诉讼是一种对抗式的"等腰三角形"结构,处于相互对立的地位上的诉讼当事人地位平等,其进行攻击防御的权利也应平等。[69] 为保持两造公平对抗的机会,诉讼法的诸多措施都具有对称性,一方当事人提出主张,另一方当事人可以反驳;一方提出证据,另一方亦可提出反证。相应地,法律对当事人的程序权利规制也应趋于平等,不能给予一方较之相对方更有利的诉讼地位。在主管竞择的规制方面也应如此。若不允许被告在首次开庭后迟延地提出仲裁主管异议,也不应直接或间接地允许原告方享有二次选择的权利。鉴于《仲裁法》第 26 条后段并未明确"视为放弃仲裁协议"的效力是否及于原告,以及该效力范围是否仅限于本案纠纷或仲裁协议整体。现行规制框架下,原告相对于被告似乎更具挑选主管机构的主动权,并可能增加原告滥用程序的风险。

现行规定下,若原告先行起诉,被告在异议期间内未提出主管异议,首次开庭后被告不能再行主张主管异议,但原告仍然可在首次开庭后以撤诉的方式将案件恢复至起诉前的状态。由于被告放弃仲裁协议被视为诉讼行为,仅在诉讼程序中产生答辩失权效果,而不及于仲裁协议本身。原告享有起诉和撤诉的程序处分权,一旦撤诉,则根据《民诉法解释》第 214 条第 1 款,撤诉将使得案件恢复到诉讼未发生时的状态,依附于诉讼程序的行为效力亦将

---

[69] 王亚新:《对抗与判定——日本民事诉讼的基本结构(第二版)》,清华大学出版社 2010 年版,第 51 页。

随之而消灭。除非法律明定，原告仍可再次起诉。在"高福友因与苏锴房屋租赁合同纠纷案"中，[70]法官认为，"撤诉是程序上对案件予以终结，双方撤回的仅仅是起诉的诉讼权利而已，对于双方当事人之间的实体权利义务并未作实质处理，撤诉后，诉讼当事人重新回到诉讼尚未开始前的状态。因此，即使双方当事人在（2016）苏1282民初1668号案件中被视为放弃仲裁协议，但该案因双方撤诉而重新回到诉讼尚未开始前的状态，双方当事人在（2016）苏1282民初1668号案件中被视为放弃仲裁协议的效力并不及于本案"。

根据《民事诉讼法》第148条，宣判前，原告申请撤诉的，由法院裁定是否准许。又根据《民诉法解释》第238条的规定，若法庭辩论终结后原告申请撤诉，但被告不同意，人民法院可以不予准许。原告在法庭辩论终结后撤诉，需征得被告同意。换言之，原告能否在首次开庭时或其后撤诉，主要由法官裁量决定。尽管原告撤诉可依靠法官裁量调控，但司法实务中的撤诉通常被法院当作结案方式来使用，存在非正当化使用的倾向。[71]相关实证研究显示，2014年全国公开上网的民事裁定书中，一审撤诉裁定占全部民事裁定总数的60%以上。[72]高企的撤诉率虽不能说明任何案件中法官均对撤诉抱以积极态度，但法官裁量管控能否有效限制原告的主管竞择行为不无疑问。

（二）规制逻辑的内在矛盾

《仲裁法》第26条（《仲裁法（修订征求意见稿）》第40条）后段的片面规制很大程度上源于该条"放弃仲裁协议"的法律效果定位模糊。在诉讼程序中通过默示行为放弃仲裁协议，究竟是仅对诉讼程序发生影响的诉讼行为，还是产生实体法律效力的法律行为，抑或两者兼而有之。学界对此亦众说纷纭。

依据《仲裁法》第26条后段的文义，"放弃仲裁协议"似乎产生仲裁协议效力终止的实体法律效果，其所产生的效果为法院继续行使审判权。[73]照此解释，将此处的"放弃仲裁协议"理解为放弃程序权利的诉讼行为更加贴合。学界也多主张该条款仅产生程序失权效果，而非终止仲裁协议的实体权利义

---

[70] （2016）苏12民终2420号。

[71] 王福华：《正当化撤诉》，载《法律科学》2006年第2期。

[72] 马超、于晓虹、何海波：《大数据分析：中国司法裁判文书上网公开报告》，载《中国法律评论》2016年第4期。

[73] 唐德华、孙秀君主编：《仲裁法及配套规定新释新解》，人民法院出版社2002年版，第282页。

务关系。[74] 如认为当事人以行为默示放弃的是整体的仲裁协议,当基础合同产生新的纠纷时,当事人无法基于原本的仲裁协议再行申请仲裁,这恐怕违背了原本协议签订的初衷,法院的司法干预有过度之嫌。[75] 因此,有学者建议第26条后段应修改为"放弃仲裁协议之妨诉抗辩"。[76]

不过,仅将"放弃仲裁协议"定位为单纯的诉讼行为,将其效力也限定在诉讼程序范围内,难以有效规制原告方挑选管辖的行为。诉讼行为是具有取得裁判之目的的行为,其效力依附于诉讼程序。[77] 这也意味着诉讼程序的变动也会随之影响当事人诉讼行为的效力。如前所述,即便被告已经默示同意放弃仲裁协议并接受法院管辖,若原告在程序进行中认为庭审结果可能对其不利,其仍能够以撤诉的方式让纠纷恢复到原有状态,并再行提起仲裁。由于被告的行为缺乏实体法上的效力,仲裁协议的权利义务关系尚未因被告的诉讼行为产生变化,原本的仲裁协议依然有效存在。在现行体制下,原告可以审时度势、作出二次主管选择。而被告的异议权仅能在法院进入实体审理前行使。即便案件进展情况对其不利,被告也不能在首次开庭后提出主管异议。此种片面规制的结构有可能扭曲激励机制,促使当事人违背仲裁协议,优先选择诉讼管辖,以便掌握程序主动权。

(三)主管竞择的规则重释

1.《仲裁法(修订征求意见稿)》第40条后段的解释框架:实体与程序法理衔接

相对于灵活易变、可随时撤回的诉讼行为,合同的目的在于为当事人提供稳定的预期和明确的指引。尤其对主管竞择而言,问题的症结并非缺乏灵活的选择权,而在于选择权利过大而引发的成本损耗。这种损耗不仅对当事人来说是时间、精力、金钱的浪费,对司法制度而言也是无谓的空耗。党的十八届四中全会明确提出建立有机衔接、相互协调的多元化纠纷解决机制。2019年,习近平总书记在中央政法工作会议上作出重要指示,明确提出要"把非诉讼纠

---

[74] 王琼妮、宋连斌:《从案例看我国仲裁法上放弃仲裁管辖权异议的效力》,载《北京仲裁》2006年第3期。

[75] 杨秀清:《协议仲裁制度研究》,法律出版社2006年版,第179页。

[76] 杨秀清:《协议仲裁制度研究》,法律出版社2006年版,第180页。

[77] [日]新堂幸司:《新民事诉讼法》,林剑锋译,法律出版社2008年版,第297页。

纷解决机制挺在前面"。随后最高人民法院、司法部、国家发改委等职能部门也相继出台文件,建立健全多元纠纷解决模式的顶层设计。"支持和鼓励仲裁发展"是"非诉讼纠纷解决机制挺在前面"的题中之义,更是司法尊重支持仲裁的有力背书。但司法对仲裁的支持并非仲裁案件的机械分流,而应引导当事人秉持善意的原则参与仲裁,共同参与建立解决争议的审裁程序。[78]我国《仲裁法(修订征求意见稿)》第4条新增"仲裁应当诚实善意、讲究信用、信守承诺"。该新增条款正是支持仲裁政策的外在展现。对仲裁协议以及仲裁法律的解释亦应以"支持、鼓励仲裁"的立场为出发点和落脚点。这一政策若要浸润个案的司法适用,并为法官的法律适用提供操作职能,就需要诉诸教义学分析。[79]

相较于普通的民事合同,仲裁协议既处分了当事人的诉权,也处分了当事人在相关争议中的实体权利义务。[80]这也导致学界对仲裁协议的属性定位学说如林、多足鼎立,涌现出程序契约说、实体契约说、混合契约说、独立类型说等争鸣观点。[81]不过,学说纷争只是问题实质的外在呈现,问题的肯綮不在于仲裁协议如何定性,而在于对仲裁协议的解释是否要兼采实体法契约与程序法契约共同的契约原理。[82]换言之,影响仲裁协议解释的法律渊源是否既包含民事程序法,又要借鉴合同法等民商事实体法。答案显然是肯定的,这也是国际国内的理论共识。[83]因此,管辖竞择的法律规制框架既包含《仲裁法》《民事诉讼法》等程序法,也需要适当借用《民法典》等基本私法原理,衔接程序法理与实体法理。

---

[78] [美]加里·B. 博恩:《国际仲裁:法律与实践》,白麟等译,商务印书馆2015年版,第80页。

[79] 卜元石:《德国法学与中国当代》,北京大学出版社2021年版,第19页。

[80] 黄进、宋连斌等主编:《仲裁法学(第三版)》,中国政法大学出版社1997年版,第77—78页。在域外,违反仲裁协议也可以产生损害赔偿责任。但我国当事人鲜少就违反仲裁协议提请损害赔偿。笔者以"违反仲裁协议"为关键词在裁判文书网中检索,共检索到27份裁判文书,其中有24份为裁定书,3份为判决书,均不涉及违反仲裁协议的损害赔偿。又以"仲裁协议违反"为关键词检索,共检索到84份裁判文书,其中79份为裁定书,5份为判决书,同样未涉及损害赔偿。

[81] 肖建国主编:《仲裁法学》,高等教育出版社2021年版,第54页;乔欣:《仲裁权论》,法律出版社2009年版,第32—40页。

[82] 肖建国主编:《仲裁法学》,高等教育出版社2021年版,第54页。

[83] See Bermann, George A. International Arbitration and Private International Law/. Pocketbooks of the Hague Academy of International Law. 2017.p.67; Paul Bennett IV, "Waiving" Goodbye to Arbitration: A Contractual Approach, 69 Wash. & Lee L. Rev. 1609 (2012).

2. 诉讼中放弃仲裁协议的行为定性

程序与实体的交叉属性也影响了诉讼程序中被告行为的定性。《仲裁法（修订征求意见稿）》第40条后段规定的"未对人民法院受理该案提出异议"应理解为单纯的诉讼行为抑或可导致实体权利义务关系变化的法律行为呢？

若将"放弃仲裁协议"理解为纯粹的"诉讼行为"，被告行为仅对诉讼程序产生效力。一旦原告撤诉，先前行为的效力也将不复存在，案件恢复到未发生诉讼时的状态。[84] 这种"恢复原状"的效力实质上赋予了原告反悔和二次选择的机会，掌握程序启动权的一方将攫取更具优势的诉讼地位。"先发优势"可能变相激励当事人违反仲裁协议，优先提起诉讼，加剧主管竞择。同时，先行起诉也将导致司法管辖提前介入，增加仲裁协议履行的不确定性，甚至架空《仲裁法（修订征求意见稿）》新确立的"仲裁前置"审查模式。这对仲裁制度的长远发展显然是不利的。因此，放弃仲裁协议的效力也应及于原告。原告提起诉讼的行为及被告在规定时限内未提出异议的行为，均可对仲裁协议设定的权利义务关系产生影响。与此同时，异议期间经过后，原被告的诉讼行为也受到限制。双方均不得在上诉或再审程序中再行提出主管异议。

综上，笔者认为不应将此行为单纯理解为仅产生诉讼法上效力的诉讼行为。[85] 被告放弃仲裁协议的行为实际上是诉讼行为与民事法律行为的复合。两者在外观上是同一行为，其构成要件与法律效果虽有所重合，但绝非完全一致。这种构造类似于生活中常见的"两块牌子、一套人马"。尽管从外观上看来，当事人仅作出了一个行为，但该行为发挥的效力、引发效力的要件均存在微妙差异。相应地，行为效力的解释也应揆诸实体与程序的共同法理。

3. "放弃仲裁协议效力"的主观范围

就主观范围而言，放弃仲裁协议对原被告双方均发生法律效力。乍看上去，《仲裁法》第26条后段"视为放弃仲裁协议"的主体是"另一方"当事人，也即被告。似乎放弃仲裁协议的效力仅对被告产生。不过，也可以将第26条理解为总分结构，即原告向人民法院起诉未声明有仲裁协议并为法院受理后，将对应两种情形：一种情形是被告在首次开庭前提交仲裁协议的，不

---

[84] 此种情况也可以通过"禁反言规则"或"诚实信用原则"予以调控，本文暂不深入展开。

[85] 如《民法典》第565条第2款规定的解除权的诉讼行使。

能视为放弃仲裁协议，除非协议无效，法院将驳回起诉；另一种情形是被告未提出主管异议的，视为放弃仲裁协议，法院将继续审理。因此，法律效果的产生是"原告起诉未声明有仲裁协议＋被告未提出主管异议"这两者共同作用的结果。仲裁协议的效力自然也及于原告。若被告明示或默示同意由法院继续审理本案，而原告在首次开庭后撤回诉讼请求，法院应征询被告意见，并结合本案审理的情况，双方参与诉讼的成本负担、原告有无违反诚信原则拖延审理或谋求更有利裁判结果的意图等因素，审慎判断。对被告而言，若其在首次开庭后主张双方间存在仲裁协议，原则上不予准许。不过，被告迟延主张主管异议的情形可能多种多样，刚性化的时间要求是否过于严苛也值得反思。

4."放弃仲裁协议效力"的客观范围

原则上，放弃仲裁协议效力的客观范围应限于系争纠纷，而不及于仲裁协议整体。《仲裁法》第26条所规定的"放弃仲裁协议"应当目的性限缩解释为放弃就系争纠纷提起仲裁的权利。仲裁权利的放弃与仲裁协议的失效、终止和放弃不同，其效力仅限于当事人诉诸法院解决的特定纠纷，原本的仲裁协议仍然有效存在。[86]若当事人嗣后又因基础合同产生其他纠纷，新产生的纠纷仍然受仲裁协议管辖。仲裁协议的效力范围原则上仅限于本案纠纷。

合同中的仲裁条款通常会约定"与本合同相关的全部争议应提交仲裁解决"，[87]据此可将仲裁协议解释为附条件合同，[88]仲裁协议以"实际产生基础合同相关之纠纷"为法律行为的生效要件。当事人之间发生与基础合同相关的特定争议时，当事人始得负有就系争纠纷向约定的仲裁机构提请仲裁之积极义务和不得向法院起诉之消极义务。[89]但是，仲裁协议的合同属性决定了其高

---

[86] Gary B. Born, International Commercial Arbitration (Third Edition), 3rd edition, Kluwer Law International, p.1010 (2021).

[87] ［美］加里·B. 博恩:《国际仲裁：法律与实践》，白麟等译，商务印书馆2015年版，第118页。

[88] Paul Bennett IV, "Waiving" Goodbye to Arbitration: A Contractual Approach, 69 Wash. & Lee L. Rev. 1609, 1668–1669 (2012).

[89] ［美］加里·B. 博恩:《国际仲裁：法律与实践》，白麟等译，商务印书馆2015年版，第80页、第84页。

度灵活的品质。[90]在意思自治的射程范围内，当事人享有变动合同的自由，可以达成合意变更、终止合同。[91]根据《民法典》第543条，当事人协商一致，可以变更合同。因此，当一方当事人违反仲裁协议的约定向法院提起诉讼时，并不直接构成违约。应将其行为理解成原告通过起诉行为发出变更仲裁协议内容的意思表示，该意思表示自起诉状副本有效送达被告时生效，且被告的异议期开始起算。[92]

至于原被告间是否达成变更仲裁协议的合意，端赖于对被告意思表示的解释。《民法典》第140条规定意思表示可通过明示、默示或沉默的方式作出。明示是指以口头或书面的话语形式明确表达意思的行为。默示通常情况下与可推知的意思表示同义，是指除口头或书面话语的直接表达外，基于交往惯例、法定或约定、肢体语言等形式可推知的意思表示。[93]沉默是指不具有意思表达意义的单纯沉默。一般在法律有明确规定的情况下，沉默才可被拟制为意思表示。或当事人明确约定了作出积极反对表示之义务，若届时保持沉默，当事人的沉默也可以被解释为同意。[94]笔者认为《仲裁法》第26条后段"未对人民法院受理该案提出异议"应包含明示、默示以及沉默这三种表示方式。当事人以书面或口头答辩的方式明确表示放弃仲裁审理，此种情况自不待言。若当事人未对仲裁主管作出直接回应，但从其言语或行动能推断出其放弃的意图，亦符合该条意旨。由被告方应诉答辩的行为可推知当事人协商一致解

---

[90] T. J. Stipanowich, "Arbitration and Choice: Taking Charge of the New Litigation", De Paul Business & Commercial Law Journal, Vol. 7, 2009, at p. 387. ("……仲裁首先是合同的产物，本质上是高度灵活的。")

[91] 杨代雄：《法律行为论》，北京大学出版社2021年版，第3—4页。

[92] 变更仲裁协议的意思表示具有一定的特殊性。其附着于诉讼程序，故可类比《民法典》第565条第2款诉讼中行使合同解除权的规定。起诉状副本的送达具有实体法与程序法的双重效力：对诉讼程序而言，起诉状副本送达意味着诉讼系属成立。对实体权利法律关系而言，根据《民法典》第137条第2款第一句，起诉状副本送达也意味着意思表示到达相对方。参见刘哲玮：《诉的基础理论与案例研习》，法律出版社2021年版，第44页。

不过，变更说的一个障碍在于《民法典》第544条规定，当事人对合同变更内容约定不明确的，推定为未变更。这意味着如果无法从被告的意思表示中推知"放弃仲裁协议"是放弃整体的仲裁协议还是对本案纠纷提起仲裁的权利，则推定为协议未变更，也即仲裁协议未被放弃。后文笔者将证明可通过限定"放弃仲裁协议"之内容解决语义模糊的问题。

[93] 朱庆育：《民法总论（第二版）》，北京大学出版社2016年版，第193页。

[94] 朱庆育：《民法总论（第二版）》，北京大学出版社2016年版，第195页。

除了合同，法院依此获得纠纷的主管权。[95]实践中，亦有法院将当事人是否"实体答辩"作为评断是否放弃仲裁主管的参考要素。[96]

争议较大的一个问题是缺席裁判的情况下是否也产生放弃仲裁协议的效力。有观点认为被告未提出异议且应诉答辩的情况才能视为放弃仲裁协议。[97]言下之意，单纯的沉默不能产生拟制效果。《全国法院涉外商事海事审判工作座谈会会议纪要》第47条持此立场。该条规定"缺席当事人未明示放弃仲裁协议的"不能当然地视为放弃了仲裁管辖。[98]笔者认为《仲裁法》第26条后段明确规定了异议期间以及期间经过后导致的失权效果，其目的就是敦促被告方积极行使仲裁权利，避免躺在权利上睡眠。若法律已经向被告课加了积极反对的义务，其消极行为就有可能被解释为同意放弃。[99]若案件受理后，法院已经向被告有效送达了相关诉讼文书，原告要求将系争纠纷诉诸法院的意思表示已有效送达，被告因其自身原因缺席判决且未及时提出异议，就应负担相应后果。除非本案为公告送达或存在其他正当事由，否则缺席判决亦应产生放弃仲裁管辖的效果。[100]归根结底，双方是否达成放弃仲裁主管合意仍取决于意思表示的解释，需要具体问题具体分析。明示反对或拒绝仲裁主管以外的一切情形，包括明示同意放弃、默示同意放弃以及沉默，均有解释为"未提出异议"的空间，并产生法院排除仲裁主管的效果。因此，增强"未提出异议"的解释弹性更有利于充分尊重当事人的真正意图，也为法官审酌具体情势、合理平衡双方利益提供了有效的解释工具。

---

[95] 唐德华、孙秀君主编：《仲裁法及配套规定新释新解》，人民法院出版社2002年版，第64页。

[96] 如"张某1、张某2因与北京住总万科房地产开发有限公司房屋买卖合同纠纷案"中，二审法院裁定认为"万科公司如果放弃仲裁条款的约束应在一审中向一审法院明确提出或者在一审中就本案进行实体答辩。本案一审中，万科公司已经在一审法院正式开庭前向一审法院提出主管异议，其并未进行实体答辩，而一审法院亦据此进行相应的处理。"【（2019）京01民终9279号】

[97] 肖建国、黎弘博：《仲裁协议默示放弃规则的重构——以〈仲裁法〉第26条后半部分为中心》，载《法律适用》2021年第8期。

[98] 《全国法院涉外商事海事审判工作座谈会会议纪要》第47条：外国法院作出缺席判决后，当事人向人民法院申请承认和执行该判决，人民法院经审查发现纠纷当事人存在有效仲裁协议，且缺席当事人未明示放弃仲裁协议的，应当裁定不予承认和执行该外国法院判决。

[99] 朱庆育：《民法总论（第二版）》，北京大学出版社2016年版，第195页。

[100] 本质上而言，该问题取决于意思表示解释。当事人虽缺席诉讼审理，但在首次开庭前已经向仲裁机构申请仲裁，诉讼中的"沉默"自然无法解释为放弃仲裁管辖。

五、结语

受"重农抑商"历史传统之影响,我国商业社会发育的基础较弱,但改革开放以来的市场化浪潮虽赐予商事仲裁发展的良机,但其发展仍不时面对行政化的掣肘。某种程度上而言,诉裁关系正是"国家—社会""政府—市场""官方—民间"等多种关系的凝缩,这也使得诉裁关系的学术研究更多关注不同社会系统间的张力关系,而忽视了单一系统下主体间的互动关系,尤其是法院、仲裁委与当事人的纵向互动和当事人之间的横向互动。

仲裁制度是市场的产物,同时也是面向市场的产物。在多元化纠纷解决的谱系中,仲裁是可供当事人选择的解纷服务。但选择的自由也必然带来选择的滥用,尤其在双方的商业博弈中,"裁审自择"的并行审查模式赋予当事人过大的选择自主权,极易沦为拖延审理、消耗对手的工具,也浪费了仲裁与法院的司法资源。这是主管竞择问题的根源所在。随着《仲裁法》的修改,并行审查模式也将成为历史,余下的制度漏洞亦可通过对《仲裁法》第 26 条(《仲裁法(修订征求意见稿)》第 40 条)的解释予以填补。不过,当事人的权利滥用可对相对方与解纷机构产生影响,机构间的多头处理,职权划分模糊亦可对当事人的权利行使带来影响。本文的部分案件中已经展露出一定苗头,法院为纾解过大的案件压力,亦可能将原本高度相关的纠纷集群按仲裁协议的管辖范围进行切割。这样的操作方案是否利于纠纷解决,是否有助于保障当事人的利益亦值得反思。若该问题现实存在,纠纷集群应统一交由诉讼审理,还是交予仲裁庭审理,就关涉到仲裁协议主观范围扩张、仲裁第三人及诉讼第三人等辅助机制。至于诉裁关系未来的发展走向如何,不妨先"让子弹飞一会儿"。

按小时费率计收仲裁员报酬的优缺点与监督机制研究

黄 帆[*]

- 摘 要

　　按小时费率计收仲裁员报酬是国际商事仲裁的常见做法，但由于我国仲裁行业存在特殊情况，仅有少数仲裁机构的仲裁规则允许仲裁员按小时计费。为探究该收费制度在我国推广的可行性，本文将梳理域内外学者研究成果，对按小时费率计收仲裁员报酬制度的优缺点与监督机制进行总结。通过对现有研究成果未解决的问题进行总结与反思，本文认为，在我国实施按小时费率计收仲裁员报酬利大于弊，且时机已经成熟，目前主要的任务是在机构仲裁中建立仲裁机构与法院依顺序参与的监督机制，并在将来可能实行的临时仲裁中建立法院主导的监督机制，让按小时费率计收仲裁员报酬制度顺利落地实施。

- 关键词

　　仲裁员报酬　小时费率　仲裁监督

　　Abstract：Arbitrators being paid at hourly rates is a common practice in international commercial arbitration. However, only a few arbitration institutions in China have issued rules allowing arbitrators to

---

[*] 黄帆，澳门大学国际商法专业硕士研究生二年级。

be paid on an hourly basis due to the specific circumstance in Chinese arbitration. In order to explore the feasibility of popularizing hourly rate system in China, this article reviews the existing researches of scholars worldwide and summarizes the advantages, disadvantages and the possible monitoring mechanisms of the hourly rate system for arbitrator's remuneration. This article concludes that the advantages of implementing an hourly rate for arbitrator's remuneration has outweighed the disadvantages and that it is now the propriate time for the system to be implemented in China. The main task at this stage is to establish a monitoring mechanism involving both arbitration institution and judicial court by stages for institutionalized arbitration, and a monitoring system lead by judicial court for ad hoc arbitration to assure a smooth implementation.

Key Words: arbitrator's remuneration, hourly rate, supervision over arbitration

一、问题的提出

仲裁员报酬是参与仲裁的各方都必须面对的一个问题：仲裁机构在制定仲裁规则时需要考虑仲裁员报酬的计算方法；仲裁员作为提供仲裁服务的一方，其获得经济补偿的权利是无可争议的，[1] 除非仲裁协议有相反的约定；[2] 而仲裁的争议当事人作为缴纳仲裁费用的一方，自然会关心实现心目中的正义需要付出多少"代价"。

一般来说，仲裁员报酬有三种计费模式：从价法（ad valorem method），固定收费法（fixed fee method）和按时计费法（time spent method）。按时计费法是仲裁员按照花费在案件上的工作时间来确定报酬的计费方法。这种计费

---

[1] Gary B. Born, *International Commercial Arbitration*, 3rd edition, Kluwer Law International 2021, p.2167.

[2] Mauro Rubino-Sammartano, *International Arbitration-Law and Practice*, 2nd edition, Kluwer Law International 2001, p.359.

方法计算的时间不仅包括仲裁开庭的时间，也包括开庭以外的工作时间，但差旅时间往往适用低的费率。按时计费一般以小时或天数乘以费率进行计算，而小时费率有时也与日费率混合适用。[3]

不同的计费模式有不同的特点，也存在不同的问题。其中，按小时计费尤其引人关注。笔者认为，这是因为我国的仲裁员报酬制度亟待改革，这一点已经有不少学者呼吁。[4] 在改革的过程中，国际仲裁实践自然就成为一个参考选项，而按小时计费这一国外仲裁机构的主流做法[5]长期以来没有在我国仲裁机构中推行。因此，按小时计费就被纳入改革选项中。但是，引入该制度之前必须认真考察按小时计费的优缺点，并采取有效措施以克服其缺点，避免"水土不服"。

由于按小时计费的模式在国外实施已久，其优缺点也已得到充分展现，因此国外学者对按小时计费的监督机制已有一定研究，一些国家的立法和司法判例中也可以找到针对按小时计费的监督机制，这些探索都是值得我们参考的有益经验。

二、研究价值

我国[6]的仲裁机构目前所面临的主要问题是"收支两条线"[7]以及仲裁机构对于仲裁员报酬的决定权过大。[8]然而，这并不代表研究按小时计费对我国仲

---

[3] Nigel Blackaby, Constantine Partasides, Alan Redfern, Martin Hunter, *Redfern and Hunter on International Arbitration - Student Version*, 6th edition, Oxford University Press, 2015, p.297.

[4] 学界呼吁的重点主要是在报酬分配上要体现出仲裁员在仲裁中的主体作用，代表性观点可参见沈四宝、薛源：《论我国商事仲裁制度的定位及其改革》，载《法学》2006年第4期，第69页。亦有学者认可现行的仲裁员报酬制度。如康明认为，我国仲裁机构对仲裁员报酬的确定享有完全的权利，虽然这不符合商事仲裁服务的原则，但可以对仲裁员起到监督作用，促进仲裁员勤勉工作，同时也能体现"多劳多得"的原则。参见康明：《商事仲裁服务研究》，法律出版社2005年版，第141页。

[5] 2000年面向72个国家共计877名律师和仲裁员的一项国际调查显示，确定仲裁员费用最通用的方法是以时间为基础的计算方法。见［美］克里斯多佛·R.德拉奥萨、［美］理查德·W.奈马克编：《国际仲裁科学探索：实证研究精选集》，陈福勇、丁建勇译，中国政法大学出版社2010年版，第236—243页。

[6] 为行文简洁，本文表述的"我国"指代"中国大陆"地区，不含港澳台地区。

[7] 赵健：《转变政府职能与我国仲裁机构仲裁费管理体制的革新》，载《北京仲裁》2006年第6期。

[8] 沈四宝、薛源：《论我国商事仲裁制度的定位及其改革》，载《法学》2006年第4期。

裁没有价值。我国仲裁正处于改革期，现行《仲裁法》的修订就是最好的证明。其中，仲裁机构的收费是改革的重点领域之一。仲裁员报酬作为仲裁机构收费的主要组成部分，就必然要经历改革。因此，按小时收费是我国仲裁机构迟早要面对的一个改革选项。目前我国已经有中国国际经济贸易仲裁委员会（以下简称贸仲）和北京仲裁委员会/北京国际仲裁中心（以下简称北仲）在其仲裁规则中确定了按小时收费，[9]北仲还发布了具体的操作指引，[10]相信这一做法会陆续出现在其他仲裁机构规则中。

仲裁费用常常是仲裁各方抱怨的焦点，而仲裁费用的主要组成就是仲裁员报酬，[11]因此针对仲裁员计费方式的处理也涉及仲裁机构与仲裁员的关系、仲裁员的地位提升、当事人提起仲裁的意愿、法院与仲裁机构的关系乃至整个仲裁行业生态的改变和仲裁行业的发展。简言之，按小时计费是完善仲裁员报酬制度，推进仲裁制度改革而必须考虑的一项措施。

三、按小时费率计收仲裁员报酬的优缺点

（一）降低成本还是抬高成本？

按小时计费能够运用市场的力量促进仲裁员之间小时费率的竞争，[12]从而降低市场平均价格，使当事人受益。但是，按小时计费的方式为不良仲裁员拖延办案提供了可乘之机。[13]从中长期看，按小时计费还可能会导致成本增加，甚至降低地区对国际商事仲裁的吸引力。[14]尽管与总价计酬相比，按小

---

[9] 按小时费率计收仲裁员报酬制度在内地首见于《贸仲仲裁规则（2015年版）》第82条；《北仲仲裁规则（2019年版）》附录1和附录2也规定了按小时费率计收仲裁员报酬制度。上述仲裁机构其后修订的新版规则均保留了该制度。

[10] 2020年9月1日，北仲发布《关于采用小时费率计收仲裁员报酬的操作指引（征求意见稿）》。2021年7月1日，北仲正式发布《关于采用小时费率计收仲裁员报酬的操作指引》。

[11] M. Schneider, "Lean Arbitration: Cost Control and Efficiency Through Progressive Identification of Issues and Separate Pricing of Arbitration Services", 10 Arbitration International 2, 119, 124 (1994).

[12] Bruno Guandalini, Economic Analysis of the Arbitrator's Function (Kluwer Law International 2020), p.132.

[13] 黄亚英:《论商事仲裁的十大特点和优势》，载《暨南学报（哲学社会科学版）》2013年第4期。

[14] ［英］维杰·K.巴蒂亚、［澳］克里斯托弗·N.坎德林、［意］毛里济奥·戈地:《国际商事仲裁中的话语与实务:问题、挑战与展望》，林枚、潘苏悦译，北京大学出版社2016年版，第16—17页。

时计费能够大幅降低大金额争议案件的仲裁费用,有效降低预交仲裁费用的资金压力,[15]但当事人可能会面临其他方面的资金压力。[16]

(二)激励仲裁员还是拖延时间?

按小时计费的方式给仲裁员提供了愿意花时间办案的动机,但也可能使仲裁员倾向于以较花费时间的方式办理案件。[17]仲裁员可能为了避免报酬减少而不去促进当事人和解,以避免案件过早结束。有学者引用自身作为律师执业者的亲身经历,证明即使在案件审理的过程中律师发现了和解的机会,按小时计费的律师也不会有动力提议当事人和解。[18]笔者认为,这种认识应当也适用于按小时计费的仲裁员,因为当事人和解意味着仲裁程序即将终止,仲裁员也就不能继续计时收费。

(三)多劳多得还是夸大收费?

在按小时计费制度下,若案情简单,仲裁员花费较少时间就能作出裁决,那么仲裁员报酬也较少。换言之,当事人不会因为一个案情简单但标的额巨大的案件而支付过多的报酬。同时,按小时计费遵循多劳多得的原则,有助于减少或消除首席仲裁员与边裁各自工作量与报酬的不平衡,因为首席仲裁员往往付出更长的工作时间,按小时计费所收取的报酬也较多。[19]但是,也有学者以自身经历提

---

[15] 黄瑞:《仲裁案件采用小时费率计收仲裁员报酬的实务问题分析——兼评〈北京仲裁委员会/北京国际仲裁中心关于采用小时费率计收仲裁员报酬的操作指引〉》,载《北京仲裁》2021年第2期。

[16] 例如,一方当事人先指定了业界声望高且费率昂贵的仲裁员,迫使另一方当事人也选任一位能够匹配的仲裁员,以保持仲裁庭成员间的"平衡"。这就促使当事人在选任仲裁员时,倾向于选择小时费率较高的仲裁员,而这种价格偏高是无效率的。参见Bruno Guandalini, *Economic Analysis of the Arbitrator's Function*(Kluwer Law International 2020), p.132. 再如,由于计时收费的仲裁费收费标准与索赔标的数额没有直接关系,往往会出现当事人在此种方式下提出过高索赔金额,甚至漫天要价的现象。参见黄亚英:《论商事仲裁的十大特点和优势》,载《暨南学报(哲学社会科学版)》2013年第4期。还有一种情况是,在仲裁庭由三人组成时,若原告与其指定的仲裁员协商确定了高昂的小时费率且被告败诉,被告就不得不按该较高标准支付报酬。参见朱铮:《国际商事仲裁中的仲裁费用问题研究及对我国的启示》,载《重庆电子工程职业学院学报》2013年第3期。

[17] Jennifer Kirby, "With Arbitrators, Less Can Be More: Why the Conventional Wisdom on the Benefits of Having Three Arbitrators May Be Overrated", 26 *Journal of International Arbitration*, 352(2009).

[18] [英]维杰·K.巴蒂亚、[澳]克里斯托弗·N.坎德林、[意]毛里济奥·戈地:《国际商事仲裁中的话语与实务:问题、挑战与展望》,林枚、潘苏悦译,北京大学出版社2016年版,第16页。

[19] Bruno Guandalini, *Economic Analysis of the Arbitrator's Function*(Kluwer Law International 2020), p.132.

出了相反的观点，认为按小时计费并不能完全阻止夸大收费的现象。[20]

（四）仲裁费用是否可预测？

按小时计费使得当事人难以预测最终的仲裁费用。一方面，面对申请仲裁院回避或管辖权争议等情况，原本拟定的时间限度可能会进一步延长，案件审理缺乏效率并产生额外费用因此无法避免。[21] 另一方面，此种不确定性难以监管：尽管有些机构规定了仲裁员小时费率的上限及/或规定仲裁员只能就合理付出的工作请求报酬，但仍然无法完全解决不可预见的问题。[22] 尽管当事人可以预知每一位仲裁员单位时间内的收费标准，从这个意义上来说按小时计费具有预见性，但单位时间费用意义有限，因为仲裁时间难以确定。[23] 因此，作为计费基数的时间都无法确定，费用总数就更无法确定。

（五）是否客观透明？

按小时计费相对客观透明，能让当事人对费用构成与用途有清晰的了解，[24] 这有利于监督仲裁员的工作。然而，按小时计费却不一定能真实反映仲裁员的实际工作量，因为仲裁员必须足够精确地记录工作时长才能做到这一点。同时，由于当事人难以核实仲裁员的时间记录，因此当事人需要给予仲裁员足够的信任。[25]

（六）是否灵活？

关于按小时计费是否灵活，学者看法不一。有的学者认为按小时计费比较灵活，费用存在变动的空间，因为当事人可以与仲裁员就单位时间内的报酬进行协商。[26] 同时，当事人在理论上有权随时终止自己不需要的服务。[27] 但

---

[20] 杨良宜、莫世杰、杨大明：《仲裁法：从1996年英国仲裁法到国际商务仲裁》，法律出版社2006年版，第247页。

[21] 张萍：《国际商事仲裁费用能控制吗？》，载《甘肃社会科学》2017年第3期。

[22] 陈希佳：《按时计费的仲裁员报酬：比较 LCIA、HKIAC、ICDR 的相关规定》，载《北京仲裁》2021年第2期。

[23] 朱铮：《国际商事仲裁中的仲裁费用问题研究及对我国的启示》，载《重庆电子工程职业学院学报》2013年第3期。

[24] 张萍：《国际商事仲裁费用能控制吗？》，载《甘肃社会科学》2017年第3期。

[25] Nigel Blackaby, Constantine Partasides, Alan Redfern, Martin Hunter, *Redfern and Hunter on International Arbitration* – Student Version（6th edition, Oxford University Press 2015）, p.297.

[26] 朱铮：《国际商事仲裁中的仲裁费用问题研究及对我国的启示》，载《重庆电子工程职业学院学报》2013年第3期。

[27] 张萍：《国际商事仲裁费用能控制吗？》，载《甘肃社会科学》2017年第3期。

是，由于当事人和仲裁员实际地位的不对等和其他对当事人不利的现实原因，随时终止服务的权利在实践中是受到削弱的。例如，当仲裁员作出裁决之后，即使对仲裁员的收费存有质疑，当事人也往往因为不敢得罪仲裁员或其他原因而不提出这样的质疑。[28]

（七）是否符合我国实际？

有学者关注到我国仲裁员整体素质的问题，认为我国仲裁员队伍建设尚不成熟，对仲裁员报酬的监督不够细致，若采取按小时计费法，给仲裁员单独列明收费标准或当事人与仲裁员约定报酬的权利，将不利于对仲裁员的监督。[29] 同时，内地仲裁员按小时收费经验稀少，这对仲裁案件管理形成新任务。[30] 此外，还有学者注意到了粤港澳之间法律服务收费整体水平的差距，认为按小时计费不利于吸引港澳法律工作人员进入内地市场。[31]

四、按小时费率计收仲裁员报酬的监督机制

（一）三种制度安排

如上所述，按小时计费的一大缺点就是仲裁费用不可预测。若仲裁耗时过长，仲裁员报酬就会过高。实践中，为了避免此种现象，主要有三条线路的制度安排：一是事前约束，即仲裁机构在规则中明确仲裁员应合理收费；[32] 二是事中约束，即仲裁庭内部的监督，如首席仲裁员可以对边裁提交的费用

---

[28] 朱铮：《国际商事仲裁中的仲裁费用问题研究及对我国的启示》，载《重庆电子工程职业学院学报》2013年第3期。

[29] 朱铮：《国际商事仲裁中的仲裁费用问题研究及对我国的启示》，载《重庆电子工程职业学院学报》2013年第3期。

[30] 黄瑞：《仲裁案件采用小时费率计收仲裁员报酬的实务问题分析——兼评〈北京仲裁委员会/北京国际仲裁中心关于采用小时费率计收仲裁员报酬的操作指引〉》，载《北京仲裁》2021年第2期。

[31] 黄文婷、冯泽华：《粤港澳大湾区替代性纠纷解决机制研究》，载《法治社会》2018年第2期。

[32] 如香港国际仲裁中心（HKIAC）2018年《机构仲裁规则》附录2第9.1条规定，仲裁员应就其为仲裁合理付出的所有工作获得按小时费率计算的报酬；第9.3条规定，商定的仲裁员的小时费率不得超出香港国际仲裁中心设定并于仲裁通知提交之日公布于其网页上的费率；第9.6.b条规定，未用于工作的旅行时间按商定的小时费率的50%计费。伦敦国际仲裁院（LCIA）2020年发布的《费用表》第2条2（i）款规定，仲裁员的最高时薪为500英镑，特殊情况下，由仲裁院确定并经当事人同意，费率可以更高。

表进行审核；[33] 三是事后约束，即当事人请求法院或指定机构[34]监督。

其中，事前约束与事后约束实际上是并行的，因为当事人一般在知晓最终费用时（一般是裁决作出时）才会就费用是否合理与仲裁员进行争论，而仲裁庭内部监督的有效性实际上存疑：一方面，让仲裁员自己核算与厘定自己收费是十分危险的做法，在英国法判例中，有法官认为仲裁员无权这样做，[35]而且让仲裁庭自己核算自己的报酬是困难且容易招怨的，特别是在缺乏可以上诉的独立审议机构时[36]。仲裁员自行审核时必须诚实，有良心并且关注双方当事人利益[37]。另一方面，仲裁员之间的监督在实践中也被证明效果有限。[38]

（二）不同法域的做法

由法院对仲裁员报酬进行监督是各法域常见的做法。由于针对仲裁员报酬的决定不是仲裁裁决，因此法院对仲裁员费用进行审查没有法律上的障碍。[39]

在机构仲裁中，如果费用是根据仲裁规则中的收费标准计算的，法院不太可能调整这些费用，因为当事人将被视为已经知道并接受了这样的收费标准。即使当事人辩称有关条款是仲裁机构滥用其较强的议价地位而强加的合同条款，这样的主张在实践中也不太可能成功。[40] 仲裁机构在仲裁规则中关

---

[33] Nigel Blackaby, Constantine Partasides, Alan Redfern, Martin Hunter, *Redfern and Hunter on International Arbitration*–Student Version（6th edition, Oxford University Press 2015）, pp.297–298.

[34] 如《联合国国际贸易法委员会仲裁规则》第41（3）条规定，任何一方当事人均可将仲裁庭如何确定收费和开支的提议提请指定机构审查。如果指定机构认为仲裁庭的收费和开支不合理，指定机构可以要求调整仲裁员收费。第41（4）条（a）项和（b）项规定，向各方当事人通知仲裁员收费和开支时，仲裁庭还应解释相应金额的计算方式，当事人也享有提请指定机构审查的权利。未指定机构的，由常设仲裁院秘书长审查。

[35] Fernley v. Branson（1851）, 20 LJQB. 178.

[36] Rolimpex v. Dassa & Sons（1971）, 1 Lloyd's Rep. 380.

[37] Appleton v. Norwich Union Fire Insurance Society, Ltd.（1922）, 13 Lloyd's Rep. 345.

[38] 杨良宜：《国际商务仲裁》，中国政法大学出版社1997年版，第430页。

[39] Gary B. Born, *International Commercial Arbitration*（3rd edition, Kluwer Law International 2021）, p. 2173.

[40] Philippe Fouchard, Emmanuel Gaillard, Berthold Goldman, *On International Commercial Arbitration*（Kluwer Law International 1999）, pp. 625–626.

于仲裁员报酬的规定一般不受法院审查，但也有例外，如瑞典。[41]

在临时仲裁中，当事人一般与仲裁员直接协商报酬，这使得当事人可能面临来自仲裁员不合理的费用要求。在法国，法院可以降低仲裁员单方确定的过高的报酬标准。[42] 英国1996年《仲裁法》[43] 第28条规定：任何一方当事人可以向法院申请审核仲裁员收费，法院在核算与厘定的基础上，可以命令仲裁员重新考虑和调整费用。如果当事人已经向仲裁员支付报酬，那么法院可以下令仲裁员退还多收的部分。葡萄牙《自愿仲裁法》[44] 第17(3)条规定，任何一方当事人都可以请求法院减少仲裁员确定的费用或开支以及各自承担的费用，法院在听取了仲裁庭成员的意见后，可以确定其认为适当的数额。北欧国家如丹麦、芬兰、挪威、瑞典也采取了类似的做法[45]。

（三）判断仲裁员报酬合理的标准

何为"适当"或"合理"的数额呢？一方面，需要判断什么是合理的小时费率。我们可以根据争端的复杂性或问题的新颖性、争议发生地、不同行业、争议金额、是否是全职仲裁员、案件时间的长短等因素[46] 来判断费率的合理性。另一方面，需要判断什么是合理的小时数，即合理的工作时长。首先，仲裁员必须要有详细的工作与花费时间记录，供法院参考。否则，就很有可能被怀疑收费不合理。[47] 其次，在审核工作时间表的时候，如何判断每一项花费的时间是否合理呢？比较容易判断的是不涉及法律专业技能的工作时间，

---

[41] Gary B. Born, *International Commercial Arbitration* (3rd edition, Kluwer Law International 2021), pp. 2167–2168, note 375.

[42] Philippe Fouchard, Emmanuel Gaillard, Berthold Goldman, *On International Commercial Arbitration* (Kluwer Law International 1999), p. 625.

[43] Arbitration Act (1996).

[44] Lei da Arbitragem Voluntária (2011).

[45] Danish Arbitration Act, sec. 34 (2005); Finnish Arbitration Act, sec. 47 (1992); Norwegian Arbitration Act, sec. 39, (2004); Swedish Arbitration Act, sec. 37 & 41, (1999).

[46] Michael J. Mustill, Stewart C. Boyd, *Commercial Arbitration*, 2nd edition, LexisNexis Butterworths 1989, p.237; SN Kurkjian (Commodity Brokers) Ltd v Marketing Exchange for Africa Ltd (No 2), (1986) 2 Lloyd's Rep. 618.

[47] 杨良宜、莫世杰、杨大明：《仲裁法：从1996年英国仲裁法到国际商务仲裁》，法律出版社2006年版，第246页。

也就是开销（expense）[48]。例如，短途旅行也要坚持订头等舱机票，甚至伴侣也要在一起飞行，理由是需要伴侣照顾；书面审理的情况下花费飞机票；由仲裁员而不是当事人来租用开庭审理场地等情况，都不属于合理的范围，有的仲裁机构的仲裁规则还会对开销的合理使用进行详细规定。[49]不太容易判断的是审理案件所应投入的时间，此时，应要求仲裁员承担解释工作量与所花费时间及其合理性的举证责任。[50]

（四）我国关于按小时费率计收仲裁员报酬的研究与实践

基于我国仲裁机构"收支两条线"的特殊情况，我国学者对于仲裁员报酬的早期研究集中在仲裁员报酬相对于仲裁机构收费的独立性，而非具体的计费模式。国际上，仲裁机构一般尽量减少仲裁员在确定仲裁费用方面的作用，[51]但与此相反的是，我国仲裁制度的改革方向是突出仲裁员的核心位置。笔者认为，解决"收支两条线"问题是仲裁员能够按小时计费收取报酬的前提条件。

基于上述特殊情况，我国仲裁学界关于如何审核按小时计费的研究成果有限，[52]关于商事仲裁监督的研究也主要集中在裁决的撤销、仲裁协议效力认定、

---

[48] 开销包括旅行费用、酒店住宿、餐饮、行政事务工作、文档费用等。参见 Mauro Rubino-Sammartano, *International Arbitration-Law and Practice*, 2nd edition, Kluwer Law International 2001, p.812。

[49] 杨良宜、莫世杰、杨大明：《仲裁法：从1996年英国仲裁法到国际商务仲裁》，法律出版社2006年版，第258—259页。

[50] 杨良宜、莫世杰、杨大明：《仲裁法：从1996年英国仲裁法到国际商务仲裁》，法律出版社2006年版，第246页。

[51] Gary B. Born, International Commercial Arbitration（3rd edition, Kluwer Law International 2021）, pp.2170-2171.

[52] 在现有的研究成果中，我国学者提出的观点与域外学者的观点和各国立法实践差别不大，同样认为仲裁机构对仲裁员报酬的监管力度不够，因此需要赋权法院审核仲裁员报酬。同时，也必须防止法院对仲裁机构的任意干涉，因此需要给予仲裁员与当事人先行协商调整仲裁费用的权利，这也是英国1996年《仲裁法》的做法。参见朱铮：《国际商事仲裁中的仲裁费用问题研究及对我国的启示》，载《重庆电子工程职业学院学报》2013年第3期。对于临时仲裁，有学者概括地指出，临时仲裁庭组成后，应当由仲裁机构对仲裁员进行适当的监督。该学者以上海自贸区为例，认为在上海自贸区允许临时仲裁的情况下，应当由上海自贸区仲裁院对临时仲裁庭组庭后的事项进行监督。参见赖震平：《我国商事仲裁制度的阙如——以临时仲裁在上海自贸区的试构建为视角》，载《河北法学》2015年2月第2期，第164页。笔者认为，仲裁员报酬当然属于组庭后的事项，因此根据该学者的观点，应由仲裁机构监督。还有学者概括地指出临时仲裁应当由法院监督。参见宋连斌：《论中国仲裁监督机制及其完善》，载《法制与社会发展》2003年第2期。

执行仲裁裁决等司法监督模式，[53]或概括地指出应当从仲裁机构、立法、行业协会等方面加强对仲裁员的监督，而很少专门涉及仲裁员收费的监督。

我国《仲裁法》对于仲裁员按时计收报酬尚无规定，也没有对于仲裁员收费的监督机制。目前，我国对仲裁员责任的立法规定只有《仲裁法》第38条指向其他条款规定的关于索贿受贿、徇私舞弊、枉法裁决、应当回避而不回避的内容和《仲裁法》其他笼统的规定，以及《刑法》第399条之一（枉法仲裁罪）中的刑事责任。[54]

在我国仲裁机构的仲裁规则中，按小时费率计收仲裁员报酬也比较罕见。虽然贸仲2015年起率先规定了国内仲裁案件可以按照小时费率标准计收仲裁员报酬，但这仅适用于仲裁员的"特殊报酬"，同时规定国内仲裁案件的收费标准也是以争议金额总额为基础按比例进行分别计算。[55]因此，贸仲的做法还不能算作完全放开实施小时费率制。北仲2019年版《北京仲裁委员会仲裁规则》（以下简称《北仲仲裁规则》）中附录1第6条规定，在当事人约定的情况下，仲裁员报酬可以按照小时费率计算。关于审核机制，《北仲仲裁规则》规定当事人可以通过北仲仲裁员工作小时复核委员会提出收费异议，即由仲裁机构来监督仲裁员收费。该机制的设立是考虑到我国法院的司法资源现状，当事人如果想就仲裁员收费寻求司法救济不太现实。[56]此外，《北仲仲裁规则》规定了小时费率的最高标准，避免仲裁员报酬和机构管理费无限扩张，帮助当事人控制成本。[57]

---

[53] 关于商事仲裁的司法监督研究可参见宋朝武：《我国仲裁裁决司法监督制度内在冲突及解决对策》，载《商事仲裁理论与实务》，杨润时主编，人民法院出版社2006年版，第107—114页；宋连斌：《论中国仲裁监督机制及其完善》，载《法制与社会发展》2003年第2期。

[54] 吴慧琼：《论仲裁员的素质》，载《仲裁研究》2009年第3期；范铭超：《仲裁员责任法律制度研究》，华东政法大学2012年博士论文，第68页。

[55] 黄瑞：《仲裁案件采用小时费率计收仲裁员报酬的实务问题分析——兼评〈北京仲裁委员会/北京国际仲裁中心关于采用小时费率计收仲裁员报酬的操作指引〉》，载《北京仲裁》2021年第2期。

[56] 黄瑞：《仲裁案件采用小时费率计收仲裁员报酬的实务问题分析——兼评〈北京仲裁委员会/北京国际仲裁中心关于采用小时费率计收仲裁员报酬的操作指引〉》，载《北京仲裁》2021年第2期。

[57] 姜秋菊：《国内仲裁收费制度的变革与发展趋势——以北京仲裁委员会/北京国际仲裁中心的实践为视角》，载《北京仲裁》2019年第3期。

五、未解决的问题

（一）按小时费率计收仲裁员报酬的缺点是否仍然成为其推广的障碍？

我国仲裁机构的仲裁规则中鲜有按小时计费的身影。这种现象可能是仲裁机构缺乏收费自主权导致，但也与按小时计费的缺点不无关系。是哪一些缺点成为障碍，导致这一制度在我国难以得到实施？

关于按小时计费，前述学者总结的主要缺点如下：（1）我国仲裁员队伍建设尚不成熟，对仲裁员报酬的监督不够细致；（2）按小时计费仲裁成本高且无法预测，降低地区对国际商事仲裁的吸引力；（3）当事人不敢质疑仲裁员报酬；（4）不利于促进当事人和解。针对以上观点，笔者看法如下：

针对第一个问题，首先，我国《仲裁法》就仲裁员任职资格采取了严格资格立法模式，与世界其他法域相比要求更高，以确保高素质人士担任仲裁员；[58]其次，相关学者提出这一看法至今已将近十年。时至今日，我国仲裁员整体素质较以往是进步的，至少在我国主要的仲裁机构当中，仲裁员素质应该不会成为实施按小时计费的障碍。相反，实施按小时计费可以增加收费的透明度，激励仲裁员认真办案，促进仲裁员职业操守和专业水平提升，[59]从而促进仲裁行业良性竞争的生态。再者，现有政策[60]的支持无疑能够进一步促进我国仲裁员的整体素质。同时，早在2006年，我国律师行业服务收费按小时计费就已经合法，[61]按小时计费早已成为我国律师行业常见的（尽管不是主流）收费做法之一，不应认为仲裁员队伍的整体素质不如律师行业。此外，没有一种仲裁员报酬制

---

[58] 宋连斌：《中国仲裁员制度改革初探》，载《中国国际私法与比较法年刊》2001年第1期；马占军：《我国商事仲裁员任职资格制度的修改与完善》，载《河北法学》2015年第7期。

[59] 黄瑞：《仲裁案件采用小时费率计收仲裁员报酬的实务问题分析——兼评〈北京仲裁委员会/北京国际仲裁中心关于采用小时费率计收仲裁员报酬的操作指引〉》，载《北京仲裁》2021年第2期。

[60] 如2022年4月，司法部、教育部、科技部、国务院国资委等部门印发通知，要求进一步做好涉外仲裁人才培养项目实施工作，到2025年，建立起与国际通行仲裁制度相适应的涉外仲裁人才培养体系。参见司法部、教育部、科学技术部、国务院国有资产监督管理委员会、中华全国工商业联合会、中国国际贸易促进委员会：《关于做好涉外仲裁人才培养项目实施工作的通知》，载司法部网站，http://www.moj.gov.cn/pub/sfbgw/gwxw/xwyw/202204/t20220411_452536.html，最后访问时间：2022年7月17日。

[61] 参见国家发展改革委、司法部：《律师服务收费管理办法》[发改价格（2006）611号]，载中国政府网，http://www.gov.cn/zwgk/2006-04/19/content_257940.htm，最后访问时间：2022年7月17日。

度是完美的,任何一种仲裁员报酬制度在实践中都会出现问题,[62]不能因为少数仲裁员的素质问题而"因噎废食"地否定整个按时计费制度。

针对第二和第三个问题,笔者认为问题的核心在于"疏"而不在于"堵",换言之,可以建立对仲裁员报酬的监督机制来应对成本上限高且不可预测的问题。只要建立适当的监督机制,就能够最大限度地避免不合理的收费。下文将对这一点详述。

针对第四个问题,笔者认为这种看法低估了当事人一方对法律问题的判断,毕竟当事人往往会委托律师代理参加仲裁。律师可以凭借从业经验和专业知识,判断和解的时机。况且,按小时计费仍然不是我国律师行业的主流做法,因此律师有动力促成和解,和解的期望不需要完全寄托在仲裁员身上。

综上,笔者认为实施按小时费率计收仲裁员报酬制度不存在仲裁员素质方面的障碍,亦不会影响当事人和解,主要问题在于如何对仲裁员报酬实施监督。

(二)建立仲裁机构与法院分情况、依顺序参与的仲裁员报酬监督机制

按小时计费下的仲裁员报酬等于小时费率与工作小时数的乘积,因此针对仲裁员报酬的监督应当包括对小时费率和工作时长两方面的监督,同时还应注意区分机构仲裁和临时仲裁两种情况。笔者将在下文中分别就这两方面的监督机制进行探讨。

1. 小时费率

实际上,小时费率不是决定仲裁员报酬高低最重要的因素。如上文所述,按小时计费导致的不合理仲裁员报酬主要是由于不合理的工作时间引起的,而不是不合理的费率,因为在机构仲裁中,费率一般会在仲裁机构的仲裁规则中事先规定,包括费率上限。虽然在三人仲裁庭中,当事人分别与其指定的仲裁员协商费率,而这些费率可能相差很大,一方当事人可能需要支付对

---

[62] 例如,从价法(按争议金额的一定比例计费)可能会导致仲裁员报酬与仲裁员工作量失衡。参见陈希佳:《按时计费的仲裁员报酬:比较 LCIA、HKIAC、ICDR 的相关规定》,载《北京仲裁》2021 年第 2 期。因此,国际仲裁的趋势是不再将争议标的额作为仲裁员报酬计算的唯一考量因素,而是将按时计费法与从价法结合使用。由于开庭时间和案件办理时间难以预测,固定收费法会增加当事人和仲裁员协商的难度,在协商结束之前案件也无法及时开庭。参见 Nigel Blackaby, Constantine Partasides, Alan Redfern, Martin Hunter, *Redfern and Hunter on International Arbitration-Student Version*, 6th edition, Oxford University Press, 2015, pp.297–298. 另外,在收取固定费用后,仲裁员可能也无法尽心尽力地工作,动力不足。参见杨良宜:《关于国际商事仲裁的讲座(一)》,载《北京仲裁》2007 年第 2 期。

方当事人指定仲裁员的高费率报酬,但这属于当事人应当承担的风险,毕竟当事人事先知道机构确定的最高费率标准。因此在机构仲裁中,小时费率很难成为监督的对象。

但在临时仲裁中,仲裁员可能会单方面确定[63]过高的收费标准,损害当事人利益,此种情况应当得到监督。由于我国《仲裁法》没有明确临时仲裁在我国的效力,因此临时仲裁在我国缺乏法律依据,[64]但根据《仲裁法(修订征求意见稿)》,未来《仲裁法》拟在"涉外商事纠纷"范围内增加临时仲裁制度。[65]对此,笔者认为应当赋予当事人就仲裁员单方面确定不合理费率诉至法院的权利,因为临时仲裁作为一种非司法性的纠纷解决机制并不具有法院诉讼天然的国家强制力作为支撑,需要国家司法的积极支持。[66]与机构仲裁不同,临时仲裁没有内部监督机制,[67]也没有机构参与仲裁程序的管理,因此法院的支持与监督往往成为临时仲裁程序得以顺利推进的最后保障。[68]关于仲裁机构

---

[63] 仲裁员报酬可以由当事人和仲裁员达成协议来确定,但是这种协议并不多见。如果没有协议,仲裁员可以在最终裁决中确定这笔费用。当事人与还可以通过援引《UNCITRAL 仲裁规则》这类程序规则间接约定仲裁费用。参见康明:《临时仲裁及其在我国的现状和发展前景》,载《国际商法论丛》2001年第1期,第702页;[英]艾伦·雷德芬、马丁·亨特等:《国际商事仲裁法律与实践》(第四版),林一飞、宋连斌译,北京大学出版社2005年版,第243页。

[64] 最高人民法院于2016年12月30日颁布的《关于为自贸试验区建设提供司法保障的意见》(以下简称《意见》)显示,"在自贸试验区内注册的企业相互之间约定在内地特定地点、按照特定仲裁规则、由特定人员对有关争议进行仲裁的,可以认定该仲裁协议有效"。《意见》被认为是为我国自贸试验区引入临时仲裁打开了制度缺口,并为自贸试验区临时仲裁合法化提供了制度依据。但是,《意见》并非由立法机关颁布,不仅与现行《仲裁法》产生冲突,也不符合《立法法》第11条第10项关于诉讼和仲裁制度的规定。参见李建忠:《临时仲裁的中国尝试:制度困境与现实路径——以中国自贸试验区为视角》,载《法治研究》2020年第2期,第38—42页。此外,各地仲裁机构和民间组织都为我国引入临时仲裁制度进行了有限实践,如2017年4月15日起实施的《横琴自由贸易试验区临时仲裁规则》、2017年9月19日生效的《中国互联网仲裁联盟临时仲裁与机构仲裁对接规则》、2020年10月1日起实施的《深圳国际仲裁院条例》第24条。

[65] 参见2021年7月30日司法部发布的《中华人民共和国仲裁法(修订)(征求意见稿)》第七章"涉外仲裁的特别规定"。

[66] 苟应鹏:《我国临时仲裁裁决撤销制度的建构》,载《北京仲裁》2020年第3期。

[67] 宋连斌:《论中国仲裁监督机制及其完善》,载《法制与社会发展》2003年第2期。

[68] 李建忠:《临时仲裁的中国尝试:制度困境与现实路径——以中国自贸试验区为视角》,载《法治研究》2020年第2期。

对临时仲裁的监督模式,笔者认为这不符合临时仲裁的本质,即不由任何已设立的仲裁机构进行正规管理。[69] 同时,由法院直接监督也符合国际实践[70]。

2. 工作时长

决定仲裁员报酬最重要的因素是工作量,[71] 而工作量决定了仲裁员办案所需要花费的时长。当事人若觉得仲裁员工作时长不合理,应当如何寻求救济?又应当如何判断工作时长是否合理?参考上文所述的各国实践和《联合国国际贸易法委员会仲裁规则》,当事人可以将有关仲裁员报酬的争议提交至法院或指定机构。笔者认为,为最大限度地维护仲裁自治,减少法院不必要的干预,也为了尽快解决当事人之间的争议,同时综合考虑我国的实际情况与国际实践,仲裁机构可规定当事人必须先将仲裁员报酬争议提交仲裁机构进行审核,当事人对仲裁机构审核决定不服的,可再将争议提交至法院。具体原因如下:

之所以规定必须先由仲裁机构审核,是因为:第一,当事人既然选择了仲裁作为争议解决的机构,就表明当事人对仲裁机构予以信任。这种信任不仅体现在实体争议的解决上,也应体现在仲裁员报酬问题上。第二,仲裁自治性要求排除法院的过度干预,法院对于仲裁只能是必要协助和正确监督。[72] 第三,将当事人的复核请求先引导至仲裁机构解决,有利于节省司法资源。第四,在审理案件的过程中,仲裁机构本身就对案件有充分的了解,而法院则需要从头开始了解案件详情、仲裁机构的收费标准、仲裁员的各项工作等,花费时间更多,同时与法院相比,仲裁机构与仲裁员的沟通成本更低,效率更高,[73] 因此能够帮助当事人节省时间,促进争端尽快解决。第五,仲裁机构是提供仲裁服务的专业机构,能够凭借经验快速且准确地判断不同案件中仲裁员就工作内容应当花费的工作时长合理范围。上述原因中,节省司法资源或许值得商榷。由于缺乏实证研究,关于仲裁员报酬的争议对司法资源的挤

---

[69] 王岩、宋连斌:《试论临时仲裁及其在我国的现状》,载《北京仲裁》2005年第1期。

[70] Philippe Fouchard, Emmanuel Gaillard, Berthold Goldman, *On International Commercial Arbitration*(Kluwer Law International 1999), pp.625-626.

[71] M. Scheneider, "Lean Arbitration: Cost Control and Efficiency Through Progressive Identification of Issues and Separate Pricing of Arbitration Services", 10 *Arbitration International* 2, 124(1994).

[72] 毋爱斌:《〈仲裁法〉引入临时仲裁制度体系论》,载《社会科学家》2022年第4期。

[73] 在办理案件过程中,仲裁机构一般都会指定一位办案秘书与仲裁员对接,办案秘书与仲裁员会就办案程序频繁沟通,彼此对案件内容都比较熟悉,因此沟通效率更高。

兑程度有待考虑。笔者认为，允许按小时计费的仲裁机构本就寥寥无几，放开按小时计费后当事人也未必选择，因此产生的争议数量恐怕也不会很多。

除了可以向仲裁机构申请审核仲裁员报酬外，当事人请求法院审核的权利也应当得到保留：首先，适当的司法监督是商事仲裁发展的充分条件[74]，有助于仲裁可持续发展。[75]这一做法考虑到了当事人对法院权威的信赖，让当事人选择仲裁时无"后顾之忧"。[76]其次，国家司法权力的监督是对仲裁最有实质性意义的监督方式，[77]司法监督能够避免仲裁机构偏袒仲裁员的极端情况。再次，司法监督仲裁员报酬的做法也符合国际实践，有成熟的操作路径可供参考。最后，法院对仲裁的全程司法监督机制[78]早已确立，当事人委托的律师、仲裁员、仲裁机构对此都比较熟悉，操作上不存在陌生的障碍。

笔者认为，当事人经过仲裁机构对仲裁员报酬的审核后，基本疑虑已经消除，同时为了使争议得到尽快解决，不会轻易再将争议提交到法院。这一做法兼顾了两种监督机制的优点，也避免了对司法资源的直接挤兑。但实践中是否容易架空仲裁机构的监督，有待落地实施后进行实证研究。

最后，仲裁机构或法院收到当事人的审核请求后，如何判断工作时长是否合理？除了上文所述的争议发生地、仲裁员所属行业、是否是全职仲裁员、争议金额、争端的复杂性或问题的新颖性等因素，笔者认为还要综合考察个案中不同的情况影响对合理性的判断，因此需要具体问题具体分析。[79]另一方面，应当要求仲裁员出具详细的工作时间记录表，仲裁机构可以提供表格模板或建立电子化系统供仲裁员记录工作时间。若没有详细记录的，可以作出对仲裁员不利的推定。此外，应当要求仲裁员在将费用告知当事人之前，仲裁员之间必须进行厘定与核算，没有厘定与核算的，作出对仲裁员不利的推

---

[74] 宋连斌：《仲裁司法监督制度的新进展及其意义》，载《人民法治》2018年第5期。

[75] 宋连斌：《论中国仲裁监督机制及其完善》，载《法制与社会发展》2003年第2期。

[76] 苟应鹏：《我国临时仲裁裁决撤销制度的建构》，载《北京仲裁》2020年第3期。

[77] 苟应鹏：《我国临时仲裁裁决撤销制度的建构》，载《北京仲裁》2020年第3期。

[78] 刘惠荣：《论法院对商事仲裁的司法监督》，载《郑州大学学报（哲学社会科学版）》2002年第4期。

[79] 小时费率和工作时长是否合理取决于很多因素，因此想要概括列举（generalization）这些因素总是不会令人满意，甚至是危险的。参见Government of Ceylon v. Chandris（1963），1 Lloyd's Rep.214。

定。[80] 作为辅助办法，还可以要求仲裁员签署责任声明。若经复核显示费用不合理，仲裁员需要承担一定的惩罚性后果，如扣减报酬，累计一定次数移出仲裁员名册等。

针对临时仲裁中关于仲裁员工作时长的争议，笔者认为应直接由法院进行监督，上文已列出理由，此处不再赘述。

六、总结

除仲裁机构监督和司法监督外，实际上还有行业监督的形式，即由我国《仲裁法》第 15 条规定的仲裁自律性组织中国仲裁协会参与监督。[81] 然而，该组织的成立曾长期处于停滞状态，使得仲裁的行业监督停留在纸面。在该协会空缺的时期，其职能曾由原国务院法制办公室行使。[82] 尽管在《仲裁法》颁布二十多年后，中国仲裁协会终于在 2022 年底成立，[83] 但其至今仍未制定协会的运行规则，具体职能尚不清晰。另外，根据《仲裁法》第 15 条，中国仲裁协会对仲裁员的违纪行为进行追究，然而在该协会空缺期间，违纪行为必须先由仲裁机构或党政机关查处，仲裁协会方可追究，[84] 这就意味着行业监督实际上取决于仲裁机构监督，行业监督必须转委托仲裁机构监督，[85] 包括针对仲

---

[80] 杨良宜、莫世杰、杨大明：《仲裁法：从 1996 年英国仲裁法到国际商务仲裁》，法律出版社 2006 年版，第 247 页。

[81] 宋连斌：《论中国仲裁监督机制及其完善》，载《法制与社会发展》2003 年第 2 期。

[82] 王小莉：《仲裁员的监督和保护问题探讨》，载《仲裁研究》2013 年第 2 期。

[83] 中国仲裁协会的基本信息可在民政部中国社会组织政务服务平台查询，https://xxgs.chinanpo.mca.gov.cn/gsxt/newList，最后访问时间：2024 年 2 月 5 日。

[84] 根据《国务院法制办公室关于切实做好仲裁员、仲裁工作人员违法违纪处理情况和仲裁裁决被人民法院裁定撤销或不予执行情况报告工作的通知》[国法（2016）81 号]，仲裁员、仲裁工作人员在仲裁工作中的违纪处理情况包括：违反仲裁工作纪律被仲裁委员会查处的情况和违反党纪政纪被纪检监察机关立案查处的情况。因此，除党政机关查处的情形外，违纪行为实际上必须先由仲裁机构认定。2018 年机构改革国务院法制办公室与司法部合并后，司法部也重申了《仲裁法》中关于中国仲裁协会对仲裁员违纪行为的监督职能，但由于中国仲裁协会的具体运行规则尚未出台，仍不能确定协会行使该职能的具体路径。参见《司法部对十三届全国人大二次会议第 7140 号建议的答复》，http://www.moj.gov.cn/pub/sfbgw/zwxxgk/fdzdgknr/fdzdgknrjyta/201911/t20191125_208145.html，最后访问时间：2024 年 2 月 5 日。

[85] 汪祖兴：《仲裁监督之逻辑生成与逻辑体系——仲裁与诉讼关系之优化为基点的渐进展开》，载《当代法学》2015 年第 6 期。

裁员报酬的监督，因此当事人没有必要通过中国仲裁协会去重复确认仲裁机构审核报酬的决定。当然，中国仲裁协会可以对不诚信计收报酬的仲裁员根据协会章程予以行业处罚，但设计监督制度时无须再引导当事人向行业协会申请审核。

伴随仲裁法改革的进程，各个机构建立符合仲裁发展方向、符合当事人需求的收费体制是必然选择。[86] 按小时费率计收仲裁员报酬固然有其局限性，但这不应当成为其落地实施的障碍。当然，在落地实施的过程中，我们应当建立好仲裁员报酬监督制度，允许当事人在机构仲裁中依顺序向仲裁机构和法院申请复核，在临时仲裁中向法院申请复核。复核应当以仲裁员工作时间表为基础，根据个案情况综合判断工作时长的合理性。允许按小时计费并不是强制要求当事人使用按小时计费制度，而是为当事人提供多一种选择，相信当事人有自主和理性的判断能力，让当事人针对自己的情况自行分析是否适用按小时计费，这也符合仲裁的本质：尊重当事人意思自治，给予当事人解决其争议的自主权和控制权。[87]

---

[86] 姜秋菊：《国内仲裁收费制度的变革与发展趋势——以北京仲裁委员会/北京国际仲裁中心的实践为视角》，载《北京仲裁》2019年第3期。

[87] Margaret L. Moses, *The Principles and Practice of International Commercial Arbitration*, Cambridge University Press, 2008, p.1.

《仲裁法》修改背景下的仲裁裁决撤销程序：立法检视、性质定位与规则建构

张喜彪[*]

- **摘　要**

　　检视我国近30年来的仲裁裁决撤销程序相关立法，只能以零星、散乱且不成体系概括之。本轮仲裁法修改虽关涉仲裁裁决撤销程序部分规则的调整，但也仅限于对部分申请事由、期限以及救济程序的修正，之于构建一个系统化、体系化、程序化的仲裁裁决撤销程序仍相去甚远。因此，应当在明确仲裁裁决撤销程序具有争讼性、对审性、效率性与非公开性的前提下，将其准确定位为一个具有诉讼特性的非典型非讼程序——特别程序。继而以特别程序为模板进一步详细设定仲裁裁决撤销程序的当事人适格、法庭调查、法庭辩论以及救济程序等一系列程序规则，并最终将散落于不同层级、不同种类法律规范当中的仲裁裁决撤销程序规则统一于民事诉讼法特别程序体系之下。

- **关键词**

　　仲裁裁决撤销程序　非讼程序　诉讼程序　特别程序　辩论原则

　　Abstract：It can only use fragmentary and immethodical to

---

[*] 张喜彪，中央财经大学法学院2021级民事诉讼法学硕士研究生。

summarize when viewing China's relevant legislation on the procedure of revocation in arbitration for the past thirty years. The amendment of arbitration law is far from enough when compared to systematic, institutionalized and procedural procedure of revocation in arbitration, although it is related to the adjustment of partial rules of procedure of revocation in arbitration, it is only limited to the amendment of partial reasons for applying, time limit and remedy procedure. Therefore, it is as an atypical non-litigation procedure precisely with the characteristic of lawsuit, special procedure, under the prerequisite that procedure of revocation in arbitration has litigation, confrontation, efficiency and non-public. Special procedure is used as the template to further set a series of procedure rules of procedure of revocation in arbitration such as qualification of litigant, court investigation, court debate and remedy procedure in detail. Ultimately, the rules of procedure of revocation in arbitration in the fragmentary legal norm in different level and kind are unified in the system of special procedure of civil procedural law.

Key Words: procedure of revocation in arbitration, non-litigation procedure, litigation procedure, special procedure, debate principle

一、问题的提出

仲裁作为一种高效率、低成本的民商事纠纷解决手段，一直以来都在促进纠纷多元化解决、矛盾的国际化治理等领域发挥着关键作用。有资料显示，《中华人民共和国仲裁法》（以下简称《仲裁法》）施行 26 年来，我国共依法设立了 270 多家仲裁机构，办理了 400 多万件仲裁案件，涉案标的额超过 5 万亿元，当事人遍布全球 100 多个国家和地区。[1] 这种"仲裁热"现象的成因是多样化的。一方面，相较于成本较高、周期较长、效率较低以及专业性

---

[1] 数据源于司法部在其官网发布的关于《中华人民共和国仲裁法（修订）（征求意见稿）》的说明，http://www.moj.gov.cn/pub/sfbgw/lfyjzj/lflfyjzj/202107/t20210730_432967.html，最后访问时间：2022 年 7 月 16 日。

较强的诉讼程序来说，人们似乎更加青睐成本较低、效率较高、周期较短以及私密性较强的仲裁程序。[2] 另一方面，是否涉诉、涉诉多少也早已成为企业信用评价的重要标准。除此之外，伴随员额制改革进程的不断加快，各级法院案多人少矛盾不断凸显，[3] 仲裁已然成为法院释压减负的重要抓手。然而，正当仲裁越发为人们所熟知、所应用的同时，"仲裁热"现象背后的合法性、正当性、公正性等问题也逐步显露出来。有相关调查数据显示，我国仲裁当事人不服仲裁裁决并请求法院撤销或不予执行仲裁裁决的比例一直居高不下。[4] 即使法院真正裁定撤销或不予执行仲裁裁决的比例并不高，[5] 这种请求法院撤销或不予执行仲裁裁决比例激增背景下的"民意"也是不容忽视的。因此，强化法院对仲裁的司法监督作用以提高仲裁的合法性、公正性以及公信力迫在眉睫。

遵照传统法学理论，法院对仲裁的司法监督大致可分为以下三种路径：其一，确认仲裁协议效力；其二，裁定是否撤销仲裁裁决；其三，裁定是否不予执行仲裁裁决。其中，法院裁定是否撤销仲裁裁决是法院对仲裁进行司法监督的最主要方式，[6] 撤销仲裁裁决程序也就成为学界研究的重点。[7] 比如，有的

---

[2] 肖永平：《内国、涉外仲裁监督机制之我见——对〈中国涉外仲裁监督机制评析〉一文的商榷》，载《中国社会科学》1998年第2期。

[3] 孟勤国：《司法改革应直面常识挑战》，载《法眼观察》2018年7月29日。

[4] 张卫平：《仲裁裁决撤销程序的法理分析》，载《比较法研究》2018年第6期。其在文中谈到，以北京为例，北京市第二中级人民法院截至2010年共受理不服仲裁裁决案件数量653件，驳回撤销申请467件，裁定撤销仲裁66件。参见谭振亚：《仲裁案件司法审查实证分析——以重庆市第一中级人民法院司法实务为样本》，载《人民司法（应用）》2015年第19期。其在文中谈到，在重庆地区，2011年重庆一中院共受理申请撤销仲裁裁决案件14件；2012年比2011年翻了一倍，达28件；2013年激增至150件（其中包括了两批集团性案件共计96件）。

[5] 谭振亚：《仲裁案件司法审查实证分析——以重庆市第一中级人民法院司法实务为样本》，载《人民司法（应用）》2015年第19期。

[6] 张卫平：《仲裁裁决撤销程序的法理分析》，载《比较法研究》2018年第6期。张卫平教授认为，此三种救济手段中，确认仲裁协议的效力仅是一种保障当事人诉权的手段，其宣示作用大于实践意义。而裁定是否不予执行仲裁裁决主要针对的是域外仲裁裁决的承认和执行，对于国内仲裁裁决的司法监督意义不大。即使其存在适用于不予执行国内仲裁裁决的情况，也大多是对于当事人忘记申请撤销仲裁裁决情况的补充而已。

[7] 张卫平：《现行仲裁执行司法监督制度结构的反思与调整——兼论仲裁裁决不予执行制度》，载《现代法学》2020年第1期。

学者从实践的角度对仲裁裁决撤销程序进行了实证研究;[8]有的学者从法律适用技术的角度给出了仲裁案件司法审查的对策;[9]有的学者从审级的角度入手讨论了在我国设立二审终审制的仲裁裁决撤销司法监督程序的必要性;[10]也有的学者从诉讼理论的角度提出了在我国确立仲裁裁决撤销之诉的普通诉讼程序构想;[11]更有学者从制度机理和深层理念的角度开创性地论述了仲裁裁决撤销程序的基本法理。[12]

通过上述学者对仲裁裁决撤销程序的全方位、多角度的研究不难发现,目前我国的仲裁裁决撤销程序无论是在理论层面还是实际操作层面均存在着诸多问题。而这些问题的解决亟须法律的修订与完善。因此,此轮《仲裁法》的修改便成为学界关注的焦点。2021年7月30日,司法部正式在其官网上发布司法部关于《中华人民共和国仲裁法(修订)(征求意见稿)》(以下简称《征求意见稿》)公开征求意见的通知。这预示着《仲裁法》即将迎来其自1994年颁布之后的第三次修订。通过对比修订前后的《仲裁法》以及结合司法部所作出的关于《征求意见稿》的说明不难发现,此次修法的内容是比较多样的,涉改法条的比例也是较高的。根据司法部的官方说明,此次《征求意见稿》相较于《仲裁法》共新增19条,涉及总则制度、仲裁机构及制度、仲裁员及仲裁协会规定、仲裁协议规定、仲裁程序规范、仲裁裁决的撤销及其重新仲裁、仲裁裁决的执行、涉外仲裁及临时仲裁等八项主要内容的修改与完善。[13]其中,针对仲裁裁

---

[8] 宋连斌、颜杰雄:《申请撤销仲裁裁决:现状·问题·建言》,载《法学评论》2013年第6期;姜建新、陈立伟《关于仲裁裁决司法审查的调查与思考——对不予执行及申请撤销仲裁审查的实证分析》,载《法律适用》2013年第10期。

[9] 谭振亚:《仲裁案件司法审查实证分析——以重庆市第一中级人民法院司法实务为样本》,载《人民司法(应用)》2015年第19期。

[10] 胡瑾:《仲裁裁决撤销司法监督失误的程序救济》,载《武汉大学学报(哲学社会科学版)》2007年第4期。

[11] 李琳:《试论撤销仲裁裁决案件的审理程序》,载《北京仲裁》2005年第2期;杨秀清、李琳:《试论仲裁裁决的撤销——兼论我国相关立法的完善》,载《仲裁研究》(第5辑),法律出版社2005年版,第52—57页。

[12] 张卫平:《仲裁裁决撤销程序的法理分析》,载《比较法研究》2018年第6期。

[13] 数据源于司法部在其官网发布的关于《中华人民共和国仲裁法(修订)(征求意见稿)》的说明,http://www.moj.gov.cn/pub/sfbgw/lfyjzj/lflfyjzj/202107/t20210730_432967.html,最后访问时间:2022年7月16日。

决撤销及其程序的修改主要体现在国内外仲裁裁决撤销情形的统一整合、撤销裁决事由的增加、申请撤销裁决时间的缩短以及裁决撤销救济程序的设定等四个方面。其中，最大的亮点莫过于仲裁裁决撤销救济程序的设定，这一规定一旦被修订后的《仲裁法》所正式确认，将标示着我国的仲裁裁决撤销从此有了法定救济程序。不过，欣喜之余，我们也应当清楚地认识到此轮《仲裁法》的修改对于仲裁裁决撤销程序的完善只是杯水车薪。具体而言，以下两个既存已久的重要问题我们并不能在《征求意见稿》中找到答案。首先，关于仲裁裁决撤销程序的性质定位问题。仲裁裁决撤销程序虽既存已久，但其究竟是一个怎样性质的程序？其到底是诉讼程序还是非讼程序？这种所谓的司法审查程序应当如何在民事诉讼或非讼程序中进行安顿？如果说其兼具诉讼与非讼特性，那么我们应当如何认识这一程序？其是否会超出现行《民事诉讼法》的既有规定？其次，关于撤销仲裁裁决的具体审理规则问题。从现行《仲裁法》来看，仅有第59条、第60条及第61条分别对申请撤销仲裁裁决的申请期限、审判期限及重新仲裁程序作出了零星规定。即使《征求意见稿》中又新增了事后的救济程序，但这远非正式司法程序的完整规则。对于当事人适格、法院的审查方式、立案标准、判决标准以及其他具体庭审细节程序规则并未作出补充完善。

因此，本文从仲裁裁决撤销程序的立法检视入手，通过对比中外仲裁裁决撤销程序的差异性规定，反思并厘清我国当下仲裁裁决撤销程序的问题现状，从而准确定位中国法语境下的仲裁裁决撤销程序的性质，继而为定性后的仲裁裁决撤销程序构建具体的申请、受理、审判及救济规则。

二、仲裁裁决撤销程序的立法检视

（一）中国仲裁裁决撤销程序的立法检视

早在我国1994年《仲裁法》正式出台前，我国便已存在仲裁制度，只不过当时实行的是国内外双轨仲裁制度，不同种类的仲裁由不同种类的部分法分散规定。国外仲裁自始便有相应的规则且一裁终局。相比之下，国内仲裁制度的发展则十分曲折。以新中国成立为基点，我国国内仲裁制度大致经历了行政仲裁阶段（1955—1966年）、"文革"中止阶段（1966—1977年）、恢复仲裁阶段（1978—1982年）、重新确立仲裁制度阶段（1983—1995年）以及现代仲裁制度阶段（1995年至今）五个发展阶段。实质上，在1995年《仲裁法》正式施行以前，我国所确立的仲裁制度其实是一种行政仲裁制度或者具有浓厚行政色彩的仲裁制度。例如，在行政仲裁阶段，当事人之间的经济合同纠纷只能通过经济仲裁委员会仲裁而不得诉诸法院；在恢复仲裁阶段，当事人之间的经济合同纠纷虽然能诉诸法院，但前提是该纠纷已经过仲裁机关的两次裁决。直到1994年《仲裁法》的颁布，这种具有浓厚行政色彩的仲裁制度才宣告终结，我国国内仲裁制度始向现代化、国际化迈进。

受制于仲裁相关法律规范数量的寥寥，规定仲裁裁决撤销程序的法律规范也是极为有限的。细分下来，大致有《仲裁法》、《最高人民法院关于适用〈中华人民共和国仲裁法〉若干问题的解释》（以下简称《仲裁法司法解释》）、最高人民法院《关于审理仲裁司法审查案件若干问题的规定》（以下简称《审查规定》）及最高人民法院的各种批复类文件等四种法律规范。按照程序运行的机理，可以从申请、审理与救济三个环节考察上述法律规范中的仲裁裁决撤销程序规则。

首先，关于仲裁裁决撤销的申请环节。其一，申请主体。按照《最高人民法院关于审理当事人申请撤销仲裁裁决案件几个具体问题的批复》（法释〔1998〕16号）（以下简称《批复》）第2条之规定，申请撤销仲裁裁决的一方为申请人，另一方为被申请人。[14]然而，对于谁为具体当事人、谁为适格当事人以及谁有权或无权启动撤销程序，从现行法律规范中不得而知。其二，管辖、申请期限及申请事由。对于此三类申请规则，《仲裁法》第58条、第59条分别作了具体规定。其三，申请费用。依《批复》第3条之规定，申请费用由申请人缴纳，标准同非财产案件。[15]

其次，关于仲裁裁决撤销的审理环节。其一，审理程序。对于仲裁裁决撤销案件适用何种程序，现行法律规范并未明确规定。其二，审判组织。根据《仲裁法司法解释》第24条之规定，人民法院审理撤销仲裁裁决案件，应

---

[14]《最高人民法院关于审理当事人申请撤销仲裁裁决案件几个具体问题的批复》（法释〔1998〕16号）第2条："一方当事人向人民法院申请撤销仲裁裁决的，人民法院在审理时，应当列对方当事人为被申请人。"

[15]《最高人民法院关于审理当事人申请撤销仲裁裁决案件几个具体问题的批复》（法释〔1998〕16号）第3条："当事人向人民法院申请撤销仲裁裁决的案件，应当按照非财产案件收费标准计收案件受理费；该费用由申请人交纳。"

当组成合议庭并询问当事人。[16] 其三，审理期限。根据《仲裁法》第 60 条的规定，人民法院审理撤销仲裁裁决案件应当在受理后 2 个月内作出裁定。[17] 其四，审判结果。根据上述第 60 条的规定，法院审理撤销仲裁裁决案件无非有两个结果：裁定撤销或者驳回申请。不过，在受理申请后作出裁定前，人民法院认为符合重新仲裁情形的，可以通知仲裁庭在一定期限内重新仲裁并暂时中止仲裁裁决撤销程序。[18]

最后，关于撤销仲裁裁决的救济环节。受制于仲裁裁决程序的性质定位不清，加之仲裁裁决撤销程序规则散落于诸如《仲裁法》《仲裁法司法解释》等仲裁相关法律规范之间，我国目前尚无仲裁裁决撤销裁定后的救济程序。不过，《征求意见稿》第 81 条倒是开创性地规定了当事人如不服仲裁裁决撤销裁定可以向上一级人民法院申请复议的救济手段，至于是否合适、能否真正落实，还有待进一步论证。

（二）外国仲裁裁决撤销程序的立法检视

相较于我国，国外的仲裁制度起步较早、发展较快，故其有关仲裁裁决撤销程序的具体规则设计似乎也更为科学、复杂，再加之大陆法系国家与英美法系国家之间存在着巨大的法律文化鸿沟，我们很难将各国仲裁裁决撤销程序的每处细节规则都一一对应，因此只能选取部分重点共性规则进行比较研究，以期为我国仲裁裁决撤销程序的性质定位与规则建构提供可借鉴经验。

首先，关于法院审理撤销仲裁裁决案件适用程序的规定。世界主流国家范围内，各国法院审理撤销仲裁裁决案件所适用的程序大致可分为四种：再审程序、上诉审程序、特别程序以及普通一审程序。[19] 其中，英国的申请撤销仲裁裁决案件适用再审程序。根据英国相关仲裁法律的规定，英国境内的仲裁实行一裁终局，依法作出的仲裁裁决具有终局效力。仲裁裁决所认定的事实事

---

[16]《仲裁法司法解释》第 24 条："当事人申请撤销仲裁裁决的案件，人民法院应当组成合议庭审理，并询问当事人。"

[17]《仲裁法》第 60 条："人民法院应当在受理撤销裁决申请之日起两个月内作出撤销裁决或者驳回申请的裁定。"

[18]《仲裁法》第 61 条："人民法院受理撤销裁决的申请后，认为可以由仲裁庭重新仲裁的，通知仲裁庭在一定期限内重新仲裁，并裁定中止撤销程序。仲裁庭拒绝重新仲裁的，人民法院应当裁定恢复撤销程序"。

[19] 李琳：《试论撤销仲裁裁决案件的审理程序》，载《北京仲裁》2005 年第 2 期。

项永久、完全不发生变更。当事人仅能就仲裁裁决有关法律上之事项提起"上诉",即我国法语境下的再审程序。法国的申请撤销仲裁裁决案件适用上诉审程序。根据《法国新民事诉讼法典》的相关规定,当事人在运用仲裁手段解决纠纷的过程中可能会忽视自身所拥有的接受审判的权利,因此即使当事人已经在仲裁协议中以明示或默示的形式放弃了事后的救济权,其仍然可以在事后向法院申请撤销仲裁裁决并向上诉法院上诉。[20] 从这一点看,法国应当是不坚持"一裁终局"这一仲裁原则的。美国亦有所不同,其仲裁裁决撤销程序适用特殊程序审理。[21] 针对撤销仲裁裁决案件的不同情形,美国法院可以分别选任新仲裁员复审、指定新仲裁员复审以及命令原仲裁员复审。若撤销仲裁裁决申请被驳回且无法修正的仲裁裁决申请正在审理,法院还应当及时作出确认裁决。由此可见,美国的这种所谓的"特别程序"实质上仍然是一种法院监督仲裁员重新进行仲裁的程序。这种程序与我国法语境下的特别程序大相径庭,似乎与我国仲裁法规定的重新仲裁较为相似。日本申请撤销仲裁裁决适用的程序是普通一审程序。在以往,日本对于撤销仲裁裁决案件通常使用"仲裁裁决撤销之诉"的概念。通过这一称谓不难推断,日本实际上已将申请撤销仲裁裁决归为具体诉讼请求的行列了。只不过,这种仲裁裁决撤销之诉实质上成为与再审之诉相类似的诉讼法上的形成之诉。虽然近年来《日本仲裁法》中不再使用"仲裁裁决撤销之诉"和"仲裁裁决撤销诉讼程序"的字样,并且将仲裁裁决撤销的判决程序改为了决定程序,但这仍然不影响仲裁裁决撤销程序的诉讼特性。[22]

其次,关于管辖的规定。管辖虽然属于撤销仲裁裁决申请阶段的规则,但与撤销仲裁裁决适用何种程序也是密切相关的。比如,德国和日本均将撤销仲裁裁决视为实体的诉并适用普通审理程序。因此,《德国民事诉讼法》规定仲裁裁决撤销之诉由仲裁协议指定的或仲裁程序地的州高级法院管辖。《日本民事诉讼法》规定仲裁裁决撤销之诉由仲裁协议指定的或有管辖权的简易法

---

[20] 李琳:《试论撤销仲裁裁决案件的审理程序》,载《北京仲裁》2005年第2期;转引自《中华人民共和国仲裁法全书》,法律出版社1995年版,第54页。

[21] 陈桂明:《程序理念与程序规则》,中国法制出版社1999年版,第296—297页。

[22] 向东春:《论仲裁裁决撤销程序之完善》,载《嘉兴学院学报》2019年第5期;张卫平:《仲裁裁决撤销程序的法理分析》,载《比较法研究》2018年第6期;转引自[日]小岛武司、猪股孝史:《仲裁法》,日本评论社2014年版,第523页。

院或地区法院管辖。即使近年《日本仲裁法》不再使用仲裁裁决撤销之诉的称谓，但这并未影响作出仲裁裁决撤销决定的管辖法院。相比之下，美国所谓的特别程序实质上是一种法院指令仲裁机构重新仲裁的申请撤销仲裁裁决审理程序，因此一般情况下仍由原仲裁机构进行重新仲裁，涉及的变更也仅关乎仲裁员，而无关法院或者仲裁机构的管辖问题。

再次，关于当事人的规定。不同于我国仲裁裁决撤销程序中当事人相关规定的寥寥，其他国家有关仲裁裁决撤销案件中当事人的程序启动权、参与权以及辩论权等规定得较为翔实、具体。比如，《法国新民事诉讼法典》中详细规定了当事人的上诉权、法院的具体审理规则以及判决事项。《德国民事诉讼法》规定了当事人在仲裁裁决撤销案件审理过程中享有辩论权。[23]反观我国，有关仲裁裁决撤销程序中的当事人适格、当事人的权利及义务等问题均未在《民事诉讼法》及其司法解释以及《仲裁法》及其司法解释中加以规定。此外，唯一涉及仲裁裁决撤销程序中当事人问题的法律规范——《批复》也仅仅是简单声明了当事人的称谓，对于仲裁庭的当事人地位并未予以说明。

从次，关于撤销仲裁裁决程序结束后当事人的救济问题。与管辖问题相类似，撤销仲裁裁决完成后的当事人救济问题也是与撤销仲裁裁决适用何种程序密切相关的。以日本为例，由于其撤销仲裁裁决适用的是普通一审程序，因此若当事人不服判决（或决定）自然可以向上一级人民法院上诉，若上诉后仍不服，符合条件的还可以申请再审救济。由于德国的仲裁裁决撤销程序适用的也是诉讼程序，因此《德国民事诉讼法》规定了对于撤销仲裁裁决结果不服的当事人可以向联邦最高法院提出抗告。[24]

最后，关于当事人申请撤销仲裁裁决期限的规定各国也不尽相同。比如，我国现行《仲裁法》第59条规定的是自当事人收到裁决书之日起的6个月内，而《征求意见稿》第78条将这一期限缩短为3个月。《法国新民事诉讼法典》规定的上诉期限是1个月。《美国仲裁法案》第12条规定的是自当事人收到仲裁裁决后的3个月内提出撤销请求。德国规定为3个月内由当事人向法院提出。日本之前（《日本民事诉讼法》第801条之规定）的规定是当事人应当在仲裁裁决作出后的1个月内提起仲裁裁决撤销之诉；而在《日本仲裁法》修

---

[23]《德国民事诉讼法》，丁启明译，厦门大学出版社2017年版，第238页。

[24]《德意志联邦共和国民事诉讼法》，谢怀栻译，中国法制出版社2001年版，第286—288页。

订后，该法第 44 条第 2 项将当事人向法院申请撤销仲裁裁决的这一期限变更为 3 个月内。

（三）中外不同仲裁裁决撤销程序的反思与评价

通过检视中外不同的仲裁裁决撤销程序及其规则，我们可以清楚地看到，无论是在整体的仲裁制度上还是在具体的仲裁裁决撤销制度上，我国与世界其他主流国家之间均存在着较大的客观差距。这种差距主要体现在质和量两个方面。首先，"质"的差距主要表现为我国既有的规则与主流国家既有规则的差距。比如，我国与外国均设置了仲裁裁决撤销程序的当事人规则。然而，我国的当事人规则仅仅是以最高人民法院某年批复中的某一条所规定；而其他国家则是在民事诉讼法或仲裁法中正式且详细地规定了当事人适格、当事人的权利与义务等问题。其次，"量"的差距主要表现为我国仲裁裁决撤销程序重大规则的缺失。经过上述检视，我们可以清楚地看到，几乎没有任何一个设置了仲裁裁决撤销程序的国家尚未设置相应的救济程序。自我国正式出台第一部《仲裁法》并设置相应的仲裁裁决撤销程序至今已经过去了将近 30 年的时间，而我国于 2021 年在《征求意见稿》中才开始打算以正式立法的形式确认相应的救济程序。除此之外，我国的仲裁裁决撤销程序仍然缺乏许多诸如审查方式、立案标准以及判决标准裁决撤销程序规则。

当然，我们并不能一味否认我国的仲裁制度建设，更不能一味地照搬照抄域外所谓的先进经验。欲进行我国仲裁裁决撤销程序的规则建构应首先明确一个最基本的前提：即我国的仲裁裁决撤销程序到底是一个什么性质的程序？只有厘清了这一问题，后续的当事人、管辖、申请期限、庭审规则以及程序救济等问题才能迎刃而解。

三、仲裁裁决撤销程序的性质定位

不同于国外对于仲裁裁决程序性质的清晰界定，我国的仲裁裁决撤销程序虽既存已久，但其性质与功能定位尚不明确，甚至存在争议。比如，有的观点认为该程序属于普通诉讼程序且应当承认仲裁裁决撤销之诉这一具体诉讼类型；[25] 有的观点认为该程序属于程序性裁判；[26] 有的观点认为该程序属于

---

[25] 李琳：《试论撤销仲裁裁决案件的审理程序》，载《北京仲裁》2005 年第 2 期。

[26] 姜霞：《仲裁司法审查程序要论》，湘潭大学出版社 2009 年版，第 188—230 页。

特别程序;[27]还有的观点认为该程序属于一种准诉讼程序,兼具诉讼与非讼特性。[28]此外,司法实践的通行做法却是将该程序简单地非讼化,实际将该程序视为一种非讼程序,与以上任一学理上的观点又有所不同。[29]因此,究竟应当如何定位仲裁裁决撤销程序的性质呢?

(一)仲裁裁决撤销程序具有某种诉讼特性

从世界范围内的国家及地区来看,将仲裁裁决撤销程序视为诉讼程序的做法并不在少数。比如《法国新民事诉讼法典》第1483条、第1486条以及第1487条就明确规定了撤销仲裁裁决的上诉程序。其中,第1483条详细规定了当事人所享有的向上诉法院请求变更或撤销仲裁裁决的双重救济权利;第1484条特别规定了当事人放弃上述上诉权后仍享有的撤销仲裁裁决的申请权;第1487条明确规定了当事人的上诉和撤销动议的审理应明确按照诉讼程序进行的程序规则。此外,日本几乎曾是将仲裁裁决撤销程序视为诉讼程序的最典型代表。在日本,申请撤销仲裁裁决被称为"仲裁裁决撤销之诉"。按照民事诉讼法学界的诉的分类标准,这种诉的类型属于形成之诉项下的诉讼法上的形成之诉,与再审程序相类似。[30]因此,这一诉所适用的程序也必然是普通民事诉讼程序。

在我国,持仲裁裁决撤销程序是诉讼程序观点的学者主要基于两点立场:其一,非讼程序的非对审制、非公开制难以保障当事人的实体及程序权利,且缺乏对法院的司法监督。在非讼程序下,直接原则、言词原则、辩论原则及处分原则都将难以有效甚至无法贯彻。在这种当事人的程序权利几乎消磨殆尽的程序下,当事人的实体权利自然无法得到保障。此外,根据我国《民事诉讼法》的程序设定,适用非讼程序的案件一般都是"一判终局",当事人一般无法上诉或复议,因此缺乏对法院司法权的有效监督。其二,法院处理撤销仲裁裁决案件的审查内容反映了法院应当适用的审查程序。从我国《仲裁法》规定的可申请撤销裁决的事由来看,该事由可能同时包含法律适用纠纷和事实纠纷。其中,对于法律适用纠纷,即使不赋予当事人充分的程序权

---

[27] 胡思博:《对撤销国内仲裁裁决活动属性的法理探析》,载《哈尔滨学院学报》2011年第5期。
[28] 张卫平:《仲裁裁决撤销程序的法理分析》,载《比较法研究》2018年第6期。
[29] 张卫平:《仲裁裁决撤销程序的法理分析》,载《比较法研究》2018年第6期。
[30] 张卫平:《民事再审:基础置换与制度重建》,载《中国法学》2003年第1期。

利,法院一般也能够作出正确的决断。这种司法自信是由我国法院的水平及法官的素质所给予的,尚有一定说服力。然而,对于对方是否隐瞒了相关证据、仲裁员是否受贿等事实纠纷的判断,仅依赖法官的自我审查恐怕是远远不够的。此外,申请撤销仲裁裁决的事由与再审事由高度相似也是该程序应当适用普通诉讼程序的有力论据。[31]

回归到诉讼程序与非讼程序最基本的区分标准,相较于非讼程序,典型的诉讼程序具有以下特征:[32]第一,解决实体争议;第二,程序结果以判决的形式作出而非裁定;第三,全程贯彻直接原则、言词原则以及辩论原则;第四,法官据以裁判的依据必须是经法定程序认定后的当事人的主张、陈述及证明;第五,公开审判。根据张卫平教授的观点,以上特征可以"三性"概括,即争讼性、对审性及公开性。[33]其中,争讼性是诉讼程序和非讼程序的鲜明区分点。"诉讼"和"非讼"的称谓直观地表明了这一点。非讼程序之所以被称为非讼,正是因为其一般不具有争讼性。以非讼程序中的宣告失踪为例,利害关系人向法院申请宣告失踪,本案中并不存在利益或立场对立的当事人。对此,一部分人可能会产生疑问:既然没有利益,为什么所谓的利害关系人还要申请宣告失踪呢?对此,应当明确的是,此处所称"不存在利益或立场对立"仅是就宣告失踪这一程序而言的,至于利害关系人是否在其他案件中与被宣告失踪人存在利害关系则是另一个问题。此外,既然仲裁裁决撤销程序中的当事人双方存在着利益或立场的对立,那么对于一些涉及仲裁裁决效力的事由审查也当然应该赋予双方当事人充分辩论的权利。因此,即使仲裁裁决撤销程序并非典型的诉讼程序,其自身所具有的争讼性和对审性等特征也决定了该程序具备诉讼特性。

(二)仲裁裁决撤销程序并非典型的非讼程序

在讨论仲裁裁决撤销程序究竟是不是非讼程序之前,我们首先需要厘清非讼程序的外延。关于非讼程序及其范围,学界并没有统一的观点。[34]传统

---

[31] 张卫平:《仲裁裁决撤销程序的法理分析》,载《比较法研究》2018年第6期。

[32] 姜世民:《非讼事件法新论》,新学林出版股份有限公司2011年版,第1—4页。

[33] 张卫平:《仲裁裁决撤销程序的法理分析》,载《比较法研究》2018年第6期。

[34] 赵蕾:《诉讼与非讼的再区分——以诉讼与非讼基本模式的差异为研究进路》,载《比较法研究》2012年第4期;赵蕾:《中国非讼程序年度观察报告(2017)》,载《当代法学》2018年第6期。

的非讼程序有广义与狭义之分。其中，狭义的非讼程序一般等同于现行《民事诉讼法》第15章特别程序的内容，但对于第15章中的"选民资格案件"是否也可归为狭义的非讼程序仍存争议。[35] 就广义的非讼程序而言，除上述第15章内容外，还应当包含督促程序、公示催告程序等《民事诉讼法》第17章、第18章的内容。不过，近期又有学者提出了一种更广泛意义上的非讼程序。即在民事领域内，凡是不属于诉讼程序的程序，均属非讼程序。[36] 比如，民事诉讼中的诉前行为保全程序也应当属于非讼程序。除此之外，立法与司法对于非讼程序的范围也存在着细微矛盾。比如，《民事诉讼法》并未使用诉讼程序和非讼程序的称谓，取而代之的是一审程序、二审程序以及特别程序等称谓。若默认一审、二审以及再审属于诉讼程序的范畴，那么执行程序是否应当划入非讼程序？反观《民事案件案由规定》（法〔2020〕346号）第十部分的规定，其虽采用了"非讼程序案件案由"的称谓，但范围却囊括了仲裁程序、人身安全保护令程序以及人格权禁令程序等案件。这一范围已经远超学界通常所认为的广义的非讼程序的范围。

　　按照目前的立法及司法技术水平，完全划定非讼程序的范畴几乎是不可能的。不过，由于非讼程序的特点是相对固定的，可以从这一角度讨论仲裁裁决撤销程序的性质。按照张卫平教授的观点，目前我国的非讼程序具有适用案件的非民事争议性、程序的非统一性、无严格对立当事人、一审终审、原则上的独任制、不适用再审程序、审限较短以及无案件受理费等八个主要特点。[37] 从民事争议性与无严格对立当事人的特点来看，仲裁裁决撤销程序虽仅是对仲裁裁决本身的审查，一般不涉及实体民事纠纷，但该程序中的确存在着严格对立的当事人。裁决撤销申请的支持与驳回将直接影响当事人双方的实体权利义务，这也正是仲裁裁决撤销程序的争讼性之所在。从程序的非统一性、一审终审、不适用再审以及审限较短的角度来看，仲裁裁决撤销程序是完全符合这些特点的。一方面，仲裁裁决撤销程序的规则不同于既有特别程序的规则；另一方面，根据《仲裁法》第60条、第61条的规定，仲裁裁决

---

[35]　张卫平：《民事诉讼法》，法律出版社2019年版，第471页。

[36]　严仁群：《人格权禁令之程序法路径》，载《法学评论》2021年第6期；邵明、康健：《论行为保全法理在人格权侵害禁令中的适用——基于解释论的视角》，载《齐鲁学刊》2021年第6期。

[37]　张卫平：《民事诉讼法》，法律出版社2019年版，第465—466页。

撤销程序的审限为2个月、一审终审且无救济程序。然而,根据《仲裁法司法解释》第24条的规定,人民法院应当以合议的形式审理仲裁裁决撤销案件而非独任制。此外,仲裁裁决撤销案件在司法实践中需要收取受理费,标准为400元/件。

因此,通过将既有的仲裁裁决撤销程序规则与非讼程序的基本特点——对比后不难发现,非讼程序的8个基本特点中,仲裁裁决撤销程序仅符合5个。故司法实践中虽常有将仲裁裁决撤销案件适用非讼程序审理的做法,[38]但这并不能抹去仲裁裁决撤销程序本身所具有的诉讼特性。本质上,仲裁裁决撤销程序并不是一种典型的非讼程序。

(三) 仲裁裁决撤销程序是一种新型特别程序

既然仲裁裁决撤销程序既非典型的非讼程序,又同时具有诉讼特性,那么到底应当如何认定这一程序的性质?其究竟是诉讼程序还是非讼程序?应当如何在我国民诉法的既有体系下安排这一程序?根据学界对仲裁裁决撤销程序的性质讨论,大致可归纳为三种认定方案。第一种是"诉讼程序说"的方案,建议在我国设置独立的仲裁裁决撤销之诉,从而使仲裁裁决撤销程序直接适用一审普通程序。第二种是"准诉讼程序说"的方案,建议在我国设立一种介于诉讼程序与非讼程序之间的独立的仲裁裁决撤销程序。第三种是"修改说"的方案,建议保持我国当下仲裁裁决程序格局,无须对其进行明确的性质定位,仅增添部分程序规则即可。以上三种方案各有优劣,并非最佳。"诉讼程序说"的方案过于保守,虽然为当事人提供了充足的程序保障,但忽视了仲裁裁决撤销案件的效率性。"准诉讼程序说"的方案虽然兼顾仲裁裁决撤销程序的诉与非讼特性,但立法、司法及普法成本过高。仅为了某类案件便要打破既有的程序格局恐有买椟还珠之嫌。"修改说"的方案虽然成本较低且更为可行,但并未触及仲裁裁决撤销程序的性质定位这一根本问题。

因此,应当另辟蹊径,将仲裁裁决撤销程序定位为一种新型特别程序。[39]理由如下:

首先,此处所称特别程序是指现行《民事诉讼法》第15章的特别程序,

---

[38] 谭振亚:《仲裁案件司法审查实证分析——以重庆市第一中级人民法院司法实务为样本》,载《人民司法(应用)》2015年第19期。

[39] 王强义:《民事诉讼特别程序研究》,中国政法大学出版社1993年版,第1—28页。

而非学理上的特别程序。在一些国家（如日本）的民诉法学理论中，特别程序是与普通程序相对应的程序，又称特别诉讼程序。与之相比，我国的特别程序的范围较广，一般认为同时包含特别诉讼程序和非讼程序（狭义）。比如，我国《民事诉讼法》特别程序中的选民资格案件即属特别诉讼程序，而其他则属非讼程序。此外，《民事案件案由规定》（法〔2020〕346号）第十部分已经明确规定了特别诉讼程序属于广义的非讼程序的一环。

其次，将仲裁裁决撤销程序定位为新型特别程序能够在保证效率的同时做到成本最小化。所谓兼顾效率其实就是兼顾仲裁裁决撤销程序本身所具有的争讼性以及对审性。对此，有人可能会产生疑问，本文所指特别程序是我国民事诉讼法语境下的特别程序，而我国民事诉讼法语境下的特别程序又属于我国民诉理论分类下的狭义的非讼程序，如此一来，仲裁裁决撤销程序仍被定位为非讼程序，是否存在前后矛盾？对此，需要进行一番说明。第一，非讼程序虽不能实现诉讼程序对审制，但依然可以实现对审制下的部分核心效能，从而保障争讼性。简言之，非讼程序并非绝对地无争讼、无辩论。第二，《民事诉讼法》第15章的特别程序属于非讼程序仅是学理上的分类，而非法定分类。在《民事诉讼法》中，并未明确说明特别程序属于非讼程序。仅以学理上的分类来限制民诉法上的特别程序作用的发挥是极不妥当的。第三，即使特别程序无法完全满足仲裁裁决撤销程序所要求的争讼性和对审性，仍然可以在今后的仲裁裁决撤销特别程序中设置诸如"法官可根据仲裁裁决撤销案件的具体情形，在审理中裁量适用普通程序的相关规则"等例外规定。[40]此外，特别程序相较于普通程序明显具有更高的效率。所谓的成本最小化则是相对于"诉讼程序说"和"准诉讼程序说"而言的。"准诉讼程序说"的立法、司法及普法成本不言自明。至于诉讼程序与特别程序的成本孰高孰低则并不容易比较。但从长期来看，设置一个新型特别程序来审理仲裁裁决撤销案件相较于设置一个新型诉的种类并通过普通程序审理此类案件还是具有低成本的优益性的。

再次，将仲裁裁决撤销程序定位为特别程序有立法体例及内容的支撑。伴随着《民事诉讼法》第15章的扩充，特别程序其实早已突破了原有的"狭义非讼程序"定位。一方面，选民资格案件一直扮演着特别程序中的"特殊

---

[40] 张卫平：《仲裁裁决撤销程序的法理分析》，载《比较法研究》2018年第6期。

者"角色。其自身的特别诉讼程序性质一直被民诉法例外规定。比如，《民事诉讼法》第 187 条末尾规定道："选民资格案件除外"。另一方面，2012 年《民事诉讼法》修改并在特别程序下新增确认调解协议和实现担保物权两类案件，这同样表明立法者欲使特别程序突破固有定位，不断拓宽丰富特别程序适用范围的立法意旨。

最后，将仲裁裁决撤销程序纳入特别程序符合当下司法实践。上文已详细论述了当下法院的通行做法是运用非讼程序审理仲裁裁决撤销案件。因此，仍将该程序规定在特别程序中也较为符合审判者的预期。

四、仲裁裁决撤销程序的规则建构

在明确了仲裁裁决撤销程序的特别程序定位之后，还应当进一步对该特别程序进行具体的规则建构。其中，具体规则的设定应坚持少删、少改、多解释、多调和、适量增的原则，尽量遵循已有规定，力求将以往散乱的仲裁裁决撤销程序规则整合统一。

（一）仲裁裁决撤销程序的启动规则

仲裁裁决撤销程序的启动规则主要包括以下五个方面的内容。

首先，关于申请主体。按照上述《批复》第 2 条的规定，申请撤销仲裁裁决的一方为当事人，另一方为被申请人。不过，对于仲裁庭和仲裁委员会是否可以作为适格当事人等问题，当下法律并未作出规定。对此，应当进一步明确申请方与被申请方的绝对当事人地位，仲裁委、仲裁庭以及案外人均非本程序下的适格当事人，更无权主动启动该程序。

其次，关于管辖法院。对于仲裁裁决撤销程序的管辖问题，《仲裁法》已作出了明确规定，即由仲裁委所在地中级人民法院管辖。对此，有学者在对比了仲裁员的任职资格与中级人民法院法官的任职资格后，认为仲裁员的任职资格标准远高于中级人民法院法官的任职资格标准。认为应将此类案件的管辖法院上升一级，由高级人民法院进行管辖。[41] 不过，从我国目前中级人民法院法官的整体素质来看，还是完全有能力胜任此类依特别程序进行审理的案件的。一方面，仲裁裁决撤销程序一般不涉及对实体法律关系的审查；另一方面，即使涉及部分事实问题的审查，也多是与证据相关的问题。因此，

---

[41] 李琳：《试论撤销仲裁裁决案件的审理程序》，载《北京仲裁》2005 年第 2 期。

由中级人民法院管辖此类案件完全可行。本轮《征求意见稿》第77条第1款也恰恰印证了这一观点。从地域管辖规定来看,《征求意见稿》第77条将现行《仲裁法》第58条中的"仲裁委员会所在地"改为了"仲裁地",是对以往民诉法及仲裁法的一次纠错,对于我国充分把握"仲裁地"概念与制度并与国际仲裁制度接轨具有较强的现实意义。此外,《征求意见稿》第7章还专门新设了涉外仲裁临时仲裁制度,该制度虽仅适用于涉外仲裁,并不适用于纯国内仲裁,但也为今后纯国内仲裁裁决撤销程序的管辖规则完善提供了宝贵经验。

再次,关于申请事由。现行《仲裁法》关于仲裁裁决撤销事由的规定集中在第58条,共6种情形。根据法条体例,大致可分为管辖权瑕疵、程序瑕疵、徇私舞弊以及损害社会公共利益等四个方面的内容。不过,这些事由存在着诸如与外国仲裁裁决撤销事由不一致的缺陷。因此,司法部关于《征求意见稿》的说明中指出,此轮仲裁法的修改将仲裁裁决撤销的申请事由作为修改的焦点之一。其中,第77条第1款统一整合了国内和涉外仲裁裁决撤销的申请事由,并增加了对恶意串通、伪造证据等欺诈行为取得的、涉嫌虚假仲裁的撤销情形。第77条第3款增加了裁决的部分撤销情形。如此一来,我国关于国内外仲裁裁决撤销程序的申请事由将更为统一、完整。今后的仲裁裁决撤销特别程序可以直接将其纳入体系之下。

从次,关于申请期限。根据上述立法检视,目前世界范围内大多数主流国家均将撤销仲裁裁决的申请期限规定为自收到仲裁裁决之日起的3个月以内,甚至之前有国家规定为1个月内。反观我国,现行《仲裁法》第59条则是将这一期限规定为自当事人收到裁决书之日起的6个月内。对比国内针对此种期限规定之差异,足以见得我国关于此期限之规定过于漫长。第一,从仲裁裁决撤销的申请事由来看,该部分内容大都是一些十分严重或者明显的错误,当事人作为利益攸关者及理性经济人,有义务及时预见或发现此类错误。第二,仲裁裁决撤销程序启动的申请期限过长,不利于仲裁裁决效力的发挥与认定,且很可能在一定程度上影响仲裁制度的权威与公正,从而影响社会关系的稳定。因此,此轮《征求意见稿》第78条将这一期限缩短为3个月,值得肯定。嗣后在构建仲裁裁决特别程序时,也应当采纳这一时限规则。

最后,关于申请费用。仲裁裁决撤销程序的申请费用问题似乎很容易被我们所忽视，因此关于费用问题的规定及深入论证并不多。按照《批复》第3条的规定，申请撤销仲裁裁决案件的收费标准同非财产案件的收费标准。根据之前的《人民法院诉讼费收费办法》的相关规定，这一标准为10元到100元不等。尔后，最高人民法院于2010年出台的《诉讼费用交纳办法》第13条第5款中将这一标准提高到了400元。不过，从当事人申请仲裁裁决撤销的现实以及司法实践来看，400元的诉讼费用仍然是一个较低的标准。近年来，通过仲裁裁决撤销程序滥诉、虚假诉讼的情况屡见不鲜。在未来，应当严格发挥诉讼费用抑制此类乱象的作用，进一步提高收费标准和程序门槛。比如，可将这一标准进一步提升（如提升到1000元），或结合案件的具体情况如实际涉案标的额等综合考量。

（二）申请撤销仲裁裁决案件的审查与审理规则

首先，法院对仲裁裁决撤销申请的审查是一个较为简单的问题。其审查的主要内容无非是申请书中的当事人的信息、请求、理由、期限等内容。审查完毕后，若符合法定要件，法院应当及时出具立案通知书；若不符合法定要件，应当及时出具不予受理裁定书；若材料有缺失，应当要求当事人及时补正。

其次，关于审理规则。仲裁裁决撤销程序的审理规则有以下四个方面：

第一，审判组织。按照《民事诉讼法》的规定，适用特别程序审理的案件一般都是独任制。不过，由于仲裁裁决撤销案件特殊的争讼性，还是应当采用合议制审理。对此，《仲裁法司法解释》第24条已明确作出了人民法院应当组成合议庭的相关规定。此外，现行特别程序中的选民资格案件也存在着适用合议制的特殊规则。

第二，审理对象。法官在审理仲裁裁决撤销案件的过程中，审理对象一般表现为程序性事项，即当事人的申请事由中的相关规定。不过，关于法院是否能够主动审理"仲裁裁决损害公共利益"这一申请事项，尚且存在一定争议。根据张卫平教授的观点，《仲裁法》第58条第1款与第3款属于不同性质的申请事由。[42]其中，针对第1款中的申请事由基本遵循"不告不理"的原则，法官一般不会主动进行审查。而第3款中的申请事由，由于事关社会公共利益，法官则有义务进行主动审查。

第三，审理流程。不同于普通诉讼程序，特别程序一般具有流程简化的特

---

[42] 张卫平：《民事诉讼法》，法律出版社2019年版，第516页。

点。比如，多数的特别程序均不设置专门的法庭调查以及法庭辩论流程。然而，鉴于仲裁裁决撤销程序的争讼性与对审性，应当在其程序流程中设置一定类似于法庭调查以及法庭辩论的环节，使当事人可以充分辩论并穷尽攻击防御方法，从而最大限度保障双方的程序及实体权利。由于仲裁裁决撤销程序多为关于申请事由相关证据的审查和认定，因此设置法庭调查环节也有利于此目的的实现。此外，个案是否具体适用相应的法庭辩论及法庭调查环节可由法官灵活裁量。

第四，审理方式。为兼顾仲裁裁决撤销程序的争讼性与对审性，法官一般应当开庭审理此类案件。至于特殊情况下能否采用书面审理，则视案件的繁简程序及当事人意愿而定。此外，由于仲裁程序与特别程序均以不公开审理为原则，因此仲裁裁决撤销程序一般也应当不公开审理。当然，如果是双方当事人合意公开审理，且不涉及个人隐私、商业秘密及国家秘密的案件，也可以例外公开审理。

（三）仲裁裁决撤销裁定后的救济程序

基于对上述各国仲裁裁决撤销裁定后救济程序设定的立法检视，足以见得此类救济程序的多样性。例如日本通过"上诉+再审"的模式进行救济，德国通过向联邦最高法院抗告的模式进行救济等。其实，在讨论我国相应的救济程序之前，应当首先明确一个逻辑：仲裁裁决撤销程序的性质定位基本决定了其嗣后的救济程序。简言之，仲裁裁决撤销程序与其救济程序是相互配套的。德日等国的仲裁裁决撤销程序本就适用普通诉讼程序，因此其嗣后救济程序也采用普通诉讼程序的救济程序。反观我国将仲裁裁决撤销程序定位为一种特别程序而非诉讼程序，因此应当遵循特别程序的救济模式。按照特别程序的规则设定，所有适用此程序的案件均为一审终审，不得上诉。不过，鉴于仲裁裁决撤销案件所具有的争讼性、对审性等特点，应当为其设置相应的救济程序，即复议程序。立法者在此轮《仲裁法》修改的过程中也注意到了这一点，并在《征求意见稿》第81条中作出了如下规定："当事人对法院撤销裁决的裁定不服的，可以自收到裁定之日起十日内向上一级人民法院申请复议。人民法院应当在受理复议申请之日起一个月内作出裁定。"

结　论

仲裁委或仲裁庭并非司法机关，仲裁权更非司法权。因此，这种权力的背后必须有相应的监督机制。时下，重新思考如何构建一个系统化、体系化、程序化的仲裁裁决撤销程序就成为当务之急。一方面，应当首先明确仲裁裁决撤销程序的性质定位。仲裁裁决是诉讼程序、非讼程序抑或准诉讼程序将直接影响其后续的申请、受理、审理、判决以及救济等一系列程序规则的建构。另一方面，在构建具体的程序规则时，应当注意协调各种散乱在不同法律规范之间的仲裁裁决撤销程序规则，坚持少删、少改、多解释、多调和、适量增的原则，最大限度维护法律的安定。可以预见，此轮《仲裁法》的修改绝非仲裁裁决撤销程序完善的终点。在未来，距离仲裁裁决撤销程序成为法定特别程序并被正式纳入《民事诉讼法》，或许还有很长的一段路需要走。

论上诉机制与 ICSID 公约和 UNCITRAL 仲裁规则的兼容性

刘文慧[*]

- 摘 要

   本文详细分析了在投资仲裁中建立上诉机制需考虑的基本问题，重点研究了上诉机制与现有国际投资仲裁制度的不相容性，同时寻求上诉机制与两个主要投资仲裁系统的协调，即与根据 ICSID 公约和 UNCITRAL 仲裁规则进行的仲裁的兼容。本文认为应当建立一个常设多边的上诉机制，上诉理由应包括由当事人提出，并且是解决争端所必需的明显的法律错误和严重的事实错误。现有撤销程序的功能可以通过将撤销理由纳入上诉理由而被上诉机制代替。上诉机制与现行 ISDS 系统在制度上的不相容性是可以解决的，可以在多边框架中以选择公约的形式引入常设上诉机制。上诉裁决可以根据《纽约公约》执行，与公共政策无关的拒绝执行的理由可以由当事人放弃，以确保上诉裁决的最大终局性。

- 关键词

   国际投资争端解决　上诉机制　投资仲裁　ICSID 公约　贸法会仲裁规则

---

[*] 刘文慧，莱顿大学 2021 级国际争端解决与仲裁高级研究法学硕士。

Abstract: This thesis provides a comprehensive analysis of the essential issues to be considered in establishing an appellate mechanism in current investment arbitration. Identifying the incompatibilities of the new mechanism with the existing regime for international investment arbitration is the focus of this work, along with a seeking of a reasonable appellate mechanism and its coordination with the two main systems, namely arbitrations under the ICSID Convention and the UNCITRAL Arbitration Rules. This thesis considers that a standing and multilateral appellate mechanism could be more consistent with the purpose of establishing such a mechanism. Only manifest legal errors and serious factual errors could be the grounds for appeal. The errors should be raised by parties and necessary for the settlement of the dispute. Besides, annulment could be replaced by an AM in which the annulment grounds are covered by the scope of appellate review. It is possible to resolve the incompatibilities of the new mechanism with the current ISDS regime and a standing appellate mechanism could be introduced in a multilateral framework in the form of an opt-in convention. Finally, a decision made by the appellate tribunal could be enforced under the New York Convention, and certain grounds for refusal of enforcement that are irrelevant to public policies could be waived by the parties to ensure the maximum finality of an appeal award.

Key Words: ISDS, appellate mechanism, investment arbitration, ICSID, UNCITRAL

1. Introduction

1.1. Background

The current system of Investor-State Dispute Settlement (ISDS) has been under challenge for some time. The legitimacy of investment arbitration continues to be criticised.[1] Those generalized criticisms include conflicting awards, time and expenses, the potential challenge to national sovereignty[2] and the independence and impartiality of the arbitral tribunal, etc. The question of 'consistency, coherence, predictability, and correctness of arbitral decisions by ISDS tribunals' is foremost among them.[3] The issues that have been raised are not new. However, the United Nations Commission on International Trade Law (UNCITRAL) mandated Working Group III respond to the concerns raised in the current ISDS regime and develop possible reforms that could improve the system. This is the first time that a large number of states have been involved in the reform of ISDS.

Among the numerous reform options proposed to address the above challenges, the introduction of some types (ad hoc, a standing appellate body, or as the second tier of a standing court) of appellate mechanism (AM) [4] is likely to get the most attention and to be one of the most significant suggestions. Some states consider that it is envisaged that an AM could review and correct the decisions rendered by ISDS tribunals, thus providing a consistent and fair decision for all parties.[5] It is also pointed by certain states that with the

---

[1] See S. Franck, "The legitimacy crisis in investment treaty arbitration: Privatizing public international law through inconsistent decisions", 73 (4) Fordham law review, 1521–1625 (2005); Also see M. Waibel, A. Kaushal, et al, The Backlash against Investment Arbitration: Perceptions and Reality, in M. Waibel, The Backlash against Investment Arbitration, Wolters Kluwer Law & Business, 2010, p. xxxvii.

[2] Arbitrators were criticised for adjudicating on a wide range of national policies. See ibid., M. Waibel, A. Kaushal, et al (2010).

[3] UNGA 'Possible reform of investor-State dispute settlement (ISDS)' (2018) UN Doc A/CN.9/WG.III/WP.149, para. 9.

[4] THE IDEA OF ESTABLISHING AN AM WAS FIRST PROPOSED IN ICSID SECRETARIAT (2004), POSSIBLE IMPROVEMENTS OF THE FRAMEWORK FOR ICSID ARBITRATION, DISCUSSION PAPER. https://icsid.worldbank.org/sites/default/files/Possible%20Improvements%20of%20the%20Framework%20of%20I CSID%20Arbitration.pdf (Last visited on July 18, 2022), hereinafter ICSID 2004 Proposal.

[5] UNGA 'Possible reform of investor-State dispute settlement (ISDS): Submission from the Government of Ecuador' (2019) UN Doc A/CN.9/WG.III/WP.175.

increased number of investment arbitration cases, the development of an AM would improve the coherence and predictability of the investment regime.[6] However, the addition of an appeals procedure, on the other hand, would undoubtedly increase the complexity of the issues under discussion, both substantively and procedurally. This reality may lead to some new barriers for countries to participate in international investment arbitration.

In February 2021, the UNCITRAL Working Group III discussed the draft provisions relating to the nature, scope and effect of an AM. The proposal for establishing an AM could more than ever be a potential solution to ISDS reform as a response to demands for a more coherent and consistent ISDS regime.

One important and complex issue is the impact of the new mechanism on the existing ISDS system, and a strong obstacle in this context is the lack of compatibility of the new mechanism with current prevailing procedures, more precisely, with the Convention on the Settlement of Investment Disputes between States and Nationals of Other States (ICSID Convention) as well as the UNCITRAL Arbitration Rules.[7] There are many discussions on the necessity and possibility of an AM in investment arbitration, a systematic and deeper examination of the question presented above is however required to ensure the interaction of the new mechanism with the current ISDS system.

1.2. Structure

This thesis is divided into five chapters. Chapter one provides the background for this research. This includes an introduction to the ISDS reform in the UNCITRAL Working Group III, the objective, research methodology and the structure of this thesis.

Chapter two looks at the existing ISDS regime and surveys the main legal issues at the early stage of the establishment of an AM. Section one focuses

---

[6] UNGA 'Possible reform of investor-State dispute settlement (ISDS): Submission from the Government of China' (2019) UN Doc A/CN.9/WG.III/WP.177.

[7] Arbitration Rules of the United Nations Commission on International Trade Law (1976)(with new article 1, paragraph 4, as adopted in 2013)(UNCITRAL Arbitration Rules).

on the two most important rules governing ISDS, the ICSID Convention and the UNCITRAL Arbitration Rules, providing an overview of the current ISDS regime. Section two explains the reason why an appeal proposal is acceptable and in the Section three, a detailed analysis and suggested elements are given to address the main legal issues in an AM.

Chapter three respectively explores the incompatibility of the new AM with the arbitration under the ICSID Convention and the UNCITRAL Arbitration Rules. Corresponding advice will also be given after the conflicts raised. Besides, Section three will introduce a possible multilateral AM to Existing IIAs.

Chapter four deals with the issues of annulment and enforcement of appellate awards. Section one examines the relationship between the AM and annulment and suggests the possible approaches to be compatible with the ICSID Convention and the UNCITRAL Arbitration Rules. Section two addresses the enforcement issues in different legal regimes. Finally, in Chapter five, conclusions are briefly reached.

2. The existing ISDS regime and a possible reform option: Appellate Mechanism

The existing ISDS regime has long been under public scrutiny. Its legitimacy crisis[8] has triggered a broad discussion on reforming the ISDS system during the last few decades. The idea of creating an AM for investment arbitration is not a new topic. Early in 2004, observing some state practice in bilateral investment treaties (BITs) that the intention of states to have an appellate review of investment disputes has been showed, [9] the ICSID Secretariat proposed that a single Appeals Facility might be created as a substitute for multiples

---

[8] See *supra* note 2.

[9] For example, in the 2004 US Model BIT, the idea was considered on a bilateral basis; See United States Model Bilateral Investment Treaty of 2004, Art. 28 (10) provides that: 'Within three years after the date of entry into force of the Treaty, the Parties shall consider whether to establish a bilateral appellate body or similar mechanism to review awards.'

AMs raised in different treaties providing for an appellate review of awards.[10] In the lack of active response from ICSID member states, the proposal was eventually suspended and was deemed as not mature enough at that stage.[11] Nevertheless, the availability of appeals mechanisms in investment arbitration is a 'recurrent feature'[12] in the debate about ISDS, notably as the number of investor-state disputes has increased significantly and so has the inconsistency of interpretation in the system. The ongoing discussion at Working Group III of UNCITRAL indicates that a number of states now have great concerns regarding consistency, coherence, predictability and correctness of arbitral decisions by ISDS tribunals.[13] Therefore, numerous reform suggestions have been made and not surprisingly the establishment of an AM has gained prominence among them.

This chapter will introduce two prevailing regimes for investment arbitration: ICSID and the UNCITRAL Arbitration Rules and then clarify the reasons for creating an AM in current system. Moreover, this part will deal with the legal issues when designing an AM and will give corresponding advice to these issues.

2.1. The current regimes in ISDS

In order to examine the question of the compatibility of an AM with the first-tier arbitral decisions, it is required to understand which regimes the AM might coordinate with, as well as the relevant rules governing the potential coordination. The current ISDS regime was established mainly through International Investment Agreements (IIAs), allowing foreign investors to directly initiate arbitrations against host states. Within the system, arbitration can be conducted in a number of institutions or under certain arbitration rules. Basically, the disputing parties

---

[10] See ICSID 2004 Proposal, *supra* note 5, para. 20, Ann. para. 1; The Secretariat forecast that by mid-2015, more than 20 nations may have signed treaties including provisions on appeal processes for investment awards rendered in ISDS under the treaties.

[11] ICSID Working Paper, Suggested Changes to the ICSID Rules and Regulations, 12 May 2005, para. 4.

[12] See C.H. Schreuer, A. de la Brena, "Does ISDS Need an Appeals Mechanism?", 2 Transnational Dispute Management, 1 (2020).

[13] See *supra* notes 6-7.

have a choice between institutional arbitration supported by a selected institute and ad hoc arbitration based on an arbitration agreement. The former is usually taken place in ICSID but other institutions not excluding investment arbitration are also eligible. The latter is most commonly conducted under the UNCITRAL Arbitration Rules. This section will introduce two main types of foreign investment arbitration: arbitration under the ICSID Convention and arbitration under the UNCITRAL Arbitration Rules.

2.1.1. ICSID

Most IIAs provide for ICSID arbitration under the ICSID Arbitration Rules, [14] but many also give a choice of arbitral rules upon the claimant, for example, the ICSID Additional Facility Arbitration Rules, [15] or the UNCITRAL Arbitration Rules. Currently, the majority of cases are brought under the ICSID Convention. By now, 164 states are signatories to it.[16]

The admissible investment disputes under the ICSID Convention require a legal nature between a member state and a national of another contracting member.[17] In addition, a membership of the Convention does not necessarily mean an establishment of ICSID's jurisdiction over the disputes relevant to them.[18] The parties to an investment dispute shall submit their consent to jurisdiction to ICSID.

The ICSID Convention provides a self-contained ISDS arbitration system. Article 53 (1) of the Convention provides that the award 'shall not be subject to any appeal or to any other remedy'.[19] The sole process by which the

---

[14] ICSID Rules of Procedure for Arbitration Proceedings (April 2006) (ICSID Arbitration Rules).

[15] ICSID Arbitration (Additional Facility) Rules (April 2006) (ICSID AF Arbitration Rules).

[16] DATABASE OF ICSID MEMBER STATES, https://icsid.worldbank.org/about/member-states/database-of-member-states (Last visited on 18 July, 2022).

[17] ICSID Convention, Art. 25 (1).

[18] *Ibid.*, Preamble, para. 7 indicates that 'Declaring that no Contracting State shall by the mere fact of its ratification, acceptance or approval of this Convention and without its consent be deemed to be under any obligation to submit any particular dispute to conciliation or arbitration …'

[19] *Ibid.*, Art. 53 (1).

effectiveness of an ICSID award could be reviewed is through the provision for annulment.[20] In other words, only in rare circumstances, [21] arbitral awards rendered by ICSID tribunals might be reviewed. In principle, an ICSID award is final and binding to the parties.

Another important feature of ICSID awards is the enforcement regime. Members of the Convention are required to recognise and enforce monetary awards 'as if it were a final judgment of a court in that State.' [22] Enforcement of an ICSID award is automatic, which means it is not subject to an additional recognition procedure in the territory of the member states. Although Article 55 of the ICSID Convention preserves the law on State immunity, [23] leaving the issue to domestic courts and causing challenges to ICSID awards, this is a general issue beyond the enforcement of ICSID awards, and the compliance has prevailed since the ICSID Convention entered into force.[24]

A distinction needs to be made between the arbitration under the ICSID Additional Facility and under the ICSID Convention. The former is governed by the ICSID AF Arbitration Rules rather than the ICSID Convention. The ICSID AF Rules mainly involves the cases where either of the parties to an investment dispute is not a contracting member to the Convention. It follows that the self-contained nature of the ICSID regime is not applicable to the arbitration under the Additional Facility. The recognition and enforcement of its awards is governed by the Convention on the Recognition and Enforcement of Foreign Arbitral Award of

---

[20] *Ibid.*, Art. 52（1）provides that either party may request annulment of an award if:（1）the tribunal was not properly constituted;（2）the tribunal manifestly exceeded its powers;（3）the proceedings were tainted by arbitrator corruption;（4）the tribunal departed from a fundamental rule of procedure; or（5）if the award failed to state the reasons upon which it was based.

[21] *Ibid.* The rare conditions are provided in the Convention in Arts. 49-52.

[22] *Ibid.*, Art. 54（1）

[23] *Ibid.*, Art. 55 'Nothing in Article 54 shall be construed as derogating from the law in force in any Contracting State relating to immunity of that State or of any foreign State from execution.'

[24] I. Uchkunova, O. Temnikov, O, "Enforcement of Awards Under the ICSID Convention—What Solutions to the Problem of State Immunity?", 29（1）ICSID Review, 200（2014）.

1958 (the New York Convention).

2.1.2. The UNCITRAL Arbitration Rules

Despite the fact that ICSID has become the main venue for resolving investment disputes, BITs usually provide other choices of arbitration outside ICSID, including ad hoc arbitration and arbitration supported by other private arbitration institutions such as the Arbitration Institute of the Stockholm Chamber of Commerce (SCC).[25] In practice, arbitrations outside the ICSID forum may take place under the UNCITRAL Arbitration Rules, or the ICC Arbitration Rules[26] or under the LCIA Arbitration Rules, [27] etc. All procedures have some rules in common like the parties' control of the composition of the tribunal.

Thereinto, the UNCITRAL Arbitration Rules are the most widely used and are considered as 'a modern, universally established set of international arbitration rules.' [28] They provide the parties with great discretion to design an administrative structure of a case. The UNCITRAL Rules could set up an ad hoc tribunal at any location as long as the parties agree. Also, an arbitration institution may apply the UNCITRAL Rules for specific cases. For treaty-based investment arbitration, the arbitration conducted under the UNCITRAL Rules may additionally subject to the UNCITRAL Rules on Transparency in Treaty-based Investor-State Arbitration (UNCITRAL Rules on Transparency).[29]

It is worth noting that national law works differently and has different impact on the control of awards in the arbitration initiated under the ICSID Convention and under the UNCITRAL Rules. As noted above, the ICSID

---

[25] UNCTAD, 'Investor-State Dispute Settlement: Review of Developments in 2017', IIA Issues Note, 2 (2018).

[26] Rules of Arbitration of the International Chamber of Commerce (ICC Arbitration Rules), revised in 2021.

[27] Arbitration Rules of the London Court of International Arbitration (LCIA Arbitration Rules), revised in 2020.

[28] R. Dolzer, C. Schreuer, *Principles of International Investment Law*, Oxford: Oxford University Press, 2012, p.243.

[29] UNCITRAL Arbitration Rules, Art. 1 (4); Rules on Transparency, Art. 1.

Convention provides a self-contained ISDS arbitration system governed by public international law and give the ICSID awards an automatic recognition and enforcement. Conversely, the validity of an arbitral award made according to the UNCITRAL Rules is subject to lex arbitri, [30] normally being governed by the arbitration law of the seat of arbitration. UNCITRAL has developed a proposal for national arbitration legislation called the UNCITRAL Model Law on International Commercial Arbitration[31] to facilitate international arbitration.[32] Moreover, the annulment, recognition and enforcement of the awards rendered under UNCITRAL Rules fundamentally differ from ICSID awards, which are subject to a national law and the New York Convention.

2.2. Reasons for an appellate mechanism

2.2.1. 'Consistency, coherence, predictability, and correctness' [33]

While the concerns raised about investor-State arbitration are manifold, the most salient are those contradictory decisions of ISDS tribunals that have undermined the legitimacy of the present regime.[34] For instance, in CMS v. Argentina, [35] Sempra v. Argentina[36] and Enron v. Argentina, [37] the arbitral tribunals rejected the argument of necessity raised by the State, whereas in

---

[30] UNCITRAL Arbitration Rules, Art. 1 (3) provides that: 'These Rules shall govern the arbitration except that where any of these Rules is in conflict with a provision of the law applicable to the arbitration from which the parties cannot derogate, that provision shall prevail.'

[31] UNCITRAL Model Law on International Commercial Arbitration 1985 (With amendments as adopted in 2006).

[32] See R. Dolzer, C. Schreuer (2012), *supra* note 29.

[33] UN Doc A/CN.9/WG.III/WP.149, *supra* note 4.

[34] N.J. Calamita, "The (In) Compatibility of Appellate Mechanisms with Existing Instruments of the Investment Treaty Regime", 18 (4) *The Journal of World Investment and Trade*, 586 (2017).

[35] *CMS Gas Transmission Co.* v. *The Argentina Republic*, Annulment Proceedings, ICSID Case No. ARB/01/8, Award, May 12, 2005.

[36] *Sempra Energy International* v. *The Argentina Republic*, ICSID Case No. ARB/02/1628, Award, Sept. 28, 2007.

[37] *Enron Corporation and Ponderosa Assets*, *L.P.* v. *The Argentine Republic*, ICSID Case No. ARB/01/3, Award, May. 22, 2007.

LG&E v. Argentina[38] and Continental Casualty v. Argentina, [39] the tribunal admitted this same defence argument. The inconsistency between the awards was due to differing interpretations of the concept of state of necessity under a bilateral investment treaty and under international customary law. So it is not surprising that there are some comments like the current ISDS regime addresses 'the integrity and fairness of the process' rather than the consistency, coherence or correctness of the outcomes.[40]

There is a general sense among some views that an AM could bring consistency to awards and thereby improve coherence and predictability, finally strengthening the legitimacy of ICSID. However, this general agreement remains being questioned. The opposite opinion argues that the current ISDS system is constructed of a number of inconsistent BITs that it is likely for similar provisions to be interpreted differently.[41] Therefore, in such circumstance, introducing an AM would not achieve the objective of enhancing the consistency and coherence of international investment law.[42] Similarly, it is said that consistency and coherence are not objectives in themselves to take the AM reform option as the underlying investment treaty regime itself is not uniform.[43]

However, the establishment of an AM is not necessarily premised on a uniform substantive law. It seems that an AM could be an important way to promote the formation of a coherent investment law. Primarily, in terms of the

---

[38] *LG&E Energy Corp.* v. *The Argentine Republic*, ICSID Case No. ARB/02/1, Decision on Liability, Oct. 3, 2006.

[39] *Continental Casualty Company* v. *The Argentine Republic*, ICSID Case No. ARB/03/9, Award, Sept. 5, 2008.

[40] UN Doc A/CN.9/WG.III/WP.149, *supra* note 4, para. 10.

[41] See generally Legum, Options to Establish an Appellate Mechanism for Investment Disputes, in K.P, Ssuvant, et al, *Appeals Mechanism in International Investment Disputes*, New York: Oxford University Press, 2008, p.231.

[42] *Ibid.*

[43] UNGA 'Possible Reform of investor-State dispute settlement (ISDS): Consistency and related matters' (2018) UN Doc A/CN.9/WG.III/WP.150, para. 8.

issue of inconsistency, it is mainly due to the different positions of the arbitral tribunal on the same issue.[44] If an AM could establish principles on the position of these fundamental issues, it would be helpful to improve the consistency of international investment law. Besides, in some inconsistent awards, the explanation of some tribunals may be more reasonable than the analysis of others on the same issue. However, there are no criteria for assessing this kind of differences without a centralised AM. In this regard, a standing AM seems to contribute more to the consistency and coherence of the ISDS system.

Furthermore, an AM could promote the correctness of arbitral awards. When the first-tier tribunal is aware that its award may be subject to appeal, the rationale for its decision would be more fully developed, hoping its findings could be upheld by the appellate tribunal. While an AM implies more scrutiny of arbitration awards, the investment arbitration mechanism would be more coherent if more correct and consistent appeal awards could be rendered. In order to meet this purpose, a similar suggestion is made that a standing character of an AM is more helpful than an ad hoc nature.

Besides, increasing the neutrality and independence of the appellate tribunal will also contribute to achieving more correct and consistent awards, therefore strengthening the predictability of awards in investment arbitration. From the perspective of procedural law, the objective of consistency, coherence, predictability, and correctness in awards must be achieved by the arbitrators who explain and apply investment law and render awards. It seems that appointing standing arbitrators would minimise the neutrality issue of arbitrators due to conflicts of interest.

In conclusion, an AM is more than a second opportunity to substantive review of a certain investment dispute. To some degree, it would facilitate the application of international investment law by rendering more consistent and

---

[44] See generally A. Joubrin-Bret, The Growing Diversity and Inconsistency in the IIA System, in K.P. Ssuvant, et al, *Appeals Mechanism in International Investment Disputes*, New York: Oxford University Press, 2008, p.137; Examples can be seen from *supra* notes 36-40.

correct awards, depending on the appeal rules. On the one hand, the appellate tribunal's authoritative interpretation of legal issues would provide references to disputing parties and arbitrators, as well as contribute to the correctness and consistency in current ISDS system. On another hand, the neutrality and independence of arbitrators in the appellate tribunal is likely to be increased to make more correct and coherent awards. Meanwhile, the creation of an AM implies a limitation on the discretion of arbitrators when interpreting legal rules and principles.[45]

2.2.2. Other reasons

Furthermore, despite the broad criticism, arbitration is still the most prevailing way to resolve international investment disputes currently. An important reason is the finality authority of the arbitral awards. It can be argued that in present finality has taken pride of place over the principle of correctness.[46] However, the alleged efficiency and economy attached to the finality character of arbitration currently is not evident. One of the criticisms on investment arbitration is timing and costs. In fact, the efficiency and economy of arbitration is not merely depending on the finality authority. The objectives can also be achieved by streamlining the arbitral process, limiting the duration of arbitration and reducing the costs, which is conceivable when design an AM.

The original and main purpose of an investor choosing international investment arbitration and excluding local remedies is to avoid litigation in the respondent state so that a fairness award could be expected. Therefore, the correctness of awards is also significant in ISDS. Most importantly, investment arbitration has a special character distinct from commercial arbitration that public law values cannot be ignored. Might for this reason, compared to commercial arbitration, the demand for correctness and predictability of awards in ISDS is

---

[45] S.W. Schill, 28 The Sixth Path: Reforming Investment Law from Within, in J.E. Kalicki, A. Joubin-Bret, *Reshaping the Investor-State Dispute Settlement System*, Leiden: BRILL, 2015, Vol. 4, p.621.

[46] C.H. Schreuer, et al, *The ICSID Convention: A commentary*, Cambridge: Cambridge University Press, 2009, p.903.

more stronger. It follows that the finality principle of arbitration could be broken down appropriately in the condition that the fairness and correctness of awards is at risk. And the efficiency and economy issue might be compensated by the approaches discussed above.

In addition, an AM proposal can accompany any other option as one part of a package of reforms that address the concerns other than predictability and correctness.[47] For instance, the criticisms of the constitution of tribunals, conflicts of interest for counsel and arbitrators and the lack of clarity regarding standards on independence and impartiality, etc. Besides, either a standing or ad hoc appeals body could preserve the structure of the existing investment arbitration mechanism. Such an incremental reform option can be relatively well adapted to existing investment arbitration regime.

Overall, in a Note of 28 August 2018, the UNCITRAL Secretariat analysed the concerns raised in ISDS,[48] and in April 2009, Working Group III agreed that those key concerns about ISDS, including the issue discussed in above section, were well-founded and serious enough to justify systemic reforms.[49] On this account, it demonstrates that an attempt to establish an AM is necessary.

2.3. Main elements in the setting-up of an appellate mechanism

2.3.1. The nature of the appellate mechanism

When considering the establishment of an AM, one threshold question is what the nature of the AM should be: ad hoc or permanent, bilateral or multilateral? Different nature will affect the design and content of the AM. There are some options for the establishment of the AM. Generally, those potential options could be broadly divided into two groups: a model appellate mechanism

---

[47] See E. Sardinha, "The Impetus for the Creation of an Appellate Mechanism", 32 (3) *ICSID Review*, 504 (2017).

[48] UN Doc A/CN.9/WG.III/WP.150, *supra* note 44; The note gave an 'illustrative list' of examples of divergent interpretations of substantive standards of protection, divergent interpretations with respect to jurisdiction and admissibility, and inconsistencies in procedural matters.

[49] UNCITRAL 'Report of Working Group III (Investor-State Dispute Settlement Reform) on the Work of Its Thirty-Seventh Session' (2019) UN Doc A/CN.9/970.

and permanent multilateral appellate body.

2.3.1.1. A model appellate mechanism

A model AM could be developed for either treaty parties, disputing parties or ISDS institutions. All of these parties and institutions could include the model in their treaties, agreements or arbitration rules. However, the AM in this case would function in a decentralized manner as the current ISDS regime. First of all, the AM could be developed simply in the form of ad hoc appellate tribunals case by case. Such appellate bodies are supposed to be constituted by parties in the context of particular disputes, following a similar way that the original arbitral tribunals were established. This kind of the purely ad hoc appeal body is mainly designed for non-treaty specific based disputes. It is conceivable that it may ensure the correctness of arbitral decisions but indeed have limited impact on the improvement of consistency and predictability.

The second form of the potential AM is the treaty-specific AM.[50] This is the appellate body in a BIT or a multilateral agreement, expressly indicating the parties' intent to establish an AM in the future. Certain investment treaties have envisaged the possibility of establishing such an appeal body. Article 28 (10) of the 2004 US Model BIT, as mentioned above, is an example of such treaty language.[51] The treaty-specific model could be either on a multilateral or bilateral basis.

Another form is to be set up as an option available under the rules of institutions handling ISDS cases, mainly under the ICSID Convention and Rules.[52] However, the precondition of such an option is that the relevant institutions would permit an appellate mechanism.

2.3.1.2. Permanent multilateral appellate body

Considering the comprehensive objectives of consistency, correctness and

---

[50] UNGA 'Possible reform of investor-State dispute settlement (ISDS): Appellate and multilateral court mechanisms' (2019) UN Doc A/CN.9/WG.III/WP.185, para. 41.

[51] *Supra* note 10.

[52] UN Doc A/CN.9/WG.III/WP.185, *supra* note 50, para. 44.

predictability, establishing a permanent multilateral appellate body has been mostly proposed, which could either complement the existing arbitration regime or constitute the second tier in a standing court.[53] It is argued that regulating an AM by formulating multilateral rules might be more efficient than doing so through bilateral investment agreements.[54]

The first choice is to establish a standalone appellate body as a complement to the current ISDS regime. Technically, it would help the current regime improve the correctness of arbitral awards, strengthen legal expectations for investment dispute settlement and establish limitations for the conduct of arbitrators.[55]

A permanent multilateral appellate body could also be designed as an integral part of a multilateral investment court. In this context, the second-tier appeals body would be constituted by professional judges and supported by a permanent secretariat. Such an option should be considered together with the multilateral investment court proposal in which arbitration might not be the preferred method to settle investment disputes and the first-tier tribunal would be replaced by the court.[56] So this option might be only amendable to new IIAs.[57]

2.3.1.3. Suggested nature of the appellate mechanism

Evidently, all the options raise complex questions regarding their compatibility with the existing ISDS system. The development of an AM would in any case require close coordination with the existing ISDS system. It follows that an AM needs to be designed to avoid unnecessary procedural and substantive confusion.

Generally speaking, in spite of the model AM available under the framework of a specific arbitration institution, a model AM in the form of ad hoc appellate tribunals or treaty-specific mechanisms is likely to be ad hoc and to present a

---

[53] *Ibid.*, para. 45.

[54] UN Doc A/CN.9/WG.III/WP.177, *supra* note 7, p.4.

[55] See Chapter 2.2.1.

[56] A.J. Van den Berg, "Appeal Mechanism for ISDS Awards: Interaction with the New York and ICSID Conventions" 34 (1) *ICSID Review*, 188 (2019).

[57] *Ibid.*

bilateral character. In the later two circumstances, multiple AMs would appear, which could actually further fragment the current ISDS regime. It can be seen from these potential types of a model AM that this proposal in general adheres to the present fragmented ISDS practice. As a result, it is less possible to improve the consistency and predictability of arbitral awards as a whole.

As concluded in Chapter 2.2.1, a well-designed AM would somewhat contribute to the consistency, coherence, predictability, and correctness in arbitral awards and to some degree foster the development of international investment. As commented that the appellate arbitral is not simply a body to bring proceedings on the same facts again.[58] Besides, the inconsistency and incoherence of awards within the ISDS mechanism is due to the fact that an ad hoc tribunal itself is not conceived to serve those purposes. Such objectives were not achieved by ad hoc tribunals before and is unlikely to be achieved in the future. Therefore, a standing nature would be more consistent with the motivation for establishing an AM.[59]

It seems that a multilateral AM is more suitable for a standing AM though it is not always the case. In other words, a standing appellate body may be conceived in a BIT and a bilateral one might be developed in a multilateral instrument. However, an AM on a bilateral basis only resolves investment disputes between the parties and may not really contribute to the improvement of application of investment law. And it would result multiple AMs as discussed above. Considering a standing AM would be a better option, establishing an AM under the multilateral agreement would be more suitable. In fact, some have pointed that any reform attempt would not be successful if the proposal does not 'achieve a critical mass to be multilaterally implemented.'[60] So it is better to

---

[58] J. Lee, 20 Introduction of an Appellate Review Mechanism for International Investment Disputes: Expected Benefits and Remaining Tasks, in J.E. Kalicki, A. Joubin-Bret, *Reshaping the Investor-State Dispute Settlement System*, Leiden: BRILL, 2015, Vol. 4, p.474.

[59] More reasons for a standing AM have been discussed in Chapter 2.2.1.

[60] M.L. Jaime, Chapter 7: Reshaping Investor-State Dispute Settlement Through an Appellate Review Mechanism, in A.M. Anderson, B. Beaumont, *The Investor-State Dispute Settlement System: Reform, Replace or Status Quo?*, Wolters Kluwer Law International, 2020, p.137.

start with a multilateral framework.

From the foregoing, a standing AM could be established through a treaty or an understanding or memorandum in a multilateral framework. However, the acceptance of the AM could be determined later by the choice of bilateral or regional free trade agreements. This approach leaves room for states and helps to reach consensus for the establishment of an AM. That is, consent to the establishment of an AM does not in itself imply a necessary consent to the jurisdiction of the AM in each case, which in practice the appeal procedures need to be applied either by the confirmation in BITs or agreements between disputing parties.

2.3.2. The scope of appellate review

Many questions need to be carefully considered when deigning the rules for an AM. Despite divergent considerations in each form, some common elements are crucial to the functioning of an AM. Working Group III has discussed some draft provisions governing the appellate procedure.[61] Among other things, the grounds for appeal and the standard of review are at the heart of the AM proposal.

2.3.2.1. The grounds of appeal

What matters could be grounds for appeal is the primary question regarding the design of an AM. Seeing the appeal practice at international courts or tribunals as well as the national courts, the issue here remains about the errors of law and/or fact. Basically, errors of law refer to the errors in the interpretation and application of laws, and errors of fact are those errors in the finding of facts in a case. Should the review of errors in the interpretation and application of the law be limited to certain types? And an error as to finding of facts could also be a ground for appeal?

Some States suggest that appeals should be limited to errors in the application of the law so that the appellate procedure could be more efficient and faster.[62] However, observing the practice of WTO dispute settlement, it is not that simple. The WTO Appellate Body (AB) was criticised for exceed its power to review the

---

[61] UNGA 'Possible reform of investor-State dispute settlement (ISDS): Appellate mechanism and enforcement issues' (2020) UN Doc A/CN.9/WG.III/WP.202.

[62] UN Doc A/CN.9/WG.III/WP.175, *supra* note 6.

panel repower as Article 17 (6) of the Understanding on Rules and Procedures Governing the Settlement of Disputes (DSU) limits the scope of an appeal to 'issues of law' and 'legal interpretations', whereas the AB has made findings on issues of fact.[63] Indeed, the AB found that the issue of fact and the issue of law cannot be separated in many cases.

Such finding could be more evident in ISDS. That is because investment disputes require, first and foremost, the determination of a large number of complex factual issues. Some provisions in BITs also need to be examined in the context of facts. Besides, certain investment treaties provide that the errors of fact and some grounds for annulment under the ICSID Convention could be the grounds of the AM.[64] Even in the current ICSID annulment process, errors of fact sometimes occur, 'appearing as a claimed failure to state reasons or breach of procedural rules'.[65] Therefore, although limiting the grounds for appeal to legal issues may speed up the process of review and effectively control the number of appeal cases, it would be reasonable for the scope of appeals to include errors of fact. An AM that addresses both legal and factual errors could ensure a comprehensive review function to achieve its institutional value.

Regarding the annulment grounds, the suggestion[66] and treaty practice[67] that these grounds could be appealable have been reflected in the draft provisions of Working Group III. The working document of Working Group III has proposed

---

[63] OFFICE OF THE UNITED STATES TRADE REPRESENTATIVE, REPORT ON THE APPELLATE BODY OF THE WORLD TRADE ORGANIZATION (2020), EXECUTIVE SUMMARY https://ustr.gov/sites/default/files/Report_on_the_Appellate_Body_of_the_World_Trade_Organization.pdf (Last visited on 18 July, 2022).

[64] For instance, the Canada-European Union Comprehensive Economic and Trade Agreement (CETA)(provisionally in force since 21 September 2017) Art. 8 (28).

[65] G. Bottini, 19 Reform of the Investor-State Arbitration Regime: The Appeal Proposal, In J.E. Kalicki, A. Joubin-Bret, *Reshaping the Investor-State Dispute Settlement System*, Leiden: BRILL, 2015, Vol. 4, p.461.

[66] ICSID 2004 Proposal, *supra* note 5.

[67] CETA, *supra* note 65.

that the grounds for annulment[68] and the grounds for refusing recognition and enforcement of an award[69] may all be included in the grounds of appeal.[70] This question should be discussed together with the relationship between the annulment and an AM. This thesis takes the view that the grounds of annulment could be covered by the scope of appeal. It will be examined in Chapter four below.

2.3.2.2. The standard of appellate review

The scope of the appellate review also raises the question is to what degree an error of law and/or fact could be review in the appeal procedure? As discussed, an inevitable disadvantage of extending the scope of appellate review to errors of fact is that it will take more time to complete the review. Furthermore, if a de novo review of all facts is conducted again during the appeal process, the appellate tribunal is more likely to reach conflicting conclusions. It is necessary thus to establish a stand of review to improve the efficiency of the appeal arbitration procedure.

A suggestion was made that the AM should only be able to review, in addition to legal questions, manifest errors in the finding of fact and a de novo review of facts is not necessary.[71] Such a position has been practiced in the EU investment treaties, for instance, Article 8（28）of CETA explicitly limits the review of facts to 'manifest errors' while 'errors in the application or interpretation of applicable law' are all permitted.[72]

As for the issue of law, however, the ICSID 2004 Proposal suggested that only 'a clear error of law' could be challenged.[73] Looking at the draft provisions, Working Group III provided two options regarding the error of law. Option 1 has limited words as 'material and prejudicial' while option 2 lists several essential concepts in investment arbitration like 'expropriation, fair and equitable treatment

---

[68] As set out in the ICSID Convention, Art. 52.

[69] As listed in the New York Convention, Art. V（1）.

[70] UN Doc A/CN.9/WG.III/WP.202, *supra* note 62, para. 59.

[71] UNGA 'Possible reform of investor–State dispute settlement（ISDS）: Submission from the European Union and its Member States'（2019）UN Doc A/CN.9/WG.III/WP.159/Add.1.

[72] CETA, Art. 8（28）.

[73] ICSID 2004 Proposal, *supra* note 5, Ann. para. 7.

and non-discrimination' without any wording limiting 'error'.[74] However, it is not difficult to see that this is only a formal difference. The application and interpretation of the listed legal standards is usually at the centre of an investment dispute and the result could be decisive for the final outcome of a case. That means an error of law on these issues is equal to a 'material and prejudicial' error.

Additionally, it is noted that the Working Group III distinguish '[E]rrors in the application or interpretation of law' (Article X 1.a) to '[A]n error in the application of the law to the facts' (Article X 1.c),[75] and there is no adjective modifying the degree of error in the latter. It seems that a discrepancy exists in the standard of review here. Nevertheless, the situation set out in Article X 1.c itself is manifest enough. Because establishing a correct connection between the facts of a case and the corresponding legal rules is the preliminary step before interpreting and applying the rules and is the most basic legal analysis. Assuming that rule of law A shall be applicable to the facts in a case, but it turns out that rule of law B shall be actually applied. There is no controversy here, but a manifest error. Therefore, in general a manifest or clear error of legal issues would be required to limit the scope of appellate review, whatever the formulation is like.

Errors of fact are more difficult to define than errors of law. Disputing parties may submit plenty of factual evidence to argue a slight error of fact for the purpose of an additional review of the case or for a delay of the game. Therefore, the ground of errors of fact should be strictly construed as the 'clearly' and 'manifest' used in draft provisions.[76] Not only for limiting the scope of appellate review but also for due respect to the findings of fact given by the original arbitral tribunal. But concerns may raise in practice of determining what kind of a factual error is a manifest one. Indeed, manifest shall be somehow serious.

It is noteworthy that as a response to the criticism of the expanding power of the AB to review appeals, two additional conditions were added to the scope

---

[74] UN Doc A/CN.9/WG.III/WP.202, *supra* note 62, draft provisions Article X 1.a.

[75] *Ibid.*, Article X 1.c.

[76] *Ibid.*, Article X 1.b.

of appellate review in the Multi-party Interim Appeal Arbitration Mechanism in WTO. The new standards are 'necessary for the resolution of the dispute' and 'raised by the parties'.[77] Such standards might be helpful to limit the scope of appellate review in the AM.

To conclude, an AM could both deal with errors of law and fact, but the scope of review should be limited to manifest legal errors and serious factual errors raised by parties, which would be necessary for the resolution of the dispute.

2.3.3. The effect of appeal

There is little doubt that the appellate tribunal may confirm, modify or reverse the decisions on appeal. The disputed issues are whether the appeal tribunal is able to annul the decisions of the original tribunal and whether it could refer the matter back to the first-tier tribunal.[78]

The issue of remand authority is complex and controversial. The answer to this question would significantly alter the structure of the potential AM. If the appellate tribunal is permitted to return the case to the original tribunal, is it possible for the disputing parties to appeal again after a remand? If there is no further appeal, then the original tribunal would make a final award. If further appeals are allowed, then the process will be repetitive and the overall duration of the proceedings will be greatly prolonged, along with the increased costs.

In the domestic litigation system, returning a case to the original court usually for two general purposes. The first is to improve the efficiency of facts-finding process. It is usually more efficient for the original court to re-undertake this obligation because the original court is more familiar with the dispute. So the grounds for remand normally include unclear or insufficient facts. Another purpose is to ensure the dispute not be deprived of any opportunity to be examined in due process. Thus, another common ground for remand is procedural errors in the first-tier review. Allowing the appellate court to send the case back is helpful

---

[77] WTO 'Statement on a mechanism for developing, documenting and sharing practices and procedures in the conduct of WTO disputes' (30 April 2020) JOB/DSB/1/Add.12, Ann. 1, para. 10.

[78] The first question will be discussed in Chapter four.

to maintain the justice and efficiency in litigation.

However, in the case of investment arbitration, even if the remand is implemented in a restrictive manner, the case may go through at least four rounds of review, from appeal to remand and back again, which would cause serious delays and eliminate the advantages of arbitration. This would somehow deviate from the purpose of establishing an AM. Therefore, considering the introduction of remand in an AM would bring the possibility of multiple tiers of review, it would be preferable not to accord an appellate tribunal the remand authority.

The appeal practice in WTO dispute settlement system offers a reference at an international level. Pursuant to Article 17 (13) of the DSU, the WTO's AB is accorded to 'uphold, modify or reverse the legal findings and conclusions of the panel'.[79] Clearly, the WTO appellate proceedings do not have a remand mechanism. And as noted above, the scope of appeal in WTO in theory shall limit to legal issues and exclude the factual matters. Thus, in the cases where the finding of facts is not sufficient or not correct, the AB cannot send the case back and on another side the AB might fail to analyse thoroughly to modify or reverse the original panel report in the absence of factual review.

The ICSID Secretariat mentioned the remand issue when an AM was first conceived. In its proposal, if a dispute remains unresolved in the appeal award, the appellate tribunal may send the case back to the first-tier tribunal or the disputing parties may be permitted to request for a new tribunal.[80] Generally, this proposal aimed to limit the grounds for remand so that avoid unnecessary applications. However, if remand is permitted in such cases, further controversy arises about the unresolvable disputes. If it is up to the appeal tribunal to decide whether a disputed is settled or not, the question in substance still relates to the review of factual issues. It is unlikely for a tribunal to state that a dispute with clear facts cannot be resolved under current legal rules and legal interpretation.

In conclusion, the intended purpose of remand as discussed before could be

---

[79] DSU, Art. 17 (13).

[80] ICSID 2004 Proposal, *supra* note 5, Ann. para. 9.

remedied by the extent of the scope of appeal to issues of fact. If issues of fact can be ascertained at the appeal stage, the primary function of the remand mechanism is no longer necessary. As clarified above, the review of facts should be limited to serious factual errors that necessary for the resolution of the dispute. By establishing a strictive standard for factual review, it is possible not only to replace the function of remand, but also to address its shortcomings at the same time. As for the function of correcting procedural errors in the remand mechanism, annulment proceedings might play the role, which will be discussed in Chapter four.

3. The incompatibility with current regimes

The issue of incompatibility of an AM with existing ISDS regime differs in different frameworks governing arbitrations. This chapter will identify the incompatibilities respectively under the ICSID Convention and the UNCITRAL Arbitration Rules and give corresponding suggestions.

3.1. Arbitration under the ICSID Convention

3.1.1. Appellate mechanism for ICSID in practice

The self-contained character of the ICSID regime establishes a closed system for the remedy of arbitral awards rendered under it. The closed system without any appeal finds explicit wording in Article 53 (1) of the ICSID Convention that the award 'shall be binding on the parties and shall not be subject to any appeal or to any other remedy except those provided for in this Convention'.[81] In the current ICSID system, possible remedies of awards are set out in Articles 49-52,[82] not including the appellate review. Besides, the exclusivity rule contained in Article 26 ICSID Convention also indicates the impossibility of any appeal.[83] It is certainly clear that

---

[81] The ICSID Convention, Art. 53 (1).

[82] The remedies include rectification (Art. 49), interpretation (Art. 50), revision (Art. 51) and annulment (Art. 52).

[83] The ICSID Convention, Art. 26: 'Consent of the parties to arbitration under this Convention shall, unless otherwise stated, be deemed consent to such arbitration to the exclusion of any other remedy'. However, it is noted that Article 53 (1) does not include the wording 'unless otherwise stated', therefore ICSID members cannot agree on an AM on the basis of Article 26; See C.H. Schreuer, et al (2009), *supra* note 47, p.1103.

an AM is incompatible with the current text of the ICSID Convention.

The Convention, on the other hands, is open to revision. Article 66 of the Convention provides one way for establishing an AM in the ICSID regime: an amendment of Article 53. A fact is that, as so far, no contracting party has submitted a request for amending the Convention. Any amendment of the ICSID Convention would be extremely difficult because Article 66 (1) requires the amendment proposal be approved by all 164 member states. Obtaining the consent of all parties is almost impossible. And even if all states parties agree to amend the Convention, the amendment may be challenged as being contrary to the purposes of the Convention.

3.1.2. Suggested approach: an inter se modification of the ICSID Convention

Another possible way to integrate an AM into the ICSID regime is that contracting parties agree to a modification inter se.[84] Relevant rules are regulated in Article 41 of the Vienna Convention on the Law of Treaties (VCLT).[85] The rules has been considered as customary international law[86] that might be applicable to the ICSID Convention. By this way of a separate plurilateral protocol, willing states can establish a special regime for an AM applicable

---

[84] C.H. Schreuer, et al (2009), *ibid.*, p.1105.

[85] 1969 Vienna Convention on the Law of Treaties, 1155 UNTS 331 (concluded 23 May 1969, entered into force 27 January 1980) Art.41:

'1. Two or more of the parties to a multilateral treaty may conclude an agreement to modify the treaty as between themselves alone if:

(a) the possibility of such a modification is provided for by the treaty; or

(b) the modification in question is not prohibited by the treaty and:

(i) does not affect the enjoyment by the other parties of their rights under the treaty or the performance of their obligations;

(ii) does not relate to a provision, derogation from which is incompatible with the effective execution of the object and purpose of the treaty as a whole.

2. Unless in a case falling under paragraph 1 (a) the treaty otherwise provides, the parties in question shall notify the other parties of their intention to conclude the agreement and of the modification to the treaty for which it provides.'

[86] N.J. Calamita (2017), *supra* note 35, p.607.

between themselves. The question arises that whether inter se modification is possible for Article 53 (1) ICSID Convention.

Noting that the modification of Article 53 (1) is not prohibited by the ICSID Convention thus the examination of Article 41 (b) of VCLT is the focus of the discussion. The subparagraphs of Article 41 (b) require the modification (1) does not prejudice the rights and obligations of other members under the ICSID Convention; and (2) is compatible with the object and purpose of the ICSID Convention.[87]

The travaux preparatoires of the ICSID Convention make it clear that the reason why Article 66 of the Convention requires the unanimous consent of all states parties is to avoid a situation in which states parties that do not consent to an amendment are forced to accept it.[88] If the Convention is amended only between certain parties, it does not in fact lead to an addition to the obligations or a reduction in the rights of other parties that are not parties to the amendment. Nor would it result in a forced acceptance of the amendment by those states which have not agreed to it. Therefore, in accordance with the treaty interpretation rules set out in Articles 30 and 31 of VCLT, the ICSID Convention should allow for an inter se modification.

Furthermore, the objective and purpose of the Convention, provided in Preamble and Article 1 (2) is to facilitate conciliation and arbitration in investment disputes. The introduction of an AM would better preserve the parties' expectations of procedural and substantive fairness and achieve a balance between private and public interests. Not only will this not undermine the objective of the Convention, but it may also actually help to improve the legitimacy of ISDS.

In fact, the consideration of such an approach originated with the proposal of the ICSID Secretariat. It was argued that an inter se modification by member states who

---

[87] VCLT, Art. 41 (b), *supra* note 86.

[88] Documents Concerning the Origin and Formulation of the Convention on the Settlement of Investment Disputes between States and Nationals of Other States, 1968 Vol. 2 (Reprinted in 2006), pp. 905–910, 940, 994–996.

are willing to accept the proposed AM might be an approach.[89] Although the ICSID Secretariat did not give any opinion on whether the conditions of Article 41 of VCLT would be satisfied in the ICSID context, an affirmative answer to the possibility of this approach has been concluded from the foregoing analysis. Gabrielle Kaufmann-Kohler and Michele Potesta also in their report stated that inter se agreements between states parties meet the conditions set out in Article 41 of VCLT. Other states parties that do not agree to join the inter se agreement are not bound by the AM under Article 54 of the Convention. They are in a situation similar to the relationship between non-ICISD states parties and ICSID awards.[90]

In conclusion, an inter se modification of the ICSID Convention is legally permissible pursuant to Article 41 of VCLT and it might be the most possible way to introduce an AM in the ICSID regime. ICSID is a multilateral forum that may be an example or even a model to establish a multilateral AM. The possibility of introducing a multilateral AM to the ICSID Convention and other treaties will be discussed at the end of this chapter.

3.2. Arbitration under the UNCITRAL Arbitration Rules

3.2.1. Appellate mechanism for UNCITRAL Rules in practice

Article 34 (2) of the UNCITRAL Arbitration Rules provides that all awards 'shall be final and binding on the parties. The parties shall carry out all awards without delay'.[91] Unlike the ICSID Convention, the parties to a dispute initiated under the UNCITRAL Arbitration Rules are able to modify the rules by mutual agreement,[92] which means the disputing parties who are open to an AM can modify the finality rule of awards. The biggest obstacle presented in ICSID

---

[89] ICSID 2004 Proposal, *supra* note 5, Ann. para. 2; The proposed AM is a single Appeals Facility, see *supra* note 11.

[90] G.Kaufmann-Kohler and M.Potestà, "Can the Mauritius Convention Serve as a Model for the Reform of Investor- State Arbitration in connection with the Introduction of a Permanent Investment Tribunal or an Appeal Mechanism?", *Geneva Centre for International Dispute Settlement* (*CIDS*), 3 June 2016, para 200.

[91] UNCITRAL Arbitration Rules, Art. 34 (2).

[92] *Ibid.*, Art. 1 (1): '……such disputes shall be settled in accordance with these Rules subject to such modification as the parties may agree.'

cases, finality of arbitral awards, is not the main problem here.

However, Article 1（3）of the UNCITRAL Rules indicates that an arbitration that takes place under the Rules is subject to a national law applicable to it.[93] The question arises here that an appeal of an arbitral award may be in conflict with the provisions of the national arbitration law at the place of arbitration.

Arbitral appeal is not prohibited in some countries like the UK. Section 58 of the UK Arbitration Act stipulates that an arbitral award is final 'unless otherwise agreed by the parties.'[94] Netherlands is another example where arbitral appeal is not prohibited. Articles 1061a to 1061l of Netherlands Arbitration Act set out the appeal rules in detail.[95] In those countries where appeal is permissible in arbitration law, the national courts will certainly play an important role in the future AM especially regarding the control of the arbitration. In this context, the decision made by an appellate tribunal would, the same as a first-tier award, be governed by setting aside provisions in the national law as well as the enforcement rules in the New York Convention in third countries.

However, an AM for arbitral awards would be fundamentally incompatible with a national law in the country where arbitral appeal is not allowed. One example is China Arbitration Act. Article 9 of the Chinese Arbitration Law confirms the finality of arbitration in the first sentence and then further clarifies that any arbitration institution or national courts shall not admit any dispute that has been arbitrated.[96] So arbitral awards governed by such rules are impossible

---

[93] UNCITRAL Arbitration Rules, Art. 1（3）.

[94] UK ARBITRATION ART, SECTION 58, https://www.legislation.gov.uk/ukpga/1996/23/section/58（Last visited on 18 July, 2022）.

[95] NETHERLANDS ARBITRATION ACT, THE ENGLISH TRANSLATION VERSION IS AVAILABLE AT https://www.nai-nl.org/downloads/Book%204%20Dutch%20CCPv2.pdf（Last visited on 18 July, 2022）.

[96] CHINA ARBITRATION ACT, ART.9, THE ENGLISH TRANSLATION VERSION IS AVAILABLE AT https://wenku.baidu.com/view/3176e324b91aa8114431b90d6c85ec3a87c28b9d.html（Last visited on 18 July, 2022）.

subject to appeal from the outset. This incompatibility cannot be resolved unless a revision of national law.

3.2.2. Suggested approach

In such case, there are two ways to integrate an AM into investment arbitration. The simple one is to avoid the potential conflict by the choice of parties. If the parties wish to reserve their rights to appeal, they are well advised to expressly choose an appropriate seat of arbitration where arbitral appeal is permissible.

The second approach is for the country to revise its arbitration law. However, this approach makes little sense if only a few countries are willing to amend their domestic laws. But predictably, it is unlikely that most countries will agree to revise national arbitration law in a limited period of time for the purpose of being compatible with the AM. Therefore, it is not an ideal choice for those countries that are willing to establish an AM in ISDS. They may tend to look for other possible options instead of amending their national law. A much simpler approach has been given before. Besides, it seems that for the willing countries, working together to establish a multilateral AM excluding the application of national law might be a more effective way than mass revision of their domestic rules to address the mentioned incompatibility. This approach will be further discussed as below.

3.3. The applicability of a multilateral appellate mechanism to existing IIAs

3.3.1. The feasibility of an opt-in convention

As suggested before, a standing nature would be more consistent with the motivation for establishing an AM and a multilateral one is better suited to a standing AM.[97] In the CIDS report, a 'Mauritius-like' approach was introduced to create an AM in the current fragmented ISDS regime.[98] The main idea of this

---

[97] See Chapter 2.3.1.
[98] See generally, G.Kaufmann-Kohler and M.Potestà (2016), *supra* note 91, Section VII.

proposal is that the Mauritius Convention on Transparency[99] can be a model for a potential AM.[100]

The model is on a multilateral basis, but it could enable itself integrated into bilateral treaties. Article 2 of the Mauritius Convention includes both 'bilateral or multilateral application' and 'unilateral offer of application'.[101] The two types of its application aim to provide a flexible way for IIAs in force prior to the effective date of the UNCITRAL Rules on Transparency.[102] As so far, 23 countries have signed or ratified the Convention.[103] However, the UNCITRAL Rules on Transparency is not only applicable to the parties to the Convention. Other countries could make separate consent that their existing investment treaties would be governed by the UNCITRAL Rules on Transparency.

Furthermore, under the Mauritius Convention, the UNCITRAL Rules on Transparency could be applied in any type of investment arbitration and are not limited to arbitrations conducted under the UNCITRAL Arbitration Rules.[104] In addition, parties to the Mauritius Convention are able to make three reservations in respect of their acceptance of the Convention.[105]

The Mauritius Convention has become effective with a lower threshold

---

[99] United Nations Convention on Transparency in Treaty-based Investor-State Arbitration (adopted on 10 December 2014, entered into force on 18 October 2017)(Mauritius Convention).

[100] The report also mentioned that the model of the Mauritius Convention could also be used to create an international tribunal for investments. See G.Kaufmann-Kohler and M.Potestà (2016), *supra* note 91.

[101] The Mauritius Convention, Art. 2: 'Bilateral or multilateral application' refers to the situation where the respondent state and the investor's State under a particular IIA are both parties to the Mauritius Convention, and 'unilateral offer of application' refers to the situation where only the respondent State (and not the State of the investor-claimant) is a party to the Convention.

[102] The UNCITRAL Rules on Transparency entered into force on 1 April 2014.

[103] https://treaties.un.org/Pages/showDetails.aspx?objid=080000028040a108&clang=_en (Last visited on 18 July, 2022).

[104] *Ibid.*, Art. 2: '... whether or not initiated under the UNCITRAL Arbitration Rules ...'; See N.J. Calamita, E. Zelazna, "The Changing Landscape of Transparency in Investor-State Arbitration: The UNCITRAL Transparency Rules and Mauritius Convention", *Austrian YB Intl Arb* 271 (2016).

[105] *Ibid.*, Art. 3 (1).

for entry into force. Although not many states have committed themselves to the Convention, it did come into force, breaking with the previous practice of requiring the support of multiple countries. It can be considered as a valuable example of a multilateral path to revise bilateral agreements. In brief, 'the multilateral instrument and the IIAs will co-exist' in this context.[106] That is to say, the existing IIAs could be supplemented by an opt-in convention with respect to an AM. All states are welcome to join the convention or use the rules providing for appeal in specific cases at any time. The consensual nature of applying an AM would be well maintained because of the flexibility of the opt-in convention. The multilateral convention would either provide the rules for arbitral appeal itself, or like the Mauritius Convention, refer to arbitration rules that are otherwise created or already exist.

In that instance, the appellate rules may be applicable to all investment arbitral awards, irrespective of the type of the first-tier arbitration. This character was early proposed in the ICSID 2004 Proposal that the creation of an ICSID Appeals Facility could apply to ICSID and non-ICSID awards.[107] The question arises that whether it is necessary to maintain the discrepancy between ICSID system and non-ICSID system in appeal, which has already existed in now ISDS regime. Or it that possible to adopt a single track for all types of first-tier arbitral awards? To put it another way, the question is in essence about a choice between the applicable law governing the appeal proceedings: retaining a margin of application of domestic law or excluding national law but only applying international law.[108]

The opt-in convention containing the appellate rules or any other instruments establishing a new appellate body should make this question clear otherwise the

---

[106] See G.Kaufmann-Kohler and M.Potestà (2016), *supra* note 91.

[107] ICSID 2004 Proposal, *supra* note 5, Ann. para. 3.

[108] See G.Kaufmann-Kohler, M.Potestà, *Investor-State Dispute Settlement and National Courts Current Framework and Reform Options*, Cham: Springer International Publishing AG, 2020, p.91; Also see G.Kaufmann-Kohler and M.Potestà (2016), *supra* note 91, paras. 193-195.

AM would be complicated and full of uncertainties. For instance, at the first-instance level, an arbitration may be governed by a national law of the place of arbitration while a treaty law is entirely applicable at the appeal stage. It is important to note that, unlike the Mauritius Convention, an AM, as a stage of dispute resolution, faces a more complex balance of interests and design of structure. Undoubtedly, drafting the opt-in convention for an AM is a tricky task.

3.3.2. Suggested framework for an appellate mechanism

In conclusion, it is not easy but possible for states to establish a multilateral AM as a supplement to the current ISDS system. On the basis of the opt-in convention, as proposed in Chapter 2.3.1 that the multilateral framework is only used to obtain the consent of states to establish an AM while the acceptance of AM could be determined in the specific case. Of course, it depends on the parties' willingness if such a statement or reservation is necessary. Such flexibilies are reflected not only in the manner of application, but also in greater freedom in the timing of the acceptance of the appeal mechanism. The parties may reach an agreement to accept the jurisdiction of the AM at several stages, either before, during or after the first-level arbitration proceedings. In short, this approach shows great respect to the consensual nature of an AM.

Furthermore, the ICSID seems to be an idea platform to introduce such an AM. Primarily, an inter se modification of the ICSID Convention is in theory permissible. The modification may be in the form of a 'Mauritius-like' approach. Furthermore, the ICSID is professional in investment arbitration, and it might be better to select a mature forum to develop an AM than creating a new one full of uncertainties. Most importantly, an AM established under the framework of the ICSID Convention is likely to adopt an Article 54- type enforcement regime, which means appeal awards would exempt from the judicial review by national courts. Besides, in this scenario, the incompatibility of an AM with finality rules of national law in UNCITRAL cases, which presented in Chapter 3.2.2, would be solved at the same time.

4. Challenge and enforcement of an appellate award

What kind of law, international law alone or also national law, would be governing the new AM is particularly important for the annulment and enforcement of appeal awards. This is because that the arbitral awards rendered under the ICSID Convention are excluded from the judicial review by domestic courts, whereas arbitrations under the UNCITRAL Arbitration Rules are subject to a potential challenge in the country of origin and to an enforcement under the New York Convention in other states.

The following sections will examine the issues of annulment and enforcement of an appellate award respectively under the ICSID Convention and the UNCITRAL Rules. And it needs to be mentioned that the below discussion is based on the conclusion that Article 41 of VCLT and the ICSID Convention in theory permit an inter se modification of the Convention and on the assumption that a standing appellate body could be created through an opt-in convention.

4.1. Relationship between an appellate mechanism and annulment

4.1.1. Appeal as a substitute for annulment

As discussed in Chapter two, the grounds for annulment are suggested to be included in the scope of appellate review in the draft provisions. The idea behind this suggestion is that an AM might serve as a substitute for annulment in current ISDS procedures. The existence of the annulment (setting aside) proceedings or not is important for the institutional arrangement of an AM with respect to the scope of review, costs, timing and the finality of awards, etc. It would be useful to start this question with the relationship between annulment and appeal.

Annulment is fundamentally different from appeal. Either the annulment grounds under Article 52 (1) of the ICSID Convention[109] or the grounds for setting aside under Article 34 (3) of the UNCITRAL Model Law[110] deal with the validity of the procedure itself. Any criticism of the merits of the correct findings

---

[109] ICSID Convention, Art. 52 (1).

[110] UNCITRAL Model Law, Art 34 (3).

or errors is not permitted.[111] In another word, annulment in principle merely deals with the legitimacy of proceedings, whereas appeal includes the review of substance of the dispute. Therefore, a narrow use of annulment is in principle and should be taken as an exception to the original award. Obviously, the remedies for errors provided by the ICSID Convention or the UNCITRAL Rules are not sufficient.

Perhaps it is the reason why in practice the border between appeal and annulment sometimes was crossed. In the first-generation jurisprudence, failure to apply applicable law could result in manifest excess of powers. Such approach attracted some criticism for blending the border between the two procedures. ICSID tribunals then became more cautious in the application of Article 52 of the ICSID Convention. That means an ad hoc committee for annulment would remain an error in the award even if it is aware of that. It is argued that such a practice 'would contradict the customary norms applicable to the interpretation of international treaties by permitting an absurd effect'.[112] From the perspective of the object and purpose of the ICSID Convention, legal errors and factual errors should have the possibility to be corrected.

Besides the fact of crossing the border between appeal and annulment and the extremely limited scope of annulment grounds, costs and timing of annulment proceedings remain problematic. On the one hand, a study has shown that from 2007 to 2012 the average time between the registration of an annulment case and the final decision is 26 months, [113] and that the length of the annulment process tends to increase exponentially. An already time-consuming arbitration can

---

[111] Klöckner v. Cameroon, ICSID Case No. ARB/81/2, Ad hoc Committee Decision on Annulment, 3 May 1985, para. 83.

[112] D.B.Gosis, 37 Addressing and Redressing Errors in ICSID Arbitration, in J.E. Kalicki, A. Joubin-Bret, *Reshaping the Investor-State Dispute Settlement System*, Leiden: BRILL, 2015, Vol. 4, p.870.

[113] ICSID, SECRETARIAT, BACKGROUND PAPER ON ANNULMENT FOR THE ASMINISTRATIVE COUNCIL OF ICSID, 27 ICSID REV.443, 36 (2012), PARA 62, https://icsid.worldbank.org/sites/default/files/Background%20Report%20on%20Annulment_English.pdf (Last visited on 18 July, 2022).

become exceedingly lengthy when annulment proceedings are initiated. The study also showed that during the period between 1971 and 2010, nearly one-third of all ICSID arbitral awards have been subjected to annulment proceedings.[114] The abuse of annulment occurs when the parties in fact use annulment as an inefficient appeal procedure.

On the other hand, the expanding functions of annulment proceedings has resulted in unnecessarily frequent application of annulment, leading a significant increase in costs. Although Article 61 of the Convention provides for the possibility of recovery of legal fees by the successful party, the ad hoc committee might generally allow both parties to share the costs equally.

Therefore, the annulment procedure could be replaced by the AM in the way of adding the annulment grounds into the scope of appellate review. Firstly, the scope and review function of annulment proceedings could be covered by the AM because the scope of appellate review is border than annulment. More than just a second chance to review the disputes, the AM would have additional functions, addressing not only errors but also inconsistencies in awards, the legitimacy of the tribunal and the application of international law, etc. Furthermore, by designing a time framework the AM could make the original annulment review process more efficient. In short, worries about the timing and costs of annulment will no longer exist. Finally, cancellation of annulment would ensure the finality of an appeal award. The co-existence of appeal and annulment would in fact result a three-tier review system, which is inconsistent with the purpose of establishing an AM. In conclusion, countries willing to accept an AM may consider replacing the annulment procedure with the new mechanism.

4.1.2. Coordination with current regimes

Following the previous assumption that the introduction of an AM would replace the annulment remedies either for the ICSID awards and the UNCITRAL awards, different approaches should be adopted to coordinate the new AM and the original annulment provisions.

---

[114] *Ibid.*, Ann. 2, p.5.

For ICSID awards, due to the closed nature of the ICSID regime, the annulment proceedings are conducted by an ad hoc committee pursuant to Article 52 of the Convention. The only thing that needs to be done is to exclude the application of Article 52 by an inter se modification of the ICSID Convention.[115]

The situation for arbitrations under the UNCITRAL Arbitration Rules is more complex. For sure, it would also require the appellate rules exclude the setting aside proceedings under domestic law. The question is how to achieve this. An approach is provided in the first CIDS Report that a waiver of judicial review of appeal awards could be included in the proposed AM rules.[116] The Annex of the UNCITRAL Arbitration Rules provides a model statement of waiver that '[T] he parties hereby waive their right to any form of recourse against an award to any court or other competent authority, insofar as such waiver can validly be made under the applicable law'.[117]

By this way the setting aside challenge under a national law might be substituted by the new AM. However, it can be seen from the wording of the waiver and the principle contained in Article 1 (3) of the UNCITRAL Rules[118] that the validity of the exclusion is subject to the applicable law. It is reported that Belgium, France, Panama, Peru, Sweden, Switzerland, and Tunisia are the examples where in certain circumstances the setting aside actions might be excluded as long as an agreement is reached by the parties.[119]

The question follows that not all the states would recognise the waiver of judicial review and thus the setting aside proceedings would remain in place. Such circumstance would result in different coverages in the two types of disputes, ICSID cases and others. To avoid this, it is suggested that the contracting parties

---

[115] See Chapter 3.1.2.

[116] See G.Kaufmann-Kohler and M.Potestà (2016), *supra* note 91, para. 197.

[117] UNCITRAL Arbitration Rules, Ann.: Possible waiver statement.

[118] *Ibid.*, Art 1 (3).

[119] See UNCITRAL Secretariat Guide on the Convention on the Recognition and Enforcement of Foreign Arbitral Awards (2016), p.21.

should affirm the effectiveness of a waiver of grounds for seeking annulment before their courts through legislation.[120] Besides, it is necessary to provide that the arbitration shall be seated in a contracting party to the AM rules. Only if those conditions are met, the AM would be compatible with the current regime and serve as a substitute for setting aside procedures. However, this approach is considered impractical as such a waiver is not commonly permitted in most countries and only seldom jurisdictions allow it.[121]

In conclusion, despite the advantages of replacing annulment with an AM, [122] the issue of compatibility of the new mechanism with annulment procedure appears in non-ICSID cases due to the governing domestic law. It is possible, in some countries, for the new AM to be compatible with the national law but the scope of such compatibility is predictably not broad. So even if the suggestion that appeal could be a substitute for annulment will be adopted by the Working Group III, the implementation of such rules might be not admitted in some jurisdictions in respect of non-ICSID cases.

4.2. Enforcement of an appellate award

4.2.1. Under the ICSID Convention

Providing that the AM would retain two legal frameworks for enforcement, in the context of ICSID, the rules of enforcing an appeal decision on an ICSID award may differ between the contracting parties to the inter se modification of the ICSID Convention and other ICSID member states.

For the contracting parties to the AM rules, by the way of an inter se agreement, they would be likely to establish a special regime for the enforcement of an appeal award like Article 54 of the ICSID Convention if they want to maintain the advantages of the ICSID automatic enforcement rules. The enforcement in contracting parties would be subject to the new rules reflecting

---

[120] See G. Kaufmann-Kohler, M. Potestà (2020), *supra* note 109, pp.91-92.

[121] See UNCITRAL Secretariat Guide on the New York Convention (2016), *supra* note 120; See also A.J. Van den Berg (2019), *supra* note 57, p.186.

[122] As discussed in Section 4.1.1.

Article 54, which means likewise there would be no place for national courts to control the ICSID appeal awards. Nevertheless, the question may appear that under the ICSID Convention, the AM would create two arbitral awards. It is contrary to the fact that an ICSID tribunal renders only one award. This concern may also be addressed in the inter se modification of the ICSID Convention for instance by interpreting the 'award' as 'award in force' or 'final award' so that the award made in the first level would not be regarded as an 'award' between the contracting parties.

However, other ICSID member states (non-contracting parties) will not be constrained by the revised rules. For the issue of the enforcement of an appeal award rendered under the ICSID framework in their territories, the situation of these non-contracting parties is similar to that of non-ICSID member states in regard to an ICSID award.[123] The result is that in this situation the appeal award could be at least enforced pursuant to the New York Convention.

4.2.2. Under the New York Convention

4.2.2.1. Meaning of 'arbitral awards'

Pursuant to Article I (1), the New York Convention applies to the recognition and enforcement of 'arbitral awards' which fall within its scope.[124] In terms of a decision rendered under the AM, the first question is that if it qualifies as an 'arbitral award' under the New York Convention. In fact, the difficulty is 'there is no universally accepted definition of arbitration'.[125]

There is no definition or explanation of 'arbitral awards' given by the New York Convention itself. But in the preparatory work of the Convention, one suggestion was made that it is up to the competent domestic court where recognition and enforcement is sought to decide when a decision is an arbitral

---

[123] G. Kaufmann-Kohler and M. Potestà (2016), *supra* note 91, para. 200.

[124] The New York Convention, Art. I(1).

[125] G. Kaufmann-Kohler & A. Rigozzi, *International Arbitration: Law and Practice in Switzerland*, Oxford University Press, 2015, p.6.

award under the New York Convention.[126] Similarly following this explanation, the meaning of 'arbitral awards' could be governed by an opt-in convention that confirm the nature of the decision made by the appellate body.

Furthermore, the UNCITRAL Secretariat gave two suggested criteria to help determine an arbitral award: 'the finality and the binding effect of an award'.[127] For the new AM, providing a waiver of setting aside action is effective in the country where the enforcement is sought to or in the case where setting aside proceedings were not initiated, the final decision rendered by the appellate body would of course meet the criteria. Besides, in accordance with Article I(2) of the New York Convention, 'arbitral awards' shall include awards made by 'permanent arbitral bodies'.[128] For the AM conceived in this thesis, a standing appellate body is created that within the scope of Article I(2).

Observing that unless a disruptive reform of the ISDS regime in which arbitration is no longer the primary means of settling investment disputes, an AM would inevitably rely on the existing arbitration rules under the current ISDS system, and in particular would not be separated from the ICSID Convention and the UNCITRAL Arbitration Rules, as discussed in the thesis. From the foregoing, the final award made by the appellate body falls within the scope of 'arbitral tribunal' in the New York Convention. So basically, appeal awards are enforceable under the New York Convention.

4.2.2.2. Waiver of grounds for refusal of enforcement

Unlike the automatic recognition of ICSID awards, Article V of the New York Convention provides the grounds for national courts to refuse a foreign arbitral award. To ensure the maximum finality of an appeal award and decrease differences in coverage between ICSID and UNCITRAL arbitrations, a waiver of grounds for refusing the enforcement of an appeal award could be considered,

---

[126] Travaux préparatoires, Recognition and Enforcement of Foreign Arbitral Awards, Report by the Secretary- General, Annex I, Comments by Governments, E/2822, p.10.

[127] UNCITRAL Secretariat Guide on the New York Convention (2016), *supra* note 120, p.14.

[128] The New York Convention, Art. I(2).

which is similar to the waiver of seeking setting aside action.

However, the same question in a waiver of setting aside arises here in a waiver of refusal of enforcement. Would third countries be willing to accept such a waiver? It seems that the answer to this question would be that it is up to the state to confirm the validity of a waiver of grounds for refusing enforcement within its jurisdiction. Yet, the effectiveness of the waiver may depend on the nature of grounds. An argument is that 'the grounds for refusal of enforcement in paragraph 2 of Article V of the New York Convention are legally not capable of being waived or contracted out of' because that the matters of public policy shall be applied by national courts themselves.[129] For other grounds listed in Article V of the New York Convention, it might be possible to waive because these grounds need to be raised and proved by the invoking party.[130]

5. Conclusion

After the discussion about the interaction of a potential AM with the ICSID Convention and the UNCITRAL Arbitration Rules, a conclusion has been drawn here that the introduction of an AM to the existing ISDS regime is legally possible. The barriers regarding the design of structure and legal elements to the establishment of an AM are not insurmountable and could be overcome through certain approaches.

For the fundamental incompatibility of an AM with Articles 26 and 53(1) of the ICSID Convention, Article 41 of VCLT provides a possible way to resolve the problem, which the ICSID member states may refer to. An inter se modification of the ICSID Convention meets the conditions set forth in the Article 41 of VCLT. Therefore, the ICSID members who are willing to develop an AM could modify the ICSID Convention between themselves to create a special regime for appeal, including the issues of annulment and enforcement of appeal awards. The special regime is only applicable to the contracting parties to the inter se modification and

[129] A.J. Van den Berg (2019), *supra* note 57, p.186.
[130] *Ibid.*, pp.186–187.

other non-contracting ICSID members are not bound by it.

For arbitrations under the UNCITRAL Arbitration Rules, the disputing parties are able to modify Article 34 (2) of the UNCITRAL Rules (finality rule of awards) to accept an AM as the UNCITRAL Rules are subject to the agreement of the parties.[131] However, he UNCITRAL Arbitration Rules at the same time are governed by lex arbitri, usually the national arbitration law at the place of arbitration. In the countries where arbitral appeal is not allowed, the AM would be not applicable. Therefore, the parties who want an appeal review of the first-level arbitral award are suggested to choose an appropriate seat of arbitration in which arbitral appeal is permissible.

Additionally, following the practice of the Mauritius Convention, states may integrate an AM to existing IIAs by an opt-in convention, which is multilateral and stand-alone. By this way the existing IIAs could be supplemented with an AM. Most importantly, the consensual nature of applying an AM would be well maintained because of the flexibility of an opt-in convention. The drafting work of such a convention is challengeable because it would face a threshold and difficult issue that to establish a single regime governing both ICSID awards and non-ICSID awards or to remain a dual track for the two kinds of arbitral awards. The answer to this question is particularly decisive to the issue of annulment and enforcement of an appeal award.

But in general, appeal is suggested to serve as a substitute for annulment under the ICSID Convention or setting aside proceedings under a national law. In the latter situation, a waiver of seeking setting aside action by an agreement of parties would be possible and recognized in several states but most countries may tend to refuse such a waiver. In terms of the enforcement of an appeal award, the inter se modification of the ICSID Convention may create a special enforcement regime between the contracting members but the new regime is not applicable to other ICSID members that are not the parties to the inter se modification. For them, the New York Convention might be applicable to the enforcement of an

---

[131] The UNCITRAL Arbitration Rules, Art. 1 (1).

appeal award in their territories. In the context of this thesis, an appeal award is within the meaning of 'arbitral awards' in the New York Convention so it would be enforceable under the Convention.

In fact, at this stage, conceiving an attractive framework may be a focus of the introduction of an AM. There is no rush to address all issues at the beginning and it might be better to leave some rules open to avoid unnecessary conflicts. However, several essential legal issues shall be carefully considered before establishing an AM. The first one is the nature of the AM. Considering that the introduction of an appeal layer not only aims to a second chance of review but also to make the arbitral awards in ISDS more coherent and predictable, a standing nature would be preferable. It follows that a multilateral AM is more suitable and acceptable in this case. Another important legal issue is the scope and the standard of appellate review. From the experience of appeal practice in WTO and the draft provisions provided by the Working Group III, the scope of review may include both the errors of law and fact, as well as the grounds for annulment. However, the scope shall be limited to manifest legal errors and serious factual errors raised by parties, which would be necessary for the resolution of the dispute. As for the effect of appeal, the second-tier tribunal may confirm, modify or reverse the original decisions, but it is not suggested to accord an appellate tribunal the remand authority because preserving remand in an AM would bring the possibility of multiple tiers of review, which could cause serious delays and derogate the benefits of arbitration.

In all, if an AM is to be established, it seems that a standing and multilateral AM, as a supplement to the current ISDS system, is preferred. And on this basis, the ICSID Convention could be the multilateral platform to develop such an AM, mainly because it is better to choose an existing and tested forum that is specifically designed for investment arbitration rather than creating a new one full of uncertainties, and the ICSID Convention may allow the appeal awards exempt from the review by competent domestic judicial institutions after awards. Besides the choice of multilateral platform, as proposed in the text before that the multilateral framework could be only used to obtain the consent of states to establish an AM while the acceptance of AM could be determined in the specific case. This approach aims to provide maximum freedom of choice for the state to facilitate the establishment of an AM at the early stage. Admittedly, a creation of an AM is not easy and a number of obstacles still remain, both legally and politically.

征稿启事

《北京仲裁》由北京仲裁委员会/北京国际仲裁中心主办，主要刊登中外仲裁、调解、工程评审等与多元化纠纷解决机制相关的民商事理论性、实践性的论文或者介绍性文章以及符合前述范围的翻译文章。本出版物每年出版四辑，下设"主题研讨""专论""仲裁讲坛""比较研究""ADR 专栏""案例评析""办案札记"等栏目。

编辑部热诚欢迎广大读者投稿，投稿前请仔细阅读以下注意事项：

1. 来稿应符合本出版物网站（www.bjac.org.cn/magazine/）的投稿要求及注释体例，并按要求写明作者信息、中英文题目、内容摘要、关键词等信息。

2. 来稿应严格遵守学术规范，如出现抄袭、剽窃等侵犯知识产权的情况，由作者自负责任。

3. 为扩大本出版物及作者信息交流渠道，本出版物已经委托博看网数字发行，并已被 CNKI 中国期刊全文数据库收录。凡向本出版物投稿的稿件，即视作作者同意独家授权出版其作品，包括但不限于纸质图书出版权、电子版信息网络传播权、无线增值业务权等权利，授予本出版物授予合作单位再使用、授予相关数据库收录之权利，作者前述相关的著作权使用费将由编辑部在稿酬内一次性给付。若作者不同意前述授权的，请在来稿时书面声明，以便做适当处理；作者未书面声明的，视为同意编辑部的前述安排。

4. 投稿方式：请采用电子版形式，发送至电子邮箱 bjzhongcai@bjac.org.cn。如在两个月内未发出用稿或备用通知，请作者自行处理。

5. 所有来稿一经采用，即奉稿酬（400 元/千字，特约稿件 500 元/千字）。

《北京仲裁》编辑部

图书在版编目（CIP）数据

北京仲裁 . 第 122 辑 / 北京仲裁委员会（北京国际仲裁中心）组编 . —北京：中国法制出版社，2024.1

ISBN 978-7-5216-4255-1

Ⅰ . ①北… Ⅱ . ①北… Ⅲ . ①仲裁－司法监督－中国－文集 Ⅳ . ① D925.7-53

中国国家版本馆 CIP 数据核字（2024）第 041214 号

责任编辑：侯　鹏　　　　　　　　　　　　　　封面设计：李　宁

北京仲裁（第 122 辑）
BEIJING ZHONGCAI（DI-122 JI）
组编 / 北京仲裁委员会（北京国际仲裁中心）
经销 / 新华书店
印刷 / 三河市国英印务有限公司
开本 / 787 毫米 ×960 毫米　16 开　　　　　　印张 / 14.25　字数 / 233 千
版次 / 2024 年 1 月第 1 版　　　　　　　　　　2024 年 1 月第 1 次印刷

中国法制出版社出版
书号 ISBN 978-7-5216-4255-1　　　　　　　　　　　　　　定价：39.00 元

北京市西城区西便门西里甲 16 号西便门办公区
邮政编码 100053　　　　　　　　　　　　　　传真：010-63141852
网址：http://www.zgfzs.com　　　　　　　　　编辑部电话：010-63141826
市场营销部电话：010-63141612　　　　　　　　印务部电话：010-63141606
（如有印装质量问题，请与本社印务部联系。）